CW00617847

Business Families and Family Businesses

The STEP Handbook for Advisers

Consulting Editors **Ian Macdonald** and **Jonathan Sutton**

Consulting editors
Ian Macdonald and Jonathan Sutton

Publisher
Sian O'Neill

Marketing manager
Alan Mowat

Production
John Meikle, Russell Anderson

Publishing directors
Guy Davis, Tony Harriss, Mark Lamb

Business Families and Family Businesses: The STEP Handbook for Advisers
is published by
Globe Law and Business
Globe Business Publishing Ltd
New Hibernia House
Winchester Walk
London Bridge
London SE1 9AG
United Kingdom
Tel +44 20 7234 0606
Fax +44 20 7234 0808
Web www.gbplawbooks.com

Printed by Antony Rowe Ltd

ISBN 978-1-905783-25-0

DISCLAIMER
This publication is intended as a general guide only. The information and opinions which it contains
are not intended to be a comprehensive study, nor to provide legal advice, and should not be treated
as a substitute for legal advice concerning particular situations. Legal advice should always be sought
before taking any action based on the information provided. The publishers bear no responsibility
for any errors or omissions contained herein.

Table of contents

Society of Trust and Estate Practitioners (STEP)

The Society of Trust and Estate Practitioners (STEP) is a unique professional body providing more than 14,000 members with a local, national and international learning and business network focusing on the responsible stewardship of assets today and across the generations.

STEP provides education, training, representation and networking for its members, who are professionals specialising in trusts and estates, executorship, administration and related taxes. Members advise clients on the broad basis of the management of personal finance.

Full members of STEP are the most experienced and senior practitioners in the field of trusts and estates.

For further information visit www.step.org or email step@step.org .

Preface

Nan-b de Gaspé Beaubien
The de Gaspé Beaubien Foundation

It is now more than 40 years that Philippe and I have been studying the issues of family business. At that time there was not a university in the world teaching the subject, even though it was – and still is – the prevalent form of conducting business. I still cringe when I remember the remark of a professor teaching at a prestigious business school who told us that "family business is not a teachable subject". The majority of people offering help were lawyers interested in tax and estate planning, but with little knowledge or understanding of the family issues. Our answer was to educate ourselves by meeting and sharing with families from around the globe.

Our greatest lesson from this experience was that all families in business have the same issues, but the way that they solve them depends on their unique blend of knowledge, history, culture and values.

As we became more knowledgeable, we began to share our experience with groups such as YPO (Young Presidents Organization) and CEO (Chief Executives Organization). More and more of these families came to us seeking help and from that demand grew the concept of starting a foundation devoted entirely to helping families deal with their issues. In the beginning, the Business Families Foundation (BFF) focused its attention solely on families working in a business, but the foundation expanded its work to include professionals when the families complained that they were not speaking the same language.

Our courses for professionals were well attended, with participants coming from different parts of the world. However, we realised that BFF was only teaching a small percentage of the many professionals working in the field and that much more had to be done if family businesses were to thrive and flourish. An important step in this direction is helping accountants, lawyers and other professionals to become aware of the particular issues in a family business and more adept at asking the right questions.

STEP has attempted to do just that by putting together a series of chapters written by professionals who have obviously had a great deal of experience in dealing with family businesses. There are helpful points throughout the book, although some chapters such as the family office with the explanations of trusts and estate planning may have a limited application for professionals not working in an English jurisdiction. I found the chapter by Burrows and Pervin especially helpful, because it gives some background to the evolution of the field as well as defining the key issues for professionals in a very succinct way.

STEP has done a service for the field of family business by publishing a good introductory book dedicated to professionals working in this area. Let us hope that many avail themselves of the opportunity to purchase it. Their family business clients will be the beneficiaries.

Nan-b de Gaspé Beaubien
Co-Chair, The de Gaspé Beaubien Foundation
www.businessfamilies.com
February 24 2009

Foreword

David Harvey
Society of Trust and Estate Practitioners (STEP)

Family businesses are not just distinct; they are different and often idiosyncratic. This differentness derives from the mixing of business imperatives, opportunities and problems with family chemistry, priorities and challenges.

Business and family drivers need not contradict; they can give strength, unity and long-term purpose, which together will grow the well-being, unity and wealth of family and business for the long term. Equally, Tolstoy's opening line of Anna Karenina is an apt warning, "happy families are all alike; every unhappy family is unhappy in its own way". There are many ways in which family businesses can come to grief as blood and business compete and clash. Apparently competing business agendas may hide family rivalries no one wishes to admit. Blithely unaware advisors may blindly treat business symptoms ignoring family problems – elephants in the room to those that can see. Elder and younger generations may be ships that pass in the night, whose assumptions about each other's aspirations and ambitions may only be an introverted mirror of personal preoccupations.

Far too many professionals and their professional bodies simply assume and advertise themselves as Mister or Miss 'Right', fit to assist family enterprises to success. Sometimes, despite the best intentions, such advice is little better than the business card marked expert, which means jack of all trades, master of none.

STEP recognises the differentness of family businesses, focusing as its 14,500 expert members do worldwide on the responsible stewardship and structuring of family assets. STEP recognises too the many skills that first-class advisors need to acquire directly or to borrow through networks, if they are to provide the service that family businesses need. The hard financial or legal skills of the accountant or lawyer, together with the management technique and experience and the soft skills of the psychologist and counsellor, are all to be called on. STEP's own Business Families Special Interest Group focuses on providing skills to STEP members, either directly or through the networks that the group creates.

While many guides are targeted at family business owners, very few address the needs of the advisor looking to develop family business practice and to consider the extra skills and networks needed to serve the family business client. This guide is intended to support any adviser who is serious about developing family business skills; it provides a first set of signposts on the road to becoming someone truly competent to advise family businesses; membership of STEP can be another part of that growth process.

David Harvey
Chief Executive, STEP
www.step.org
January 20 2009

Family businesses and business families

Ian Macdonald
Wright, Johnston & Mackenzie LLP

Internationally, family businesses are the biggest untapped market for professional services. Most professional advisers are likely to be dealing with family businesses already, but few fully appreciate the complex structures and relationships in the family business system. This first chapter sets the scene for the distinctive types of advice that family businesses require and the ways in which it can be provided.

We will define 'family business' and 'business family', assess why family businesses are important and different and explore the complex systems found in all family businesses.

1. What is a family business?

There are a number of commonly used definitions of family business, all of which capture something of their unique features but none of which is universally accepted. Some examples follow:

The majority of votes are held by the person who established or acquired the business (the founder) or by their family members and at least one representative of the family is involved in the management of the business.

In a publicly quoted company, the founder or their family possesses 25% of the right to vote through their share capital and there is at least one family member on the board. The founder or their family own more than twice as many shares as the next largest shareholder.

More subjective criteria are needed in many cases, especially in smaller businesses, and it may be enough to ask those running the business whether they consider it to be a family business or want it to be one. Family control or influence can often be exercised through relationships or management structure just as readily as through votes.

If all else fails, try the 'elephant test' – an elephant is difficult to describe but easy to identify when you see one, so if a business looks like a family business then it probably is one.

You will see that none of these definitions refers to any of the more common classifications of business by reference to size, structure (sole trader, partnership, limited liability company), market sector or public listing. Family businesses are found in all these categories and we must not try to advise them in the same way as we would non-family businesses that have the same structure, ownership or activities.

2.   **What is a business family?**

If we can identify a family business, defining the business family should be easy but uncertainties await us here also. The business family obviously includes the people directly involved in the business and their immediate relatives; but should it also include all generations including those too young to be involved, spouses not related to the founder by blood, and others connected to the family in less formal ways? Essentially, the answer should be "yes", because the single most important lesson that advisers should learn when dealing with a family business is that we should take into account the interests of the business and of all the members of the family system. To do less than this will almost certainly produce solutions or structures that do not address all the issues of the business or family – and that as a result will probably not be adopted by the clients, no matter how much work and expertise has gone into them and how technically sound they may be.

It is also worth noting that a family can still be a business family even if there is no longer a business directly involved – the family business may have been sold, but the family may wish to continue or adapt the principles and structures that were in place for the trading business to deal with the resulting wealth. To take this even further, many of the techniques described in this book can readily be applied to families who wish to remain connected through the ownership and enjoyment of assets even where there has never been a family business as such.

3.   **Why are family businesses important?**

It is a common misconception about family businesses that they are just small or medium-sized, owner-managed, inefficient, badly run and unlikely to endure.

In fact, the world is full of family businesses of all shapes and sizes; they generally outnumber non-family businesses and have been shown to outperform them and last longer as well. A recent survey in the United Kingdom for the Institute for Family Business found that family businesses produce more than 30% of national gross domestic product and make up 65% of the country's private sector businesses.

Other research has shown that the statistics in the United States and Canada are similar to the United Kingdom, while the proportions of family businesses are even higher in Europe, South America and Asia, probably for cultural reasons.

In the United Kingdom, most family businesses are privately owned – including one-third of the country's largest private businesses; but only 6% of the publicly quoted companies in the FT All-Share Index are family businesses. This is an unusually low proportion. In most other countries the percentage is much higher – in France, for example, it is 50%.

And the importance of family businesses is not confined to economic contribution: family businesses are often able to take a longer-term view, are a crucial breeding ground for entrepreneurial activity and provide employment and stability in many communities.

4.   **How are family businesses different?**

In a business that is not family-owned, the overriding objective is shareholder return. The owners of family businesses are, however, likely to want more than simply a financial return from their enterprises, because they are part of the family's vision. Family businesses benefit from the commitment of the owning family and this often means that business decisions are taken with a longer time horizon than in other businesses. Add to this the fact that the owners are identifiable and communication between the business and the owners should be easier.

But there are challenges as well. There does not have to be a business involved for advisers to know the huge number and variety of issues that can arise in families. And in any economic climate the challenges facing businesses are huge. Put the two together and the situation becomes highly complex, so a different approach is clearly going to be required. There must be a trade-off between outright shareholder return and the many other priorities that the family will have in running the business. Business decisions taken without taking into account the emotional influence of the family could seriously damage the relationships involved; but, equally, decisions taken mainly for personal or family reasons are unlikely to be in the best economic interests of the business.

The business and family aspects are always going to be present, so there is no point in advisers trying to provide solutions and set up structures that address only one set of issues. What appears to be a business issue may have its roots in the family and the adviser's first challenge is to tease out the real issues.

It will be one of the recurring themes of this book that "you can't take the business family out of the family business", so advisers must find ways of addressing the different factors that arise in family businesses. Fortunately, there are a number of tools which can help advisers manage the complexity inherent in family businesses.

5.   Family businesses are complex systems

The starting point is to identify the range of interests and concerns that can exist at any time in a family business (regardless of its size, structure or activity).[1]

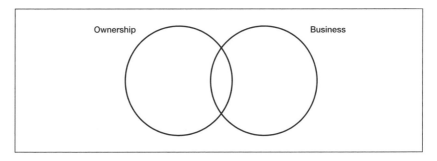

Ownership   Business

In any business involving more than one person, there are two principal categories of people to be taken into account in business decisions and planning: the owners and those running the business. If each of these groups is shown as a circle (see diagram above), there can be three different categories of people involved: those

---

[1]   Ken McCracken, "The family business client – managing the complexity", *The Family Business Client*, Vol 1, Issue 1.

who own the business but do not work in it; those who work in the business but do not own any part of it; and those who do both. Much of company law in most countries regulates the relationship between these groups.

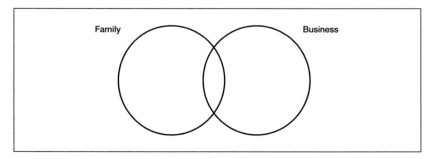

In family businesses, it was thought that the 'ownership' circle could simply be replaced by a 'family' one (see diagram above). The business system is likely to be objective and outward-looking and its priority will be to maximise production, make a profit and adapt to market changes. The family system, on the other hand, is based on emotion, inward-looking and may have different values with more resistance to change.

The intersection of the family and business circles is where things get interesting, especially when any stress is applied to one system or the other. When this happens, the system under stress will normally begin to dominate. If this is the family system, business perspective is lost, attention turns inwards and the business may fail to keep up with developments in the marketplace. If, on the other hand, the business system has the upper hand, family communication, loyalty and emotions are damaged and relationships can quickly break down. The business is seen as the obstacle to family well-being and both will suffer.

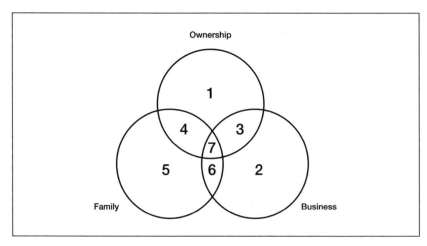

In their research at Harvard University in the early 1980s, Tagiuri and Davis[2] identified the importance of a third subsystem – ownership – which overlaps with the other two but has a distinctly different purpose and agenda, because not all owners are necessarily members of the family nor will all family members own a part of the business. Their three-circle model helps to identify the complex range of different interests present in a family business by showing the family business as made up of three independent but overlapping systems – ownership, management and family.

Introducing the third circle vastly increases the complexity of the model, but now any person in a family business system can be placed in one of the seven segments that have been created (see previous diagram). The location of each person can explain and even predict their expectations, fears and behaviour. It also helps to explain why conflict arises in so many family businesses – quite simply it is inherent in the structure because the family and the business have limited resources – of time, money, expertise and even love. In competing for those resources, everyone has different needs and sees the world from their own perspective.

Owners, family and business want different things and need access to the business and the wealth it generates for their different needs. By assessing the likely interests of different members of the family business system, advisers can manage the complexity and conflicts that result.

5.1 External investors (segment 1)

Those who own part of the business but do not work in it and are not members of the family could include venture capitalists, banks, business angels, and, in quoted companies, institutional and private shareholders. They will be concerned mainly with the return on their investment and will expect business decisions to be clearly separated from family dynamics. Those in this segment should realise that by investing in a family business they will be subject to different issues for those in other companies and they may need to take a more active interest in family issues including succession.

5.2 Management and employees (segment 2)

Those who work in the business, whether as directors, managers or more junior employees, but are neither owners nor family members will be concerned about career prospects and job security. They will be wary of nepotism, which could favour family members when appointments, salaries and promotions are being considered, and they will want to know that the strategic direction of the business is being considered in a businesslike way. If a family business has a reputation for 'putting the family first', it may find it difficult to recruit the best managers and employees.

5.3 Non-family working owners (segment 3)

Sometimes the response to the problem of recruiting and retaining the best non-family managers and employees is to give them shares or other rewards linked to equity. This segment will be concerned about the dividend and capital return on

---

2 R Tagiuri and JA Davis, "Bivalent attitudes of the family firm", *Family Business Review*, Vol IX, No 2.

their shares but the stakes offered are usually small and, in private companies at least, will be strictly controlled and not easy to sell. The value of such shares is difficult to establish and will be affected by what happens elsewhere in the system.

5.4 Non-working family owners (segment 4)

In many cases when ownership of a family business (usually a company) passes from the founder to the next generation, some of the new shareholders do not work in the business. Their interests tend to be a mixture of the expectations of external investors and non-family owners tempered by family responsibilities. Younger family owners in particular may want information about the prospects of employment with the family business in the future and whether they are likely to acquire more shares. All those in this segment need to consider whether their shares are primarily a source of wealth or whether the inherited family values include a responsibility to pass these holdings to the next generation.

5.5 Family members (segment 5)

Even if they do not own a share of the business or work in it, every member of a business family has at least an emotional investment in the business. The family will almost certainly make sacrifices to keep the business going, but a balance between the needs of the business and the needs of the family is important. They may be interested in the business for lifestyle reasons because of the wealth it creates, or there may be prospects of future employment or ownership for themselves or their children.

It is for this reason more than any other that any attempt to solve the challenges of a family business purely from the point of view of the business without reference to the family is doomed. You cannot leave the business family out of the family business.

5.6 Family employees (segment 6)

Family members who work in the business but do not own shares will be concerned with career development in the same way as segment 2, but they might have different expectations about the future – "one day this could all be yours".

One area of possible conflict well illustrated by the model is between those in this segment and the non-working family owners in segment 4. The family employees' hard work and determination to grow the business may be tempered by the fact that their efforts will reap financial rewards for their relatives who do not work in the business. The employees may feel that the profits they have helped generate should be retained and reinvested in future growth, while the non-working owners will expect a healthy dividend as well as provision for growth.

The family element here blurs the distinction between rewards for employment and return on investment. Both expectations are equally appropriate, but any discussion may become personalised.

5.7 Working family owners and business leaders (segment 7)

Someone who shares ownership of the business with their family and works in the business with some of them will have the interests of all the other segments. This is particularly so when they are the managing director or other leader of the business as well as being a parent and an owner who will thus face many conflicting choices, especially when it comes to succession. Should they do what they consider best for the business even at the expense of family harmony? Can the future of the business and everyone who has a stake in it be put at risk by decisions influenced by family sentiment or expediency?

It is little wonder that leaders in family businesses often feel lonely, because it is not easy carrying all these interests and responsibilities on your shoulders while having to deal with people in other parts of the system who complain when their needs and responsibilities are not being met. Truly "the buck stops here" and it is little help when the family dimension is ignored by advisers or seen as part of the problem rather than as part of the solution.

No other type of business enterprise has this structural form. The three-circle model explains the complexity that goes with having a family system, a business system and an ownership system linked together through not only the family business but also wealth, legal structures, employment structures, and emotional and relational bonds. Such a complex mix may appear daunting and undesirable, but we can learn from family businesses that have prospered over many generations how these overlapping interests have been managed and indeed put to their advantage.

The three circles illustrate the wide range of views and opinions that can exist in any family business and they may help everyone involved, including their advisers, realise that these different views and the conflicts that will naturally result may be as much to do with the position of individuals within the family business system as they are to do with their personalities.

The model also highlights that it is almost impossible and perhaps even dangerous to advise one part of the family business system without taking into account the impact elsewhere in the system. It follows that the family business adviser must remain neutral and not be, or be seen to be, biased in favour of any one person, group or part of the system. The adviser will not be able to do this if technical help is being sought on the basis or expectation that the family has to be separated from the business.

So the three-circle model offers the following themes relevant to business owners, leaders and advisers:

- Family businesses – whatever their size, structure or business – represent *families in business*. Do not try to take the business family out of the family business.
- It allows advisers to discover valuable information about the business and the family in a sensitive way and to build relationships with the client. Who else would ask these questions?
- The advisers can identify where the power lies in the system and ensure that they talk to all the right people and do not get trapped in one part of the system ("I only advise the business/the family").
- Technical expertise is important when advising family businesses, but they are more demanding and expect their advisers to help them find solutions that achieve a balance between the business family and the family business. The best way to do this is to create a governance structure that embraces and balances the interests of family, owners and business.

6. Family businesses change through time – time changes everything[3]

The three-circle model is an essential tool for every family business adviser – and their clients – but it is incomplete because it is a snapshot of the family business system at a particular moment in time. Family businesses, like any businesses, are always developing, so we have to supplement our understanding of the family business system with a model that shows the changes that happen in the ownership, business and family segments of the three circles.

The three-circle model not only helps those inside and outside the system to appreciate the complexity of the system and the likely needs and attitudes of those in different parts of it; it also helps predict what the consequences may be if anyone in the system changes their role or place in the structure. The model not only tells us where the family business system is now and how it got there but – even more interestingly perhaps – helps us see where we are going next.

It is inevitable that people will move around the system. For example, when a founder retires and passes on his shares he may move from segment 7 (owner-leader-family) to segment 5 (family only); the successor may move from segment 6 (manager-family) to segment 7 (taking over as the next owner-leader-family).

It follows that the changes that will inevitably take place in people's roles, needs and interests can be planned for. Planning involves the emotional challenge people face as their lives change as well as the technical challenges to construct efficient structures from a corporate, financial and legal perspective.

Building on the concept of family businesses as systems that must be able to respond to change if they are to survive, we now need a framework for understanding the pattern of predictable changes that will take place in family business systems. Changes taking place in the lives of individuals, families, ownership groupings and businesses profoundly affect the types of structures (organisational, legal, financial and family) that are used to hold the family business system together.

It is the task of those advising family businesses to help create and modify these structures, but it is important to realise that every family business already has its own natural organic structures without which it could not continue to function. These structures are, however, unlikely to be able to cope with the changes that take place through time. The adviser's job is to adapt and develop those structures to reflect and manage those changes, not to ignore or jettison what is already in place.

In the business circle, a structure that is not suitable for doing business and surviving the real world will eventually fail. Advisers may see this happen where senior generation leaders are unable to let go and cling to their way of doing business, despite the reality that the world has moved on.

In the ownership circle, inappropriate ownership structures that keep family members' wealth and inheritance locked into the family business will fail if shareholders feel that, to achieve liquidity, they must refuse to support the strategy of the firm or decide to sell out.

---

3   Dr Barbara Murray, "The developmental model for understanding change over the life cycle of a family business", *The Family Business Client*, Vol 1, Issue 1.

In the family circle, families who use the family business to keep the family together (fearing that the family may disintegrate or that some family members may not be able to make it in the employment world outside the family business) will place too high a strain on individual family members who feel their life is unsatisfactory or is being subordinated to the family business. Often, family members who want to have their own lives are cut off by the family for 'rebelling'.

7. The developmental model

Changes are going to take place, therefore, in the ownership, family and business circles as life goes on and it will be helpful for anyone with an interest in the family business system to know in advance what these are and how they might affect the system. We will look briefly at the life-cycle stages that each of the sub-systems of a developing family business can expect to go through if it continues through the natural evolutionary process.

In each sub-system, the projected stages of development are less precise than the circles themselves and different family businesses will follow different courses. Some will recycle themselves back to an earlier stage of the model, some may skip a step and some will disappear altogether, but the developmental model[4] is a useful guide to the way in which many family businesses will or can change through time.

8. Development of the ownership system

The ownership structure can take many forms at different stages but, because the key people in the system will get older and families tend to expand in size and complexity, most fall into one of three basic forms:

- controlling owner;
- sibling partnership; and
- cousins' consortium.

Not all families will move ownership in line with this model. Some may never get beyond passing shares to one controlling owner in the next generation, even if this means that other siblings lose out, and there are many other ways in which businesses can rearrange their ownership among siblings and cousins.

8.1 Controlling owner (CO)

This is often the structure by which entrepreneurial owner-managed businesses start up. They may become family businesses when more family members are recruited into ownership or management although in reality the family will probably be closely involved from the outset, even if only emotionally. CO firms are characterised by ownership control being concentrated in the hands of one individual or couple.

The main challenges at this stage are to do with how this power and control is managed, given that others are likely to have a stake in the business as family or non-

---

4   KE Gersick, JA Davis, M McCollom Hampton and I Lansberg, *Generation to Generation: Life Cycles of a Family Business*, Harvard Business School Press, 1997.

family managers or possibly other owners. Sooner or later the entrepreneur will need to access other expertise and advice, but may not be willing to listen to it or risk implementing it.

CO firms may also be undercapitalised. The founders will have invested long hours in the business and may not want or be able to share the returns with others – even if growth and investment are curtailed.

However, the main challenge faced by the CO structure when there is to be a next generation of family ownership is how to choose the right ownership structure for the next generation – one that will be workable for those who will be involved in the future ownership and management of the business and for the family as a whole.

8.2   Sibling partnership (SP)

If ownership of the business is passed to more than one sibling in the next generation, it becomes a sibling partnership. This is fundamentally different from the CO stage, because power and control are now shared by a group of relatives, some of whom may not actually work in the business.

Siblings in ownership have to learn how to share effective control of the business and particularly to decide how any non-working owners are to be treated, given that they are investing their inheritance in the business under the siblings' leadership. Some siblings may wish to exit ownership, so proper systems for liquidity are needed to ensure that this can be done at all and that the business is still properly capitalised if equity is removed.

And not everyone wants to be in business with their siblings. Often they find themselves in this structure as a consequence of their parents' wish to ensure that the business continues, or that their estates are divided equally and to save tax. As time passes, some or all of those who are involved in the firm as owners or managers may in turn seek out roles in the firm for their children. Differences in age and experience can cause problems at this stage, and if sibling factions develop these can cause real difficulties when the offspring (cousins) take over.

8.3   Cousins' consortium

This is the most complex of the family business ownership structures and some large family businesses have ownership spread out over hundreds of cousins. By this stage ownership has been considerably diluted; it may be in the hands of many minority shareholders, each with a different view on the security and value of their 'investment' depending on whether they work in the business and on the extent to which they feel connected to, and are kept informed about, the progress and prospects of the business. Cousins' consortium structures may by this time be led by non-family chief executives, so issues may emerge about how family control can be retained and how senior non-family personnel can be motivated if ownership is unlikely.

Because of the number of cousins who may be involved, it is vital that the right organising mechanisms are in place to manage the expectations of family, ownership and business stakeholder groups. Even more than with the sibling partnership structure, some owners are likely to want to cash out, so planning should involve the creation of an internal family business capital market suitably funded.

9. **Development of the business system**

Any business that is not growing and adapting to meet changing market conditions is going backwards and is unlikely to survive. Family businesses are no different. A typical progression of the business system would be as follows:

- start up;
- expansion;
- formalisation;
- maturity; and
- diversification.

Entrepreneurs set up business ventures to create something and to make money, not to become managers; but if the business is successful, it is inevitable that additional employees will have to be recruited and administrative and management structures will be required. The business can cope with the extra costs and complexity involved in this if the underlying enterprise is sound.

What is more difficult is to respond to changes in the marketplace, although there is evidence that family businesses are able to do this at least as well as, and to survive longer than, non-family businesses. These market forces may account for many of the oldest continuous family businesses internationally being in the more stable (and indeed essential) sectors of food and drink and hospitality – and undertakers!

Many family businesses will have to diversify their activities, set up new spin-off ventures and regenerate themselves, often at least once in each generation. These changes are more likely to be successful if they do not occur at the same time as a transition in the ownership and family sub-systems.

10. **Development of the family system**

The family itself will also change through time as everyone grows older and new generations appear. While again there is no automatic pattern, the natural progression could be:

- nuclear family;
- multigenerational family; and
- network of families.

The family structure has to adapt to changes in the parents' 'marriage enterprise' as their children are born, grow up, leave home, marry and have children of their own. The physical, social and emotional development of the children – and subsequent generations – takes place within the context of the business family and each person has a place in the circles previously described.

As they grow up, enter the business and work together with the senior generation, the next generation develop into people with different needs, opinions and outlooks. This can be difficult for parents to accept and the major challenge they face is learning how to relate to their children as adults. Letting go can be as difficult with children as it is with the other valued offspring, the family business.

11. Summary

This chapter has attempted to introduce some of the distinctive challenges of family businesses, to explain why family businesses are a worthwhile area for professional advisers and to describe some of the tools and models that have been developed by family business advisers over the last 20 years or so to address the issues that arise.

The rest of this book deals with these issues and others in more detail and gives comprehensive guidance on how to tackle the challenging world of family businesses and business families.

Roles, relationships and responsibilities

Judy Green
Family Firm Institute Inc
Jane Hilburt-Davis
Key Resources LLC

1. Family business professionals

Families in business are hardly a new phenomenon – they can be found in all cultures, all periods of history, in literature and drama, and more recently in the analyses of GDPs around the world. And it is undoubtedly safe to assume that such businesses have always relied on advisors of some sort. Yet it was only at the end of the twentieth century that a distinctly new profession emerged – that of the 'family business professional'. At first, this term referred essentially to family business advisors and consultants; then family business researchers and educators were added. Today, the term also includes family wealth advisors and consultants. Put them all together – advisors, consultants, researchers and educators – in the family business and family wealth fields and you have what have come to be known as family business professionals.

How did these professionals come into existence?

1.1 Establishing and growing the profession – the first 25 years

In the mid-1980s, a group of professionals and family business executives in the United States recognised the need for interdisciplinary collaboration in advising family-owned business and, as a result, founded the Family Firm Institute, Inc, in 1986.

The original founders envisaged the Family Firm Institute (FFI) as a 'three-legged stool' aimed at serving a membership encompassing consultants, educators and family business owners. They determined that FFI would carry out its mission in the following three ways:

- by hosting an annual conference to bring together members from across the nation (now from around the world), to share knowledge and research in the field of family enterprise;
- by organising regional study groups and workshops, so that members could be involved in 'grassroots networking' with their peers and discuss common problems and challenges in the family business arena; and
- by publishing a journal – the *Family Business Review* (*FBR*). This publication would combine research findings and their implications, conceptual ideas, contributions on practice and theory, and actual case studies on family-owned businesses.

1.2 Identifying core disciplines and organising knowledge

In 1995, FFI established a body-of-knowledge committee to determine the skills and expertise needed for professionals in the family enterprise field. This group identified what has come to be known as the 'core disciplines' – law, finance, management science and behavioural science (which were initially called 'the four buckets'). Identifying the core disciplines added new focus to the annual conferences and led to the development of spring seminars, in the United States and Europe, to further the education of family business professionals. In turn, in 2001, these seminars led to the creation of a certificate programme with two offerings: a Certificate in Family Business Advising and a Certificate in Family Wealth Advising.

As the field evolves, and as professionals expand their skills, they are also faced with deciding whether or not to make the transition from the role of advisor to that of consultant. An advisor is a professional who remains essentially in his/her original field but brings to the work a wide knowledge of the complexities of family businesses. The professional who becomes a family business or family wealth consultant is one who leaves his/her original profession and works full-time as a consultant to family enterprises.

(See Annex 1 to this chapter: Resources for family business professionals.)

2. What is unique about this profession?

Traditionally, advisors and consultants work in one of the three systems of a family firm (see below), often as if the systems were separate from one another. What distinguishes family business consultants is that they work in the interface of the three systems (circles), within the shaded area. Family business consultants may help a family in conflict decide who does what in the business, define job descriptions, and compensation and benefit packages. Without the skills, training, and experience to maintain a systems perspective and work with all three systems, the consultant will not be able to create lasting changes or any changes will be short-lived. A family business consultant has no choice but to work in the interface of the three interacting circles and must be prepared to deal with issues in each.

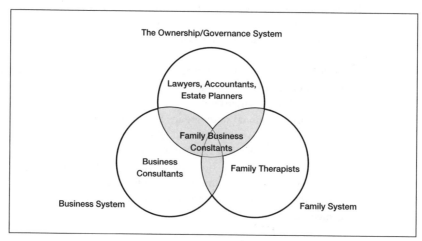

2.1 Systems thinking

Systems thinking is about creating structures to manage the interactions between systems. It involves working with multiple levels of the client system and the complex web of relationships. The family's reality has been constructed over time by their interplay and interactions. As they learn how to build new ways of dealing with each other, they develop more effective methods of solving problems. Much of the work consists of building structures, processes, and procedures, such as family councils, family employment policies, shareholder agreements, and codes of conduct to manage and monitor the interaction between the systems. It involves creating healthy boundaries, not barriers, between the family and the business.

2.2 Process/content

In working with family businesses, the consultant must be able to provide information as well as manage the change process. Content and technical expertise *and* knowledge of change management is needed to work with family businesses. The advisor must know the difference between process and content, understand the importance of each and use not one but *both* as the situation requires. For example, the consultant working with a business family must be able to answer specific questions about the estate plan, transfer of ownership and management issues in the succession process, as well as manage and guide the change process. Most change efforts in family businesses are not likely to succeed unless there is an appropriate combination of content and process, creating outcomes as well as process improvement.

2.3 Interdisciplinary consulting teams

Teams are essential when working with family businesses, since no single professional has all the content information and process skills needed. Improvements on the technical side, such as defining a sound estate plan or clear roles and responsibilities, promote healthier relationships that in turn support good business practices. It is unrealistic, for example, for any one professional to be expected to understand all the complexities of estate planning; but it is critical that, if they work with family businesses, they understand the tax consequences of not having an estate plan, or the potential family consequences arising from trusts and the selection of trustees. 'Process' consultants, such as organisation development consultants and family therapists, should have familiarity with corporate and governance structures, and financial terminology. 'Technical' consultants, such as accountants and lawyers, should be familiar with key psychological issues, such as family developmental life cycles and the impact of crises on family dynamics.

3. Key elements of working in an interdisciplinary team

As indicated throughout this chapter, family business advisors and consultants come to the field from a variety of different professional backgrounds, especially law, finance, behavioural science and management science. Each of these professions has a body of knowledge and provides its practitioners with expertise that is critical to helping family enterprises. The complexities of family businesses can overwhelm those who have worked independently. Nonetheless, since clients are increasingly expecting their advisors to work as a team, it is important that professionals understand and master the benefits of the team approach.

There are several models of teams. These models depend on how often teams work together, the level of coordination, the members' commitment to the team, and how often and how they work together. There can be:

- a *consulting (interdisciplinary) team* – a pre-existing team that is hired by the client;
- a *collaborative (multidisciplinary) team* – advisors from different disciplines who meet in a study group forum, get to know each other's work, and bring one another into client situations on an as-needed basis, or in a 'shadow' consulting function;
- *accidental interaction* – advisors who meet and connect only through the client, and coordinate their efforts only in their work with that particular client; and
- *dysfunctional interaction* – advisors unknown to one another, even if working with the same client, with no coordination.

Despite the recognition that consulting teams offer more comprehensive advice, they also pose challenges. Team members must deal with the following questions before beginning their work together:

- Who will direct the team's activities?
- Who will see that the work is coordinated?
- How will the billing be handled?
- How will differences of opinion be managed?
- Who will liaise with the client?
- How will the client be sold on the interdisciplinary team?
- How will competition for the best idea or the best recommendation be dealt with?
- How will everyone find the time necessary to plan for the tasks of team maintenance as well as meeting the client's needs?

The ethical issues of each profession will also need to be addressed. Here are a few examples of questions that might be raised by each advisor on the team:

- Lawyers will ask: Who is my client?
- Therapists will ask: What are the issues of confidentiality? What are the boundaries? For example, can I have lunch with my clients?
- Advisors from financial fields will ask: What are the financial priorities and how do they fit into the family priorities and values? How are the intangible assets of the family included in the valuation?
- Everyone: What are the consequences of my advice on the other areas of the family business system? For example, what are the consequences of my legal advice on family dynamics?

(See Annex 2: Sample code of ethics for family business advising and consulting.)

4. What roles do advisors play?

Family business consultants play many roles in their work and these include those set out next.

4.1 Coach

As coach, the consultant works with individuals to teach new ways of communicating, setting personal and career goals, and determining whether these goals are compatible with the goals of the family business. A coach may also provide leadership training and assist with problematic relationships, keeping boundaries between family and business clear. Coaching also involves referrals to other professionals, such as a therapist, career counsellor, or financial advisor.

4.2 Conflict manager

In this role, the consultant works with members of smaller groups in the family or business who have the most difficulty working together, or who are trapped in a conflict that blocks the work. This effort will include dialogue building, conflict resolution, negotiations, and improving communications.

4.3 'Container' or holding environment

Introduced by DW Winnicott, who studied the nature of the mother/child bond, the 'holding environment' provides a balance of safety and challenge, of protection and vulnerability for the infant. Eventually, the child internalises these elements and develops a robust sense of self. Key to healthy development, with implications for the ability to grow, learn, work, and love, is the quality of the holding environment. To provide this, the consultant must be able to tolerate ambiguity and anxieties while the system and the individual change.

4.4 Transitional object for change

This role is similar to that of 'container' and requires that the consultant is able to stay calm and manage his/her own feelings during the change process, while encouraging the client and being available for support and encouragement. In order to employ this ability to identify and manage the effect of the family's strong emotional pull, family business consultants learn to use the genogram, a valuable tool (see the next chapter), first for themselves and then for the families they are working with. This role requires an ability to differentiate between normal anxiety associated with change and signs of pathological reactions. For example, if during the succession process the founder's anxiety increases, this is normal. If, however, during this process there are clear signs that the succeeding generation is unable to take over, or the founder continues to sabotage the process by staying actively involved in work, the consultant must be more than a transitional object but must take an active role in helping the family business to find solutions. For example, he or she might assess whether the successors are capable of taking over and willing to do so; or he or she might help the owner to let go and move on.

4.5   Teacher

The family business consultant teaches throughout the process. At one of the first meetings, a short teaching module (Family Business 101) on the uniqueness of a family business and some of the statistics of success and failure help to normalise the situation and assist the family to see that they are not as unusual as they fear. The three-system model is useful for families to see the complexity of their situation. Teaching and education is an integral part of the entire consultation, from issues of healthy communications, fair compensation, and how to run a family council meeting, to setting up a board of advisors or addressing the needs and concerns of non-family business managers.

4.6   Critic

The consultant must ask tough questions – the ones that open communications. ("Why do you think that dad/president doesn't feel he can retire at this point? What was the reasoning behind the salary discrepancies?"). Introducing this concept at the outset is critical. The family should be cautioned that this is a part of the process, as well as creating a safe, structured environment to discuss the difficult issues. Circular questions are a variation on this technique. A circular question encourages systemic thinking, exploring the interconnections and interactions. For example, the above question asked as a circular one would be: "What do you think your daughter imagines is your reasoning for your not retiring?"

4.7   'Process cop'

As soon as work starts with the client, and the consultant has established trust and a set of ground rules for interaction between family members, the consultant continues to help the client by:

- *clarifying communications*. For example, each person speaks for him/herself and differentiates between "what you think, what you feel, and what you know for a fact". The consultant may initially repeat what he/she has heard each individual say;
- *encouraging a positive problem-solving approach*. For example, if there is a disagreement, the family decides at the first meeting how to make decisions. This could be by majority vote, consensus, whoever is most affected decides, and so on. An agreed process for managing conflicts can be a foundation for solving the larger issues of management transition and company ownership;
- *challenging the family's way of perceiving problems and proposing solutions*. This might include regular family council meetings, executive management meetings, learning how to conduct effective meetings, and making fair decisions. By establishing agreed ground rules for interactions, the family will begin to solve their own problems; and
- *creating structures*. Structures are an integral part of the consultation process. They can provide security and predictability for rebuilding the trust that is necessary for agreements and consensus. Building and enforcing structures in each of the systems – family, ownership, and business – generates healthier interactions, enforces healthy boundaries, and offers methods and

mechanisms for planning, solving problems, and managing conflict. The ongoing dialogue, negotiations, compromises, exchanges of ideas, and collaboration between the family and the business should sustain both the firm and the family over the long term. These mechanisms may include an 'off-line' conflict coaching session with the consultant, a fish-bowl dialogue during the meeting with coaching from the consultant, or stopping the conflict with a "deal with that outside the meeting" admonition. In the ownership system, the structures may include an outside board of directors; in the business system, performance reviews for family members and fair compensation mechanisms are other examples.

5. What do contracts look like?

5.1 Engagement letter

The proposal or engagement letter is designed to clarify the relationship and nature of the contract between the consultant and the client. This letter requires the consultant to identify the client – that is, the family business system. The letter should outline the work to be performed and the expectations that the consultant has of the client. The time, money, and effort to be expended are described, along with the method of payment. Finally, the letter should describe who will undertake liaison (administrative, scheduling, meeting, preparations, and so forth) between the client and the consultant. (See Annex 3: Sample engagement letter.)

5.2 Fee structure

How to bill clients is a subject that is not often written about (due to a combination of reasons including vulnerabilities, competition, and criticisms of fee setting), but is discussed frequently by consultants. Because the field of family business consulting comprises professionals from several professions, there are differences in methods of charging for services.

Guidelines for choosing a fee schedule are set out below. Consultants should:

- choose the method that fits their values, skills, bookkeeping, and comfort level;
- be clear with their clients exactly what they are paying for and stick to it. Renegotiation should be around the work and not the fees;
- be consistent with charges; know what the going rate is in the area and, if consultants choose to travel, know what the going rate is elsewhere. Charge for travel time, as well as expenses. This does not mean one size fits all, but rather that a decision will be made in advance as to what fees will be charged for different sizes of companies, geographic areas, and levels of consultancy skill and experience;
- choose cases that they want to work with;
- where money is a concern, discuss with the client and come up with a mutually agreed list of priorities;
- remember that this is about value as well as pricing;
- always be clear about their contributions and why they are agreeing to the

work if they are providing services voluntarily (eg, because the work is challenging, adds to society or community, or will eventually lead to more work and/or bigger contracts); and

- when working in a team, decide beforehand if the team will bill as individuals or as a team. This is usually a function of how the team works together. Teams composed of consultants from the same discipline will generally submit one bill, while individuals in interdisciplinary teams will often submit bills separately.

Consultants will have to decide for themselves what works best for them or their team.

(See Annexes 3 and 4 for billing practices and additional guidelines for fee structures.)

6. Evolving issues

6.1 Public information

The need for clear and intellectually informed public information has followed the development of professional advisors. In the early 1980s one had to persuade the press (and educate it) on the economic impact of family-owned business. Today one can hardly pick up a major newspaper without seeing an article on family-owned business – often describing dramatic and atypical family and business situations! Easy access to information on family business via the internet has also increased awareness of the role of family business in economies worldwide and the various services that have grown up around it.

6.2 Globalisation

If the membership of the Family Firm Institute is an indication of trends worldwide, the family enterprise professional is increasingly a global phenomenon. In 1992, the membership of the FFI was 90% US-based. Today, 35% of the membership is outside the United States and a variety of groups worldwide are trying to create or leverage existing programmes to educate family business professionals.

In addition to globalisation in the field of the family business, there is the globalisation of family members themselves. Younger generations are routinely educated, at least partially, outside their own countries. Moreover, in-laws and extended family members are frequently global in extent.

7. Implications of the new profession for the management of family-owned enterprises

7.1 Unique characteristics

Family business and family wealth advisors and educators are unique in several ways:
- they are committed to an interdisciplinary approach to the client;
- they recognise the need for additional education beyond what was received in the core disciplines; and

- they realise that collaboration among and between advisors, consultants, researchers and educators is necessary if the global economic engine known as the family business is to remain vibrant.

7.2 Pool of uniquely educated advisors

There now exists an ever-growing pool of qualified educator advisors that family enterprises can turn to for advice. These advisors can provide their family enterprise clients with solid, individualised and refined responses to the issues of succession, liquidity, wealth creation and so on. Hopefully in the near future, family enterprises will routinely inquire about the family business professional's educational background, not just their education in the core disciplines or 'buckets' referred to earlier.

8. Conclusion

Today, advising, consulting, education and research relating to the family business are recognised as legitimate, unique professional endeavours worldwide. In addition to the Family Firm Institute (which is currently the only professional association exclusively for family enterprise professionals), there are various professional associations from the core professions that offer specialised tracks in family business advising at their regional and annual conferences, thus further extending the concept of family business advising as a distinct field. In less than 25 years, a profession has developed that provides family enterprises with a wider variety of choices, and with domestic and international advisors, who have had specialised training in the complexities of this field, who understand the importance of collaboration, and who can provide the kind of services these unique systems require.

Annex 1: Resources for family business professionals

Anyone working as a family business professional needs to be acquainted with the resources that have been created to extend and maintain the field. Selected lists follow next.

Books

- Aronoff, Craig, Joseph Astrachan, John Ward, *Family Business Sourcebook*, 3rd edn (Family Enterprise Publishers, 2002)
- Astrachan, Joseph and Kristi S McMillan, *Conflict and Communication in the Family Business* (Family Enterprise Publishers, 2003)
- Bork, David, Dennis Jaffe, Sam Lane, Leslie Dashew, Quentin Heisler, *Working with Family Businesses, A Guide for Professionals* (John Wiley & Sons/Jossey Bass Publishers, 2003)
- Carlock, Randel and John Ward, *Strategic Planning for Family Business* (Macmillan, 2001)
- Gersick, Kelin, *The Succession Workbook: Continuity planning for family foundations* (Council on Foundations, 2000)
- Gersick, Kelin (ed), *The Best of FBR II* (Family Firm Institute, 2006)

- Gersick, Kelin, John Davis, Marion McCollom Hampton, Ivan Lansberg, *Generation to Generation: Life cycles of the family business* (Harvard Business School Press, 1997)
- Hilburt-Davis, Jane and W Gibb Dyer, *Consulting to Family Businesses: A practical guide to contracting, assessment and implementation* (Jossey Bass/Pfeiffer, division of Wiley, 2003)
- Kaslow, Florence, *Handbook of Family Business and Family Business Consultation: A global perspective* (Haworth Press, 2006)
- Lansberg, Ivan, *Succeeding Generations: Realizing the dream of families in business* (Harvard Business School Press, 1999)
- Leach, Peter, *Family Businesses: The essentials* (Profile Books, 2007)
- McGoldrick, M, R Gerson and S Shellenberger, *Genograms: Assessment and interventions* (Norton Publishers, 1999)
- Miller, D and I Le Breton Miller, *Managing for the Long Run: Lessons in competitive advantage from great family businesses* (Harvard Business School, 2005)
- O'Hara, William, *Centuries of Success: Lessons from the world's most enduring family businesses* (Family Business Consulting Group, 2004)
- Ward, John, *Perpetuating the Family Business: 50 lessons learned from long lasting, successful families in business* (Palgrave Macmillan, 2004).

Conceptual resources

As part of any educational programme relating to family business and family wealth advising, advisors and consultants will be exposed to these key concepts, which will underpin their work with family enterprises:
- systems theory;
- three-circle model: working at the interfaces;
- consulting model;
- interdisciplinary mindsets;
- cross-generational thinking; and
- genograms.

Organisations

In the last 25 years, a number of organisations have grown up around the world for the education of family business professionals. Key organisations are as follows:
- Family Firm Institute (FFI): www.ffi.org
- Canadian Association of Family Enterprise (CAFÉ): www.cafecanada.ca
- Attorneys for Family-Held Enterprise (Afhe): www.afhe.com
- International Family Enterprise Academy (IFERA): www.ifera.org
- Family Business Australia (FBA) (www.fba-me.org)
- Grand Valley State University: www.fobi.gvsu.edu

Journals

FFI was fortunate in that, early in its existence (1988), it secured Jossey Bass as the publisher for *Family Business Review* (*FBR*). This internationally known publisher provided instant credibility for the new journal. Now, 20 years later, *FBR* remains the only scholarly journal in the world dedicated exclusively to family business research. It is currently published by Sage. In 2007, its international reach was extended by the publication (in Spanish) of the *Clasicos de FBR en Espanol*.

Although the Family Business Review remains the only scholarly journal in the world devoted exclusively to issues and opportunities relating to family-owned enterprise, research on family enterprise is now entering its second generation as other high-quality journals feature articles and issues on family business and family wealth advising (eg *International Small Business Journal, Turnaround Management Association Journal, The Journal of Corporate Renewal, Journal of Entrepreneurship, Journal of Family and Economic Issues, Harvard Business Review*).

Family Business Magazine (see www.familybusinessmagazine.com) and *Families in Business* (see www.campdenpublishing.com/default.asp?ptid=3&pid=13&pgid=1) are two other relevant publications.

Annex 2: Sample code of ethics for family business advising and consulting

Code of professional ethics (© Family Firm Institute 2001)
Adopted April 2001

Purpose
Members of the Family Firm Institute are obligated to maintain the highest standards of professionalism. Members of FFI come from a variety of professions of origin, many with their own codes of ethics. Membership in the Family Firm Institute, however, represents a willingness to adhere to the standards of professional conduct outlined below. When a member's specific professional discipline's code of ethics calls for a standard of conduct different from the following, whichever code or guideline is the more stringent or more extensive or demands the higher standard and sensitivity will apply.

Clients
At the outset of an engagement, the family business advisor will state in writing whose interests he or she is representing during the course of the engagement. Should the need arise to revise the definition of 'client' during the engagement, this need will be communicated to and negotiated with all appropriate parties and confirmed in writing.

Members, their organisations and professional associates will keep client information and the identity of the client confidential and will not disclose it without the written consent of the client.

Professional conduct
- Members will not represent their education, training, experience, professional credentials and competence, or areas of skill and expertise in a deceptive or misleading manner.
- When a member refers a client to another party, the member will disclose to

the client the nature of any business relationship between them or their organisation and whether there will be any referral fee or other fee sharing.

- Members agree not to misrepresent their affiliation with the Family Firm Institute, nor to imply that being a member of FFI holding a Certificate in Family Business Advising implies either credentialing or endorsement by FFI.
- Members will avoid real or perceived conflicts of interest whenever possible and will disclose them to all affected parties.
- Members have an obligation to provide a client with all information obtained in the course of conducting their engagement which is pertinent to the decisions the client is contemplating.
- Members have a duty to keep current in their professional practices through self-study and regular attendance at family business-related conferences and courses.
- Members, in their professional activities, will treat all persons fairly regardless of their race, creed, color, national origin, religion, gender, age, marital status, sexual preference, physical condition and/or appearance.
- Members will recognise and respect intellectual property rights including providing specific acknowledgment of the original authorship and source when publishing or publicly representing another person's work.
- Members will assist other members in their professional development, where possible and appropriate, and support them in complying with this Code of Professional Ethics.
- Members will respect the development and growth of the field of family business and will take positive steps to promote the field.

Fees

Members will disclose in writing and at the outset of every engagement the basis of their fees and expenses and provide an estimate of the total cost of the service whenever possible.

Research

Members who do research will carry out the research with respect and concern for the dignity and welfare of the people who participate. It is the members' responsibility to be adequately informed, and abide by, relevant laws and regulations regarding the conduct of research with human participants. Individuals entering into research must do so voluntarily and with adequate information.

Annex 3: Sample engagement letter

Dear: XXXX

It was a pleasure meeting with you on XXXX. At your request, I am enclosing/attaching a proposal for a work plan specifically tailored to your needs. The purpose of this is to outline a step-by-step approach for our work together.

The context

Your company was founded by your father approximately 55 years ago and continues to be a family owned and managed business. You are beginning to plan for the process of transitioning to the next generation. Your father's present intention is to step down in 2015, if all goes well. You were clear that the success of the business is a priority. To deal with succession, I recommend that you consider a combination of initiatives in order to deal with the present and plan for the future.

The issues that you are raising and facing present an excellent opportunity to examine what is important to the family and the firm's future, and to use this time to make the appropriate changes going forward. You six are to be commended for undertaking and seeking assistance in this process. Any consultants you engage should have the education, experience, and skills in working within the boundaries of the personal, business, and governance systems; to be sensitive to family issues as well as business and ownership issues. To address your issues, I have found it useful and effective to think of the consultation as a process (not an event) and should be considered in phases. And I believe that, for the best chances of success, a commitment of time and resources is critical.

I suggest the following for your planning process.

Phase I Assessment, planning and design

1. Individual interviews and data gathering

This would include a series of individual interviews with the six of you; your uncle who is an executive in the company; your spouses; the three other non-family executives; and the five non-family members of the Board of Directors. Concurrent with these meetings, I would review any relevant material – for example, any previous consultants' recommendations and reports; the organisational chart; the family agreements book that you referred to; and relevant financial material. This, along with the interviews, allows me to have as complete a picture as possible, in order to build a realistic action plan and time line. It is important to have this 'whole systems view' before we move to the next phase.

2. Summary report

After the interviews and material review, I will prepare a brief summary report with recommendations that will serve as a guide for our next steps together. It will also serve as a working document for the short-term and long-term steps in the consulting process. We will together review this report prior to any implementation of it. As I mentioned, this is a collaborative process between us and we will continue to evaluate the progress as we go along.

Phase II Implementation of proposed changes

All of the work in Phase II is determined by the assessment and planning session(s) in Phase I. It may include but not be limited to:

- developing a family council;
- facilitated discussions between generations 1 and 2;

- establishing an objective, fair process for choosing the successor(s);
- facilitating the succession process and getting a buy-in from the family;
- keeping the process on time and on track: setting and implementing the established goals;
- if needed, managing the relationships among family members before, during and after this process in order to preserve the family values, culture, and legacy and manage effective communications; and
- coordinating efforts with other advisors.

Phase III Follow-up and assessment

It is difficult to establish an exact timeframe that would allow for an effective follow-up, once we agree that the work is accomplished. Typically within 18 months, I find it useful to convene a meeting to review the progress. This component of the work will assess the overall accomplishments and reinforce positive changes that have occurred. It would also be a time to decide on the next steps, if any.

Fees and billing arrangements

The fees for my professional services are XXX per day (XXX per hour) plus expenses. Travel time is billed at half rate. I estimate that the scope of services for the *first phase* outlined to be between XXX and XXX. The analysis of working time is broken down as follows:

- Initial interviews (XX family members; XX non-family managers; XX advisors) – XX hours (approximately 1.5 hrs/interview);
- Review of written material – XX hours;
- Analysis and preparation of Summary Report – XX hours;
- Feedback and planning session – XX hours.

This is an estimate and includes all activities related to my professional services outlined above and all administrative services, report preparation, minor reproduction and general phone and mailing expenses. I do not add any additional administrative or management fees to the project budget or expenses, so your resources are used for the specific work of this engagement. The change process – in organisations in which family and business interact in particular, where so much is at stake – does not usually happen in a linear manner. It is necessary, however, to understand fully the issues and perspectives and to build a sound data-based foundation in order to be prepared for surprises, emerging events, and seemingly random occurrences. This plan builds that foundation.

My standard practice is to request a retainer that will be applied to the first bill(s). Therefore, to get started, I ask that you pay to XXX an initial retainer fee of XXX. Upon receipt of the signed engagement letter and the retainer, I will begin the work. I invoice monthly in relation to time and expenses incurred in the engagement. (A finance charge of 1.5% per month will be added to invoices that are outstanding beyond 30 days.)

Indemnification clause
Place for the indemnification clause.

Discussion
I hope that this outline provides you with my thoughts on the process and the means by which we could proceed. To get deep and lasting changes, I have found the best way is not to skip any of the necessary steps. This proposed work plan involves consultation that includes both process and content. Each is important in developing an improvement process and getting all involved to 'buy in' to the work. For that reason and, because I consider the family business system to be my/our client, I request that all of you sign below. You are to be commended on your willingness to look ahead strategically for the next steps in both the life of the business and the family, and to move forward in a thoughtful, strategic, and timely manner. I welcome the opportunity to work with you. Please indicate your approval of this proposal by returning this signed letter of engagement and a retainer of XX (payable to XX). Please call me if you have any questions.

Sincerely,

Annex 4: Billing practices
(Adapted from Hilburt-Davis and Dyer, *Consulting to Family Businesses* – see Annex 1)

	Method	*Advantages*	*Risks*
Per hour	The client pays for each hour you work. Adopted from the legal, accounting, and therapy professions.	Clear; simple; amount of time can be renegotiated; the work for the client, either face to face or the pre- or post-work, is recorded and paid for. Some clients feel	limited in their contacts, especially if money is concerned, ie the clock is running.
Per day	For each day of work, the consultant is paid a day's pay	Clear; simple; paid for the days worked for and with the client.	Same as above; the amount of the initial contract often has to be renegotiated since family businesses are rarely simple to fix. *continued*

	Method	Advantages	Risks
Per project	The client pays for a certain project or amount of work, ie a family retreat, a family business assessment, or building an outside board.	Based on the consultant's experience, an educated guesstimate of the amount it will take to do a certain piece of work for the client. Client knows upfront what the project will cost.	Consultant is paid the same amount no matter how many hours of work to finish the project. With family businesses, with unique and complex systems, this is often more time, rather than less.
Retainer	The consultant is paid a given amount for a certain period of time to be available whether or not the client uses the services during this period. Should specify a certain number of months, for example.	Gives client access to the consultant and services; usually happens after the consultant has a proven track record of effectiveness; good if consultant is involved in several projects or client voices concern over consulting fees or client wants priority time with you: meter is not running.	Consultant can be overused without built-in agreements about the best use of time and talents; should specify "subject to mutually convenient schedules" and understood that client gives as much notice as possible. *continued*

	Method	Advantages	Risks
Per product	The client pays for a product (workbook, etc).	Simple; clear; provides additional income from a product that is separate from the work and time spent with the client	Under or over priced; appropriate training or explanation of product is not heeded or given.
Results based	Based on output, rather than amount of time worked with and for the client. Measurable results agreed to at time of contracting. Results can be in sales, profit, or cultural, ie number of new ideas from teams, promotions from within.	Consultant participates in the improvements or gains in the organisation; meter is not running. Cost to client is fixed at the beginning; output or improvement is arrived at collaboratively with client; builds the relationship; defines the goals clearly. It is a great exercise for the family, as well as the business, to objectify results.	Results may be a moving target in the family business, with so many variables and an emotional component; sometimes difficult to define output; results may change as the consultation progresses; results have to be objective, not subjective. (An interesting discussion of 'value-based fees' can be found in Alan Weiss' The *Ultimate Consultant*, Jossey Bass, 2001)

Understanding the business family

Christine Blondel
The Wendel International Centre for Family Enterprise at INSEAD

"We had lived in perfect harmony for years, and suddenly we were all fighting, destroying the family and putting the business at risk."

"What is nice in our family is that we can disagree at work, and still be on very good terms on personal levels."

Good family relationships are a real asset for the family business. But questions of ownership, power and perceived lack of fairness can lead to painful and dangerous conflicts. In my work as a family business consultant, whatever the situation at hand, my job first and foremost consists of understanding the dynamics at play in the family and improving communication.

1. Mapping family history: genograms

When working with a family, a first step is to understand its history, as this helps explain current relationships. People take certain stands because they view the world from a particular position. This position can be very different from one family member to another. Genograms are a sort of family tree which is very useful to map the family history and understand relationships.[1]

Let us use a real family business case to draw the family genogram, and start understanding the family relationships in this case. The case is set in the United States:[2]

When Laura hung up the phone, she could hardly believe what her mother, Anne, had just told her. Without prior warning, Anne was asking her children to give their approval to sell the business within two weeks! A large company had just made an unsolicited offer and Anne felt that the opportunity could not be missed. Laura was astonished and felt betrayed ...

Laura was a member of the third generation of the Bolles' family, who had managed a beautiful hotel in the South of the United States for almost 80 years. Her grandfather, Charles, had bought the Resort to provide a milder climate for his wife who suffered from tuberculosis. However, she died shortly afterwards and he remarried – this time to a pianist,

---

1   I owe much to professors Manfred Kets de Vries and Randel Carlock, who both held lively classes on the topic of family relationships and the family business at INSEAD. With Liz Florent, they authored the book *Family Business on the Couch* (Wiley, 2007).
2   Summary of the case "The Resort in Pueblo Valley", INSEAD case by Christine Blondel (purchase possible through ECCH). The case was awarded the ECCH 2008 award in the Entrepreneurship category.

Maggy, also a strong woman (Laura's grandmother). But Charles died five years after his wedding with Maggy, leaving a one-year-old child, Charles Junior. Charles Junior was raised on the property, which Maggy managed with the help of non-family managers. When he grew up, he developed a passion for planes, studied engineering and worked in the aerospace industry. At age 70, Maggy called him, asking him to come and help her with the Resort – otherwise she would sell the business.

Charles Junior listened to family loyalty and pride and joined the business, putting his visionary mind and energy into renewing the property. He had a strong sense of business and was highly regarded in the business community. Like his father, he married twice, his first wife having died tragically. But unlike his father, he had four children, two with his first wife (Charlie and Kathy) and two with his second wife (Laura and Jessie).

The drawing below, called a genogram, is a way to show the family tree with some codes to help 'read' the family history.

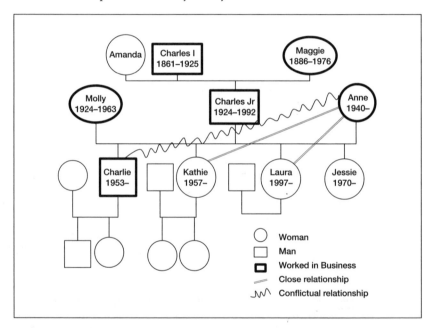

The dates in the genogram show that Charles Junior grew up without a father (Charles Senior died in 1925; Charles Junior was born in 1924). We can see that Charlie and Anne have a conflicted relationship, for which the genogram provides a possible explanation: Charles Junior remarried only 13 months after the death of his first wife (Charlie's mother), when Charlie was only 11 years old.

Charles Junior was unable to talk about his succession with his children, and died of a heart attack on the day when he showed the Resort to a potential non-family manager.

His own experience of succession was simple: his mother had taken over when his father died. Years later, she had called him, her only child, when she started to feel tired. Without siblings, he had not experienced the difficult path of having to decide who would take over leadership, and how to distribute roles. Faced with his own succession, he had to invent everything – and in effect left the task to his wife.

Charlie seemed to have particular expectations in terms of succession, given his position as oldest child and only boy. He was very disappointed to learn that he inherited equal shares with his sisters – worse, his father had initially planned to give him more shares but had levelled the distribution between the siblings without making it known. Charlie was certainly unhappy to discover that the majority of shares and all voting rights went to his stepmother Anne.

History reinvents itself, and leadership, for the second generation, went to the leader's widow.

Anne managed the business, Charlie continued to work in the business, Laura and Kathy stayed involved in advisory roles. Charlie and Anne's relationship was tense and when Anne received an offer to sell the Resort to a large hotel chain, she was ready to accept.

The business was ultimately sold, and it is quite possible that the difficulty of the relationship between Charlie and Anne, added to a tradition of poor communication, played an important role in the sale.

2.   Using genograms in consulting assignments

When I work with business families, I like drawing a genogram of the family from the creation of the business, and linking it to the history of the business and of the ownership. I often start the genogram during my first meeting with the family, asking people present to position themselves on the family tree with post-it notes on a big paperboard. During the course of the interviews with the family members, I complete the genogram. This first step outlines important points in the history of the business family: *

- *Number of generations since the start of the business:* the questions at hand will be quite different whether the business is in its first to second generation, with two parents and three children – or in its third to fourth generation, with 10 cousins and 30 second cousins.
- *Culture of the family:* the family culture can be reflected, among other things, by the number of children, the religion (some families produce several priests or nuns), studies, entrepreneurship and other factors.
- *Family preferences:* in some families the older son is expected to be the successor. Or the only daughter may be treated as the "little darling". This has a clear influence on relationships in the family business.
- *Age and situation differences:* a significant age difference between siblings or cousins can give them a very different perception of their position in the generations. Similarly, if some cousins have lost their parents while others still have them, they may feel totally differently in terms of their

responsibilities and autonomy, which can create conflict.

In the A family, the family members were Luigi and Anna, brother and sister, whose parents had both died of cancer, and Paul and George, their cousins, whose father was leading the business. Because they no longer had their parents, Luigi and Anna wanted to have a say in the management of their affairs (they were well beyond 40), while Paul and George felt that this showed a lack of respect for their own father.

- *Life cycles:* each family member is in a different stage in his or her life cycle. Those in their thirties are busy building their families and careers. Those in their sixties and seventies are facing the issue of their retirement – often bringing that of their mortality. And members in their forties and fifties may wonder whether the paths they have taken so far are the ones they wish to follow for the second part of their lives.

- *Composition of the family – number of children and gender, birth order:* in previous generations, and in some cultures, the older son was expected to take over the business. However, it often happens that a younger son, or a daughter, actually has the ability and the drive to lead. This change of patterns can create unease in the family.

In the very traditional European B family, the CEO had three daughters and no son, and had to reconsider the past paths of succession.

- *Divorces and stepchildren:* as we saw in the case of the Resort family, a divorce has a significant influence on family dynamics, and relationships between stepchildren and stepparents can be a challenge.

- *'Branches':* some family members have a very strong perception of belonging to a certain branch (ie, descendants of one of the founder's children). In some countries, separate family holdings contribute to the separation of the branches, which almost look at each other as different families. This can be detrimental to the business when the branches expect a proportional representation on the board of directors, but also in operational jobs in the business, sometimes regardless of the performance of family members.

- *Presence of the 'chief emotional officer':*[3] the grandmother, the mother, a cousin or a sister may play the role of the 'glue' for the family, organising family gatherings and ensuring that family members feel comfortable. In some families, a divorce, a grandmother's death, a mother's lack of interest, or any other reason, may deprive the family of this role – sometimes with dire consequences for the quality of relationships.

- *Presence of a 'wise man':* some families have a non-family person playing the role of a confidant to all family members. This person can be the family office manager or a former employee. He or she knows the family well and has earned its trust over the years.

- *Existence of family members who exited from ownership:* the family history may have led to the exit of one or several family member from ownership, and to the de facto exclusion of his branch from the business family. Sometimes several versions exist of the same story, as in the example below.

---

3   *Source:* Randel Carlock (see n1).

In the C family, older brother Alain sold his shares 50 years ago. Some members of the family believe that Alain sold because he needed money to sustain an expensive lifestyle. Other members of the family believe that Alain sold because his younger brother wanted sole leadership in the business and was keen to buy his shares at a discounted price. The family is divided over whether or not to offer Alain's children the option to become shareholders.

- *Networks and loyalties:* some family members can belong to common networks (eg, a football club, a hunting group, a specific community and so on), which create closer ties. Special bonds can also exist between godparents and their godchildren in some families.

- *Adoption:* in some families adoption is used as a solution for succession and for name transmission. In other families, adopted children are not considered as 'full' blood-family members.

   In the D family, the grandfather adopted his grandson to give him his name and to designate him as his successor in the business.

- *Other family events:* handicapped children, miscarriages, early deaths, addiction, violence, abuse, extramarital relationships or children – all these have a big influence on family relationships and are not always discussed in the open.

Often, and particularly in the case of sensitive family issues, I like to discuss the genogram with a family therapist to understand the implications on family dynamics and on my work. The therapist is not in contact with the family, but works with me on the analysis of the anonymous genogram.

3. Application: looking at succession in an Indian family firm[4]

In this Indian family, two brothers, Ashok and Krishnakant developed a tool business with their father. Each of the two brothers has two living children.

Krishnakant is a mild-mannered man, heads the finance and government interface, and acts as the family patriarch. His brother Ashok is an engineer by profession, is widely respected, and heads production and commercial. He joined the business halfway through his undergraduate engineering studies. He seems to place business before family.

Shravan, the older cousin, is 38 years old. He was educated in Mumbai, with a degree in mechanical engineering. He was very involved with the plants from childhood. His dream was to pursue a PhD in the United Kingdom but his father and uncle visited him there and told him that he was needed in the business; hence he could at most complete his Masters before coming back to India. He joined the family business at age 23, after his Master of Science in the UK. He is now a successful production manager (five manufacturing plants) and reports to his uncle Ashok. He has some frustrations because he thinks that radical change is needed in the business and feels that the brothers are not receptive to his ideas.

Binal, his sister, moved to the United States with her husband. Both are consultants with international firms, and have no intention of returning.

---

4   Summary of the case "Niraj: successor's dilemma in an Indian family firm" by Niraj, Tom, Christine Blondel and Ludo Van der Heyden, INSEAD case (available through ECCH).

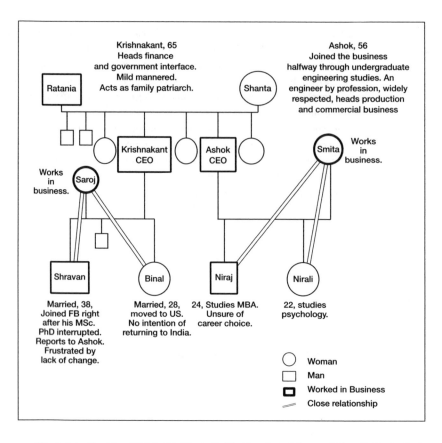

Krishnakant, 65
Heads finance
and government interface.
Mild mannered.
Acts as family patriarch.

Ashok, 56
Joined the business
halfway through undergraduate
engineering studies. An
engineer by profession, widely
respected, heads production
and commercial business

Ratania

Shanta

Krishnakant
CEO

Ashok
CEO

Smita — Works in business.

Works
in
business. — Saroj

Shravan

Binal

Niraj

Nirali

Married, 38,
Joined FB right
after his MSc.
PhD interrupted.
Reports to Ashok.
Frustrated by
lack of change.

Married, 28,
moved to US.
No intention of
returning to India.

24, Studies MBA.
Unsure of
career choice.

22, studies
psychology.

○ Woman
□ Man
■ Worked in Business
═ Close relationship

Niraj, Ashok's older child, is 24. He studied in Mumbai at the prestigious India Institute of Technology and in Maryland, and worked one year in a high-tech firm before taking an MBA in Europe. He was less involved than Shravan with the business in childhood – there was more prosperity when he grew up. He is getting along very well with his uncle Krishnakant. His father and uncle told him that they expected him in the business, but Niraj is unsure of what he wishes to do next. He feels some pressure to join, and at the same time is attracted in international careers in consulting. He is concerned that he may be too young and inexperienced and that father and uncle may have unreasonable expectations. He is also afraid that he might not be able to work with Shravan (potential conflicts).

His sister Nirali, 22, is studying psychology.

Saroj and Smita, the brothers' wives, are involved in the business.

The case shows no particular family issue. All children were raised in the same house and relationships are warm. The genogram helps us look at the dynamics of succession. The two brothers are 10 years apart, which should allow Krishnakant to retire and leave Ashok in charge. Because of his retirement, Krishnakant is worried about having sufficient income for him and members of the family. He is starting to be risk averse. His son Shravan sacrificed his dream of a PhD to join the family business and is all the more frustrated when he feels that the elders do not take his suggestions seriously.

Niraj is 14 years younger than his cousin. The family he was raised in is not the same as Shravan's, in the sense that the business was successful and the family was more affluent. His father and uncle ask him to join the business, but he has more freedom to choose another career first. Niraj is afraid of not getting along with his cousin if he joins the business. When he starts communicating with him, he realises the pressures his cousin has been through and starts to appreciate him. However, in a first step he decides to work in an international consulting firm.

In Indian society, daughters are expected to join their husband's family, hence they are not expected to take a role in the family business. However, we see that the wives have an active role, supporting their husbands in tasks requiring a large amount of trust.

Looking at the genogram together may help the different members of the family understand each other's viewpoints. It is a great way to map the family history, and to visualise why the family is in its current stage.

4. The evolution of business families: changing patterns[5]

The story of the Danssen family shows how succession decisions can lead to family conflicts and feelings of unfairness.

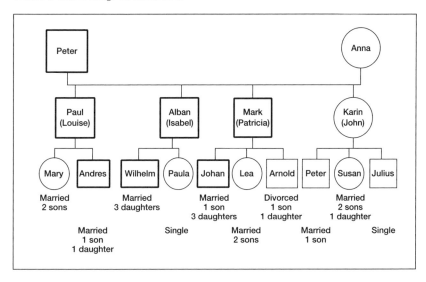

The business had been started after World War II by Peter Danssen, who had had the idea of importing hearing aids from the United States. His initial motivation was to help his mother, who was losing her hearing; but he soon realised that there was a market for the devices in Denmark. The business grew very successfully and he was joined by his three sons who took different responsibilities, learning to work as a team: Paul worked in manufacturing (once they had started their own production), Alban in finance and

---

5   Extracts of the case "The Danssen family: initiating family governance" by Christine Blondel, INSEAD (available through ECCH).

administration, and Mark in marketing and sales. Mark demonstrated outstanding leadership abilities and took over from Peter in what seemed to be a smooth transition.

Their sister Karin was not involved in the management of the company. Peter decided to give more shares to his sons (30% each), and to give Karin 10% of the company shares and compensation in the form of real estate.

When the time came for the third generation to join the business, the brothers felt that they should keep one management position for each of their branches (each branch being composed of their respective descendants). Hence, Andres, Wilhem and Johan, the eldest sons of Paul, Alban, and Mark, joined the business and learnt from their fathers and uncles. Wilhem proved to be an excellent leader, while Johan had a great interest and talent in human resources, and Andres in production like his father.

In 2002, Wilhem, aged 44, officially took the position of CEO. Paul, Alban and Mark retired from operations but remained as board members.

While management had been transferred to the third generation, ownership had not, and there were a lot of unexpressed questions in the family about how it should be transmitted. The second-generation owner-managers felt that the family managers needed to have more shares in order to be able to take decisions more easily.

The third generation had different viewpoints. They could see that Karin's branch felt a bit like second-class citizens as far as business decisions were concerned. The business had expanded in significantly greater proportion than the value of the real estate she had been given, and though the latter was much more tradable, Karin's children felt that they were deprived of opportunities that their cousins had access to. Aside from the potential issue of wealth, they could not envisage working in the business, despite having successful careers, given the past pattern of succession.

Johan could feel frustration among other members of the family as well. His younger brother Arnold had never quite accepted the fact that he did not have a chance to work in the business. Wilhem's younger sister Paula had mentioned on many occasions that she would have loved to work in the company – she was a very successful executive in a famous Danish design company.

Perhaps it was time for the third generation to revisit the rules established by their predecessors?

In many business families, past patterns of succession are similar to that of the Danssen family. Daughters received real estate and liquid assets, while sons received shares in the business. In the Danssen case, Karin's family is in the uncomfortable position of being owners without really having a say – no position in the board of directors, no position in operations. In most families, the issue is not so much the distribution of shares (when daughters were compensated with other forms of assets), but the lack of empowerment that comes as a consequence and the feeling of not having a voice.

Giving all members a voice, as we will see further, is the first starting point for solving the issues. The Danssen family held a family meeting where they asked everyone to list their issues, they created work groups to work on governance, communication and values, asked an external moderator to interview all family members in order to bring to the open the family members' feelings, and appointed

Karin's daughter, Susan, to the board. They also changed the rules for family members to work in the business.

5.   Fairness and families: distributive justice, procedural justice

A family lost more in attorneys' fees than the value of their inheritance, even though the latter amounted to several hundred million dollars.

A family member preferred to sell his shares for a lower price to a competitor, rather than selling to his brother.

In family firms, where money and power are in ample supply to fuel conflicts, the issue of their distribution is essential. We have seen a case of family members splitting a painting and its frame in order to distribute them. Some tests show that people take the risk of losing everything, rather than let a competitor beat them!

Faced with decisions regarding ownership or leadership in the family firm, one is inevitably confronted with issues of justice and fairness. These questions arise in any human context, but are of particular importance in the context of family firms. Family firms are at the same time places where fairness is greatly needed, and yet where it is often difficult to assess. Is it fair to manage the business because one was born first, and thus ready to take responsibilities earlier? Is an equal split of the shares among shareholders fairer than giving the one who is going to manage the firm a majority of these shares?

These questions are of significance to most family firms. There is rarely an obvious single answer. However, families will live with their choices for years, if not generations, and unhappy family members will lose commitment and sometimes even seek retribution for decisions to which they were subjected and which they perceived as being unfair.

Our work at INSEAD[6] focuses on issues of fairness in family firms and we argue that the fairness of the process through which the distribution takes place is even more important than the fairness of the distribution. Fair process can guide advisors to family firms in their approach. We would like to expand on notions of fairness.

Three types of *distributive* justice are usually referred to:

- *Equality:* the outcome is evenly distributed between all. Equality is often used as a basis for distribution for wealth succession, with the same amount of wealth given to each child. More generally, equality is typically the norm among shareholders: rights and duties are the same for all owners (and proportional to their share), regardless of their business acumen.
- *Equity:* those who deserve more receive more. This notion underlines most career management systems. Those who perform better will have higher salaries and more promotions than others. Equity is generally the norm in business.

---

6   "Fair process: striving in justice in family business", Van der Heyden, Blondel, Carlock, in *Family Business Review* 2005. The article received the 2006 FBN research honours for the best published research article on family business practices. We here reproduce extracts from the article.

- *Needs:* what people receive is based on their needs. This would typically be applied in a family, where parents try and give to their children what they need: for instance, more time to the one who has learning difficulties, more money to pay for art lessons to a gifted family member, and so on.

There is rarely one single right way to distribute outcome, and often discussions about outcomes require the resolution of different perceptions about the way distributive justice should be applied. Moreover, in family firms, the interaction of ownership, family and business makes it all the more complex. The difficulty of exercising distributive justice underlines the importance of paying attention to the fairness of the process – rather than focusing on the fairness of the outcome. One of the key elements of fair process (further described below) is to engage involved people and seek their input. Hence, they are more motivated, better solutions can be found and will be better implemented. Importantly, a decision reached by a fair process will be better accepted by participants, even if it is not favourable to them.

Research done in courts of justice has shown that the fairness of the procedure played a major role in people's assessment of the fairness of a trial's outcome. These ideas were applied to other organisational settings. We posit that many of the common difficulties faced by family firms are rooted in a lack of *fairness* in decision-making *processes* governing these business families and their associated firms. Conversely, improvements in fairness can be expected to improve the firm's performance as well as the commitment and satisfaction of those involved with the firm, whether as managers, owners, or family members.

6. Fair process: a framework

We offer a dual framework for characterising fair process in family firms. This construct encompasses both a clear description of the steps defining the decision-making process, and five characteristics these steps ought to possess in order for the process to be perceived as fair.

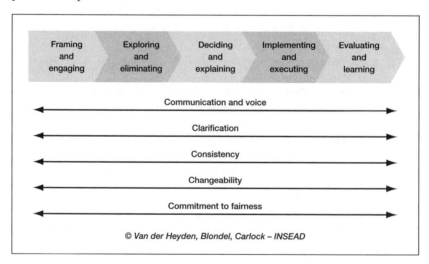

© Van der Heyden, Blondel, Carlock – INSEAD

The five characteristics are described further thus:

- *Framing and engaging:* the first step of a well-formulated managerial process consists in understanding the various facets of the issue at hand. The viewpoints of those responsible for the issue or having a stake in it, and consultation with individuals who have expertise on the issue, are particularly relevant at this stage and ought to be probed.
- *Exploring and eliminating:* the second step consists of creatively generating a list of available options, and evaluating the implications on the constituencies of the options thus generated.
- *Deciding and explaining:* having examined the pluses and minuses of the various options, the process needs to come to closure by selecting a decision for implementation. This is also where the manager will set expectations with regard to the effective execution of the decisions reached.
- *Implementing and executing:* the process needs to include the translation of the decision into action.
- *Evaluating and learning:* one of the recent contributions of the decision-making literature has been to underline the importance of evaluation as an integral part of decision-making process. Short of executing this step, there will be no learning over time, improvement will be limited, and mistakes risk being repeated.

The full framework results from the introduction of fairness characteristics in the description of the process. Five principles are proposed that, taken jointly, aim to characterise fair process in family-firm planning and decision making. These are:

- *Communication and voice:* the first principle of fairness in decision-making processes is giving those concerned with the outcome of a decision a voice, so that they can have their views heard. This will enrich the generation of options, and increase engagement and motivation.
- *Clarity:* an important family business theme is the need to clarify individual, family, and management expectations in a way that includes all family members, in-laws, and non-family managers. To be sure that they understand each other's goals, families must gather facts and evidence, and disseminate accurate information. The clarity of the 'rules of the game' is also important.
- *Consistency:* consistency is particularly important in the context of a family business, to counteract perceived or real feelings of injustice. Consistency means in particular that the same rules will apply to all, and over time.
- *Changeability:* all family businesses must be prepared to address changing business conditions, new information, or family life-cycle transitions. For instance, what was true for the former generation may not be relevant for the next generation.
- *Commitment to fairness:* A real effort to improve processes continuously, to listen and to speak sincerely, to involve family members in the preparation of meetings and to send minutes to all is important for fair process to be carried out.

Having a charter, or family 'law' can be an important support of fair process. As in a court of law, where decisions are taken within the framework of the law, so in a family, decisions are eased by the existence of family policies. These typically cover careers of family managers, ownership rules including dividends, selling and valuation of shares, and even a statement of family values.

Best practices observed in successful family firms increase fair process. Family meetings increase communication and clarity. The 'outside world', be it represented by outside board members, non-family managers or employment outside the family firm, forces consistency and may also induce change. Finally, family policies ensure clarity and consistency, and provide the necessary framework for reference.

7. Fair process in consulting to business families

My consulting practice is based on the application of fair process. Very often, issues arise in families because of the absence of fair process. The leaders of the family manage the business without realising the importance of 'managing the family'. Family owners generally trust the leaders; and if they ask questions, they may receive the comment: "You do not trust me". When generational change arrives, or if the business is not performing very well, any lack of clarity and communication from the past can give way to strong expressions of resentment. It is important then, as in the case of the Danssen family, to understand that patterns from the past may have been justified but need to be changed.

A possible consulting approach is to follow the steps of fair process. After a meeting with the family, I start individual interviews – if the family is very large, these can take place in smaller groups – and listen to family members. With their input, I report back to the family, and we start, together, to list the next steps and engage family members in groups to actually work on the issues together. This usually creates a very positive dynamic, where everybody feels that his or her voice counts. It does not mean that any family member can make comments on the business operations, but that they can participate in the construction of a more balanced business family; they can give input to design the governance and to write the family agreements; they can each contribute to closer family relationships.

Tools enabling participation in family meetings include the use of a code of conduct for the meeting (desired behaviour to have a respectful and fruitful meeting), the use of a 'talking stick' (the one handling the stick is talking, others listen – I use a teddy bear), post-it notes to post everyone's ideas, and evaluation forms capturing the main idea that each participant took out of the meeting.

Last but not least, consultants are usually called in by one person but can make it clear that they work for the good of the whole family and the business.

8. The risk of transference

Consultants must be aware of their own stories to avoid projecting them onto the client family. For instance, someone whose family sold the business may be influenced either to push a family to sell, or to push them to keep the business, depending on how this particular advisor perceived the sale of the business in his own case.

Another risk is for a consultant to feel that the case at hand is very similar to a case he previously saw, and to try to apply the same solutions. Having encountered similar cases certainly gives confidence and an idea of the approach to be taken. However, humility should always remind us that family dynamics are unique and that listening is an invaluable tool.

Building a family business advisory team

Aron R Pervin
Pervin Family Business Advisors Inc
Jonathan Riley
Michelmores LLP

"It was, perhaps, one of those cases in which advice is good or bad only as the event decides."[1]

The true value of advice is sometimes not clear until events have developed. The same might be said of advisors. However, if advisors are chosen well and managed effectively, their presence can help a family business prosper in a way that might otherwise prove difficult. Indeed, one might argue that the objectivity that can be achieved by using external advisors means that in the context of a family business, advisors have a particularly important role to play.

Is there anything to be gained from giving thought to building an advisory team? Many might say that such a team surely develops organically and according to need. Additionally, owner managers may be confident that they know what is best for their business without the need for external (and often expensive) input. In a small family business that might be an accurate view (or an economically necessary one!); however, a business does not need to be terribly large before the need for external advice arises and, like it or not, as a business grows advisors will inevitably become part of the team. The development of an efficient advisory team is likely to be a gradual process. However, when the need for an advisor *does* arise, those involved in the appointment process should bear in mind a number of guidelines. Set out below is a (by no means comprehensive) list of what these guidelines might be. This chapter also sets out a cast of players, some of whom might comprise the family business advisory team.

1. Considerations when building a team

1.1 Defining the advisor's role

This, arguably, is one of the most important elements to bear in mind. Advisors need to understand precisely what they have been asked to achieve. This can be a particular issue given the dynamics of a family business:

> *Providing inter-disciplinary family business advice is a relatively new concept when it comes to professionals and family business owners alike, so it is essential to carefully consider how the various professional advisors deliver their services.*[2]

A clear brief for advisors that sets out precisely what is expected of them will help

---

1 Jane Austen, 1775 to 1817: *Persuasion* (1818).
2 Mark Evans, Head of Family Business and Philanthropy, Coutts & Co, London, December 2008.

all those involved to understand what is expected. There are a number of obvious reasons for this: avoiding the duplication of effort; clarifying responsibilities; ensuring the correct information is provided to the decision makers; and avoiding 'mission creep' whereby an advisor looks to increase their remit where it is not wanted! Typically, a summary of an advisor's expected role would be set out in an advisor's 'retainer' letter. However, the business might usefully decide to take this further and set out in a less formal way any other important expectations regarding the advisor's role. For example, this might address the question of whether the advisor is expected to be proactive or simply reactive. It might also set out the expected lines of communication, identify the circumstances in which the advisor may alter the personnel involved (and those when they may not) and make clear any other points that are significant for that particular business.

In a growing business the absence of a firm demarcation of roles is likely to increase the risks of confusion both internally and externally and the risk of matters inadvertently not being addressed.

1.2   Understanding the business

Advisors should be educated as to how any particular family business operates. This is of course important on a practical level, but advisors should also take time to understand as much as possible about the particular family dynamics surrounding a family business. Why are the family members in business together? What motivates the family? Where does the family want to take the business? As a consequence of doing so, advisors should be better able to understand their role and what is expected of them. This in turn should mean not only that advice is accurate, but also that it reflects the particular characteristics and values of the family concerned.

This process is arguably more important when a business is supported by a *team* of advisors. By achieving a common understanding of what is required, a family business advisory team should be able not only to enhance communication among the participants in the family business, but also advise with a greater confidence and efficiency than might otherwise be the case. This 'family brief' may typically be included in a family constitution or similar document.[3] If necessary, the brief should be discussed and agreed by the family members (with the help of advisors if required) to clarify precisely the family vision – it would not be uncommon for this vision to differ from member to member at the outset of the process.[4]

1.3   Breadth of advice as well as depth

Management questions can often be best approached if they are considered by advisors from a number of different disciplines. Mark Evans again (December 2008): "Often, if you focus on one area only, it impacts on others, so you may need to consider the overall picture."

This can be illustrated in the context of advice regarding succession planning.

---

3   For a fuller explanation, see Part V on "Governance and management".
4   It is interesting to note that the provision of a comprehensive brief to advisors is not a modern notion – in the words of Abu Bakr (Muslim ruler 632 to 634): *"when you seek advice, do not withhold any facts from the person whose advice you seek"*.

Professionals advising in this area must always be alive to the fact that a business should not lose flexibility or any other advantage as a result of the planning – even though significant estate tax savings may potentially be achieved. Henry Krasnow comments as follows:

> Lawyers and accountants, like people in all other professions, often feel most comfortable focusing on things they understand and minimizing those they don't. Because many lawyers and accountants are not taught and rarely understand the importance and subtleties of management and its implications on the future of a business's profitability, many estate plans save the maximum taxes while creating stock ownership that destroys or discourages the future success of the business.[5]

With this in mind, consideration should be given to whether advice that is received should be balanced by another view. This might be done by asking the advice provider to copy their advice to another of the family's advisors involved in a different discipline, or by the advice being passed to a suitably experienced member of the family for critical review.

It is often helpful to view the estate planning process as primarily a business process rather than a personal one. It would then seem a natural step for advice on the subject to be reviewed not only by the family but also by other members of the family advisory team; in this way the planning outcome should meet the personal needs of the family whilst retaining an appropriate business structure.

1.4   Advisor selection

This is clearly crucial. There are two distinct points that should be borne in mind here and these are set out below.

(a)   Select advisors who can work together

When technical specialists come together to work in a team environment, it invariably takes some time before they function efficiently as a team. An advisory team that comprises members who have an element of professional 'chemistry' is likely to be one that is able to communicate freely and one that can offer candid analysis and assessment. By contrast, the efficient functioning of an advisory team can be stifled by fragile egos that need to be managed, or toes that are prone to be trodden on!

(b)   The appointment decision

It is up to the family to choose their advisors carefully, bearing in mind among other matters the need for cooperation among their advisors. Appointing advisors only after a 'beauty parade' (rather than simply on recommendation alone) should go some way to achieving this. As well as working among themselves, advisors should also have the buy-in of the family. As the managing director of one family business observes, "It is important that the advisor has the respect of family members and can get on with them."[6]

In many ways this appears a straightforward point; however, it is a key one to get

---

5   Henry Krasnow: *Family Business Review* Vol XI, No 3.
6   James Staughton, managing director, St Austell Brewery, Cornwall, January 2009.

right. Owners might also consider whether advisors should be on a 'virtual probationary period' at the end of which the board might consider whether or not the advisor is 'one of us'. The inconvenience of replacing an advisor who does not blend well should be minor, compared with the benefits brought about by an efficiently functioning team.

Surprisingly, family businesses often fail to ask the right questions before they hire an advisor or consultant.[7] If the appropriate questions are not asked, nor proper checks made on the advisor's professed areas of expertise, the business runs the risk of incurring time and expense in retaining the services of an advisor who is not equipped to deal with its particular characteristics. A useful step for any business might be to find out whether the advisor has previously worked in a similar team with other professionals and approach the members of that team on an informal basis to obtain their views.

The composition of a business advisory team should be reviewed regularly and if necessary aligned with the changing needs of the business as the business's circumstances, priorities and tax laws change.

A family business should be alive to the potential of one (or more) advisors exerting significant influence over the family or over one particular member. A consequence of this might be that the business maintains its problems, but with the illusion of progress. For example, an advisor might have a long-standing relationship with a family business, and perform many activities for them. However, whilst the family may appear to listen, the damage is that no sustainable change or progress is achieved. In this situation the advisor can fall into the trap of becoming 'a member of the family' and in so doing allow the reliant business family member a way to escape responsibility for his or her performance, actions or problematic events.[8] With a view to avoiding this (and other potential perils), a family business would do well to review regularly (at least annually) its business advisory team against measurable performance indicators as part of a formal performance review process. It must be remembered that "… advisors should always be seen as impartial; they are not there to represent the interests of one family member."[9]

1.5   How should advisors be retained?

On occasions there may be no choice as to the arrangement under which an advisor is retained. For example, an advisor who is an employee will be retained under a contract for services with their employer. Equally, circumstances might present opportunities for alternative arrangements: an advisor might be engaged as a consultant, offered a more permanent secondment, or taken into the business as an employee. There are of course costs and benefits to each arrangement. An agreement under which an advisor is retained as an external consultant (on a rolling short-term contract, for example) should bring a flexibility that enables the advisor to be easily replaced if the service is unsatisfactory. On the other hand, an advisor who is

---

7   See for more information the Family Firm Institute's article "Choosing a Consultant" available at www.ffi.org/default.asp?id=250.

8   Many thanks to Ron Sparrow of SourceLine (www.sourceline.ca) for his wisdom on this subject.

9   James Staughton – see note 6 above.

retained under a longer-term arrangement might show a greater commitment to the role and take more time to understand better the business and all its subtleties. Whatever arrangement is reached, the business should keep these arrangements under review as circumstances change. Indeed, expanding the management tier by retaining on a full-time basis advisors who are formally under contract might bring collateral benefits by developing the business structure. As Geoffrey Dovey of Dovey Premium Products comments in relation to the circumstances of his own business:

> ... we needed to bring into the company a number of external specialist managers, to augment the family skills sets, and provide a platform for growth. This necessitated a more formal reporting structure.[10]

As an alternative, a family may look to a "family office" to manage their family's affairs. The family office is usually seen as having more of a personal role than a business role; however, the provision of services to the family business by members of a family office can be attractive for a number of reasons including familiarity, confidentiality and flexibility.

1.6 Non-executive directors

The subject of non-executive directors is relevant when building an advisory team, for two reasons. First, non-executive directors are sometimes viewed as something of an 'external consultant' and the remit they have will need to be dovetailed with the role given to non-director providers of advice. Secondly, non-executive directors can present an objectivity[11] that can usefully be used to benchmark the impartiality provided by an advisor. It appears that the use of non-executive directors as advisors to the family business is increasing, at least in the United Kingdom.[12]

Non-executive directors are also a potential interface between an advisory team and their principals. With the best will in the world, the relationship between an advisor and their principal might not run smoothly all of the time. Involving non-executive directors in the process of developing and operating an advisory team can be a useful way of managing communication between that team and those that retain them.

2. The members of the family business advisory team[13]

Possible members of the team (in alphabetical order) and their probable roles are as set out next.

2.1 Accountant

Generally, accountants provide business, financial and management advice and, at times, help with the training of worthy successors. As a group, they deal with tax

---

10   "Planning to Succeed", *Generation*, Issue 6, Spring 2008, p 25.
11   See the Association of Chartered Certified Accountants research report number 63: "The role of non-executive directors in United Kingdom SMEs" (Berry and Perren, 2000).
12   The United Kingdom PricewaterhouseCoopers Family Business Survey 2007/2008 (www.pwc.co.uk/eng/publications/business_families_2007.html) reported that British firms are more willing to rely on external management than those in other countries, with 34% of those businesses that had drawn up succession plans indicating that they intended to appoint non-family members to all the senior roles in the business (compared with a global average of 17% that intended to do this).
13   For more information, see "How to Choose and Use Advisors" by Ward and Aronoff, 1994, ISSN: 1071-5010.

planning, preparation of returns and other aspects of financial management and reporting, including the design of new systems and the interpretation of financial statements. They often help with business-transfer, succession, estate, personal financial, retirement, and family-legacy planning. They may also assist with compensation situations. The accountant is typically the closest advisor to the owner and his or her family.

2.2 Banker

Bankers make loans, set up operating lines of credit and assist where appropriate to meet demands for liquidity. At times, bankers will also assist in the financial learning process for next-generation participants and sometimes prompt timely discussion about business succession, family estate planning and wealth management. (See also Section 2.9 below.)

2.3 Executive coach

Executive coaches can be retained to provide an ongoing partnership to help business owners produce fulfilling results in their personal and professional lives. A coach can also help people improve performance and enhance the quality and balance of their clients' lives. Coaches are trained to listen, to observe and to customise their approach to individual client needs and, in so doing, provide support to enhance the skills, resources, and creativity that the client already has. Employing a coach is often seen as an alternative to sending a family member on a course. Whilst many courses are beneficial, a coach can provide a level of bespoke assistance that is often more relevant and that provides a more intensive and efficient way of educating team members.

2.4 Family business advisor

These practitioners typically work with business families who want to get better at what they already do well. Typically, their role is to help family businesses negotiate transitions of ownership or management.

A family business advisor will often help with the creation of family and corporate governance systems, processes and structures as well as help families achieve their aims at many stages of the life cycle of a family or a business. Family business advisors are also trained to develop results-based outcomes within the business family's capacity for change – for example, an owner's exit strategy and entry strategy. In most cases, a family business advisor will also help organise, negotiate, mediate and improve family dialogue and meetings, encouraging family unity, communication and cooperation. They can also advise in connection with common family business challenges such as family compensation and liquidity issues. In many situations, they encourage the family to embrace ongoing learning, documenting a constitution, professionalising and organising the firm and the ownership situations, helping to build independent outside boards or developing private philanthropy. A family business advisor will typically have a more relationship-based engagement than a technical one.

2.5 Financial advisor

These consultants can work with family members to address the liquidity and capital needs of the business. They can help identify appropriate investment strategies and educate the business family about financial management and corporate finance.

The members of a family may not necessarily be employees in any of the enterprises owned by a family; indeed, the family members may not have a professional interest in the business that generates family wealth. In this situation the advisor required might be less a financial advisor and more a wealth advisor. The financial advisor may assist in placing the funds on behalf of the client but may also help the family members better understand the issues of wealth management, their family values and its effect on investment choices, and may guide the making of strategic investment decisions. In some instances a wealth advisor will also assist in establishing a family office.

2.6 Health professional

Family members' health is an important facet of being able to face facts, manage relationships, organise resources, regulate emotions and make decisions. Medical doctors, psychologists, psychiatrists and family therapists are often overlooked in this respect but can become an addition to the team that can add real value. At times, a health professional is the appropriate referral when unexplained depression or anxiety is observed, substance abuse is suspected and/or other stress episodes appear to undermine general health and a positive family connection.

2.7 Human resource consultant

Human resource consultants typically bring organisational development skills and in so doing can help build teams, create a cohesive working environment, improve communication and help a family ensure that their values are indeed driving the business and its culture. Human resource consultants may also help identify and recruit key non-family managers and directors, including hired hands who are brought in on a short-term basis, for example as interim CEOs. Human resource consultants may also develop compensation and performance management systems, help in designing career learning paths, and develop training programmes for management and staff.

2.8 Insurance professional

Insurance professionals help business owners protect themselves against large, unpredictable demands for cash to pay taxes or to confer financial security at death or disability. Insurance is one of the most useful methods to ensure that a business is not dependent upon the health of a shareholder or partner.

2.9 Investment banker

These individuals deal with mergers and acquisitions as well as valuing assets and businesses. They may also help in dealing with outside investment and designing shareholder redemption programmes.

2.10   **Lawyer**

Lawyers help determine the form of business ownership and capital structure and will help negotiate contracts and other shareholder documents. They often assist in governance issues and review board-level transactions. Like accountants, lawyers can also sometimes assist in the development of next-generation leaders. Lawyers can be valuable in helping to resolve disputes, either between family members or on behalf of the family business. Lawyers can also prepare estate plans, wills and trust documents and review them regularly as well as preparing marriage, employment and other appropriate agreements and provide counsel as needed when new family members enter the business. The lawyer is typically one of the closest advisors to the owner and his or her family (along with the accountant).

2.11   **Marketing consultant**

Marketing is an essential part of a business and a marketing consultant can help advertise the business, generate increased client awareness and as a result increase the volume of work received. They can help develop positive publicity for the business through highlighting work achieved and charitable endeavours undertaken. They can also help generate loyalty in employees by developing a brand that is easily identifiable and of which the employees can be proud.

2.12   **Mentor**

A mentor is someone who is experienced in the relevant business field and who can help assist and advise on problems encountered. More friendly and informal than executive coaching (see Section 2.3 above), mentors can help increase confidence by passing on the knowledge that other people have been through the same experience.

2.13   **Trustee**

These individuals (or trust corporations) will administer trusts and manage trust assets for the benefit of beneficiaries. Depending on the circumstances, trustees can act as wealth-preservation advisors and assist the family to review their estate, gift and investment-planning decisions as well as evaluate the performance of a business that might also be held in trust.

2.14   **Valuer**

It is occasionally important to know the true value of a business, for example during a transition period or when setting up certain types of stock programmes. A valuer places a true market value on the business in order to establish a buying or selling price. A professional valuation is also important when estate planning, so that steps can be taken with confidence.

3.   **Conclusion**

The composition of a family business advisory team will vary from business to business; one cannot be prescriptive as to how the team should be built. However, all family businesses should be alive to possible opportunities and pitfalls when building a team. This may take a little more time, but it should prove to be time well spent. The successful advisory team is one in which the members not only add value individually, but collaborate effectively and together represent a value greater than the sum of their parts. The rewards of building a successful team are likely to be reaped over a long period.

The effective management of a family business often requires a light touch[14] and a keen awareness of when adjustments to an organisation are required. This will include the continued assessment and management of external advisors, so they work as efficiently as possible and so that their value is maximised.

---

14   An old Chinese proverb implores: "Govern a family as you would cook a small fish – very gently ...". Many would agree that a similar principle would occasionally apply to managing the family business.

Philanthropy and private foundation readiness

Malcolm D Burrows
Scotia Private Client Group
Aron R Pervin
Pervin Family Business Advisors Inc

"It is more difficult to give money away intelligently than it is to earn it in the first place."
(Andrew Carnegie)

The literature available on private or family foundations[1] primarily – and rightly – focuses on charitable mission. The emphasis has been on effective granting, charitable programmes, and evaluation, as well as the related issues of foundation management, family involvement, and succession planning. The assumption in this body of work is that the foundation already exists and philanthropic programmes are established.[2]

There are also extensive resources on how to create a private foundation, primarily specific to the laws of their respective countries.[3] Far less has been written about the establishment of private foundations in terms of suitability – to the founders (typically husbands and wives), their family, and to the intended philanthropic mission. What happens at that moment of transition when affluent individuals have the funds and motivation to make a large charitable gift? What happens when they are considering their philanthropic options?

This chapter addresses that moment of altruistic transition. Our intention is to provide perspective to advisors about how and why private foundations are established. What are the issues and options that need to be addressed at the moment of transition? Just as important, we want to examine the question of who should establish a private foundation and what the foundation should look like. Advisors often see the planning utility of private foundations, and can sometimes miss the message and core values. Therefore more attention needs to be paid to the future success of the foundation as vehicles of 'mindful philanthropy™'.[4]

We provide a brief summary of private foundations and philanthropy at the time of writing, to provide a context. The decade since 2000 has been characterised by a period in philanthropic activity worldwide not seen since the beginning of the twentieth century in the United States, with extraordinary wealth being created and dedicated to philanthropy.

---

1   We use the terms 'private foundation' and 'family foundation' interchangeably throughout.
2   An excellent example is Gersick, Kelin F, *Generations of Giving* (2004) Lexington Books.
3   *First Steps in Starting a Foundation*, 5th edition (2007) Council on Foundations; *Starting a Foundation* (2004) Philanthropic Foundations Canada.
4   A philosophy of giving developed by Burrows and Pervin in 2008.

Although private foundations remain the philanthropic standard for affluent individuals and families, often they are not the right choice. If that is the case, other options should be explored, and consequently we have provided a brief review of the alternatives. The heart of this chapter is 'the private foundation readiness checklist', a 10-question tool for advisors and would-be private foundation philanthropists to assess readiness. Throughout the chapter we have included anecdotal case studies to provide a counterpoint to the main text. Some of these case studies address the creation of a private foundation, and others deal with the downstream issues that emerge within family foundations over time. Finally, we should note that we are Canadian advisors, and although we draw upon international sources, the majority of our data and experience is with Canadian philanthropists and business owners. We hope advisors and philanthropists in other countries find our Canadian experience to be valid and helpful.

1. Philanthropy in context

Philanthropy in the industrialised world reflects trends in demographics, wealth, and family make-up. The same phenomena driving the global wealth management business are influencing philanthropy:

- Greater wealth is more concentrated in fewer hands.
- Families are smaller in the industrialised world, leading to situations where there is excess wealth for family needs.
- The nexus of individualism and consumerism has (perhaps) weakened social bonds and increased the desire for personal expression. While this seems like a strange point to make in this context, large-scale private philanthropy often has strong elements of wanting to shape and express a personal vision in the public sphere. If taxes are an anonymous way to participate in and contribute to society, philanthropy is a highly personalised public action – even when done quietly.
- There has been a material reduction in tax rates in the major industrial countries, and in many jurisdictions, a corresponding increase in tax incentives for charitable giving. US-style tax incentives – tax deductions, extra savings for donating certain asset classes, and increased contribution or claim limit – have become more prevalent internationally. The United Kingdom, for example, eliminated capital gains tax on public securities donated to charity and introduced hybrid structures, such as the community interest company. Canada has overhauled its Income Tax Act since 1996 to provide more than 20 new incentives to promote donations of assets. Singapore has a generous double-deduction system.
- Philanthropy has become a powerful ideal. Embodied by examples such as Bill Gates, Warren Buffett and Li Ka-Shing, philanthropy is being held up as the socially responsible path and, for many affluent individuals, a way to express their values through their wealth and to make a lasting contribution to the betterment of the world. 'Philanthrocapitalism' has arrived, and although there will be ongoing debate about its aspirations, appropriate role and failings, it is a concept that is likely to stay and thrive in

the long term.[5] And, of course, there will be numerous lower-profile and more traditional private foundations that reflect this trend.

These factors have driven a decade-long growth in charitable giving that is unprecedented in recent memory. For example, from 1995 to 2006, Canadian tax-receipted giving increased from C$3.6 billion to C$8.5 billion, an increase of 133% over an 11-year period. By comparison, the Canadian economy, which has been one of the stronger G8 economies, grew at half this rate.[6] The number of Canadian donors has been in decline, dropping to 24.7% of tax-filers in 2006 from 25.1% in 2004. In summary, there are fewer donors giving more – and many of those donors are giving disproportionately large gifts from business assets. The global financial crisis of 2008 may affect elements of this dynamic, but the general trend is likely to persist over the long term.

2. The philanthropic moment

There are two pockets from which we can give to charity: the income pocket and the asset pocket. The income pocket funds donations from cash flow or annual income. It is the source most people draw upon when donating to charity. Income donations will range in value in proportion to the donor's income. Typically, there are a number of charities a person supports, and for many of these charities the support is recurring. Gifts from income are the most common kind of donations, but they are not typically the type of donations that fund private foundations. In some cases, the model of giving from income is so entrenched that it is hard for donors to imagine utilising their capital to support charities.

Second, there is the asset pocket, which is funded by net worth. These are the assets that people live on and live in, and for business families they are often tied up in an operating business. Far fewer people give from the asset pocket, and when they do, it is often connected with major life events such as retirement, sale of a business, or death. In the words of David Dunlop, one of the pioneers of major gift fundraising for education in the United States, these donations are 'ultimate gifts'.[7] A donor of a significant gift from assets, such as a bequest, needs to be more mindful about the donation, both in terms of personal planning and intended effect and outcome. The philanthropic moment is the time of transition, when assets are released and become available for redeployment. Frequently this philanthropic moment occurs later in life, often after the building and acquisition phase. Despite the media focus on a generation of young philanthropists who have come out of high tech, the more typical first-generation philanthropist with a private foundation is aged 55 or older.

The worldwide philanthropic growth over the last decade has primarily been funded by the deployment of business assets. Private foundations have always

---

5. Michael Edwards "Just Another Emperor? The Myths and Realities of Philanthrocapitalism", Demos: A Network for Ideas and Action and The Young Foundation, 2008.
6   Canada Revenue Agency.
7   David R Dunlop, "Major Gift Programs" in *Educational Fund Raising: Principles and Practice*, ed Michael J Worth (1993) Oryx Press/American Council on Education, pp 97 to 116.

existed alongside family businesses, and many have been funded by annual donations, which typically represented a portion of annual profit. This cash-flow model of funding private foundations, however, is being supplanted by event funding – major infusions of capital often at times of maximum liquidity, such as a business sale. These sums are often considered to be too large to contribute a single charity; hence the desire to establish a holding entity that will enable the future funding of many charities. Often these sizeable asset donations create endowments that are invested to produce annual income to fund grants.

One of the biggest challenges for would-be philanthropists is moving beyond the model of annual funding and beginning to think about charitable giving as an integral part of their estate. The lifelong habit of giving income often fosters a transactional mindset, while dedicating capital to charity, especially a private foundation, requires a strategic mindset. A significant asset donation will impact the overall estate plan and family wealth, and it also raises the stakes for philanthropy.[8]

3. Philanthropic options

Significant philanthropy can be divided into two categories: direct gifts to charity and gifts to intermediary charitable containers, such as private foundations and donor-advised funds.

3.1 Direct gifts

It is important to recognise in any discussion about philanthropy that direct gifts to operating charities represent the majority of donations. Donors give directly to the charities that are doing the work. Deep trust and confidence exists and no mediation is required. Direct gifts perhaps reflect a mode of giving that is typically more spontaneous than foundation giving and reflects a strong personal relationship or psychic attachment between the donor and the charity. Witness the increasing prevalence of seven- to nine-figure gifts to institutional charities, especially universities. Internationally, there have been headline-grabbing gifts like the C\$1.5 billion bequest by Joan Kroc, widow of McDonald's founder Ray Kroc, to the Salvation Army in 2006. What limits the value of direct gifts is often the capacity and perceived accountability of the charity. Large gifts are donated to established capable organisations. If the intent is to seek out smaller, younger charities, the methods of engagement change and the gift size shrinks. Often the intended gift is simply too large to give away effectively at one time. There may also be concerns that the gift is irrevocable and, once given, cannot be significantly modified.

Case study 1: Shifting motivations – from corporate to family foundation
My family company was very visible – both in our industry and the community. For years we had given personally to major charities, and our company underwrote a college training programme that was industry specific and provided skilled workers to the firm. The founder, my father, began searching for additional ways to minimise the amount of tax he had to pay to the government. Our advisors

---

8   Interestingly, this describes the beneficial essence of our mindful philanthropy™ advisory service.

suggested a private foundation. For 15 years, the business-integrated stories about the company and the foundation appeared interchangeable. The foundation never held any money; rather, it was funded based on business commitments and corporate profits, and the money was disbursed annually. When Dad died, he made a significant bequest to capitalise the foundation. Soon after I remember John, Mom and Dad's lawyer, explain the gifting policy: "When the request folder was two inches thick, it was tax planning time". Out of the six of us, I was the only family member working in the business, so it made sense for Mom to separate the business giving from the family giving. She wanted to continue the informal way of responding to community needs, but away from the firm. Mom had never participated with Dad in this gifting process, and I had only been at one meeting. So, the seven of us decided to develop a focused mission for the foundation. Although we are making some headway in creating our own direction, I recently overheard Mom tell Aunt Jane that this foundation has been helpful in providing unity to her family. Interestingly, my siblings and I might describe the situation differently: "We are intimidated from speaking due to the constant presence of John, Mom's lawyer. His interest in protecting Mom seems to undermine our participation, but we are getting better at managing the old coot and directing the money to projects that we think are worthy."

3.2   Charitable containers

'Charitable container' is a generic term for entities such as donor-advised funds and private foundations. These are intermediary entities that exist to receive and manage charitable funds and, typically, they serve as funders of 'doing' charities. (Of course, not all private foundations are limited to granting, a purpose that we address below.) Charitable containers are ideal for long-term philanthropy because they typically allow the donor and his/her family to continue to be involved in charitable decisions after the gift has been made. From a planning perspective, charitable containers are invaluable because they separate funding (the gift or gifts) from the ultimate use or distribution of charitable funds (grants). Containers provide planning certainty and time to develop a long-term strategy. Containers are useful when the gift is of a relatively large value to the donor and there are multiple charitable goals to achieve or charities to fund. They also separate the gift from the ultimate charitable use, buying time for thoughtful distribution of funds.

Donor-advised funds are to private foundations what mutual funds are to the traditional segregated investment portfolio. They offer similar benefits, such as donor direction and flexibility, and because they are offered through public charities, they also offer ease of establishment and management. As the name implies, the donor advises the master foundation on the use of the funds (and sometimes the investment), but does not have legal control over the entity. Often donor-advised funds are promoted as offering all the (obvious) benefits of a private foundation without legal costs or the administrative burden. With minimum donations of as little as C$10,000, the donor-advised fund is a democratic structure that enables long-term, self-guided philanthropy.

In the North American environment, community foundations and commercially sponsored foundations have criticised private foundations that market donor-advised funds. Casting private foundations as the straw man to sell another philanthropic option is unfortunate, and occasionally quite misleading. In many cases, the donor who is considering a donor-advised fund should not be considering a private foundation. The scale, structure and responsibility are different, despite certain functional similarities. Implicit in the endowed donor-advised fund model at a community foundation is the assumption that the founding family will not be around to guide granting in the future; hence, there is a default to the mission of the foundation. That said, a donor-advised fund is an excellent solution for a large number of donors. Some donors are seeking the granting insight and collective vision of community foundations. Others value the service and convenience. New models that offer the ability to create a limited-term container may serve the specific goals of sophisticated philanthropists better than private foundations. Indeed, some philanthropists utilise donor-advised funds in coordination with private foundations. If there is a congruence of goals and values between the donor and the foundation holding the donor-advised funds, the gifts can be as great as those to a private foundation or a large institution.

3.3 Private foundations

Private foundations are an outgrowth of medieval charitable trusts. In most common-law jurisdictions, a foundation can be formed either as a corporation without share capital, or as a trust. Typically, they are standalone charities where the majority of directors or trustees are not at arm's length from each other and the funding has come from a single source. Legal control of the assets by the directors or trustees is attractive to the business owner or executive, or indeed anyone who desires a high level of engagement with the philanthropic activities of the entity. Private foundations are an individual, as opposed to communitarian, model of philanthropy.

Perhaps because of the legendary US private foundations such as Rockefeller, Ford, Mellon and more recently Gates, private foundations are considered the 'gold standard' of charitable structures for wealthy individuals.[9] In the United States, it has been estimated that 75% of the 400 wealthiest families have private foundations.[10] In Canada, private foundations have been the fastest growing category of registered charities in the past decade. Although less than 5% of registered Canadian charities, private foundations hold C$13.14 billion in assets or 19.3% of the total assets in the sector. Private foundations have also been the recipient of 22.5% of new investment assets in the sector between 2002 and 2006.[11]

What are the qualities of a private foundation that no other charitable structures offer? Private foundations have the following primary characteristics:

- They are separate legal entities.
- They are typically tax-exempt registered charities, operating within the laws of a particular national jurisdiction.

---

9   Silk, Roger D and Lintott, James W, *Creating a Private Foundation* (2003) Bloomberg Press, p 1.
10 *Ibid*, p 1.
11 Canada Revenue Agency.

- Many jurisdictions offer tax benefits for donating to charity, including private foundations.
- The funding derives primarily from a single source.
- The directors or trustees are normally not at arm's length. In many cases, they are family. Directors/trustees are typically related to the primary donor and, in the case of the first generation, the donors are often also the director/trustees.
- They provide a high level of control for the donor within a regulated environment. ('Control' may be translated as compliance and individual oversight.)
- They may be both grantor and/or operating charity. In other words, private foundations may fund other charities as well as operating their own charitable programmes.

When reviewing these characteristics it is easy to see similarities with family businesses. Often the qualities necessary to be a successful entrepreneur translate to the social sector and to private foundations. The experience of operating a business, dealing with family dynamics, and identifying markets are applicable to private foundations. They also provide a structure to transfer and segregate wealth in the family. The ownership structure shared by family businesses and private foundations, although not entirely analogous, is characterised by a strong sense of personal responsibility. A private foundation requires active management, and unlike other charitable structures cannot survive on trust and passive participation. This is one of the reasons retiring business founders often see their private foundations as their next business venture.

At the progressive end of the spectrum, some entrepreneurs are attracted to the concept of 'social entrepreneurism', a concept pioneered by Bill Drayton and the Ashoka Foundation, which applies the energy and focus of the business entrepreneur to social problems.[12] In a family foundation context, sometimes this approach takes the form of strategic granting – searching out and backing promising and passionate social entrepreneurs – and other times the foundations aspire to do the work itself. This kind of iconoclastic, deep engagement is best suited to a nimble, high-control structure such as a private foundation. Typically, the goal is high impact rather than longevity. The Young Foundation in the United Kingdom is a current leader in the social innovation field, and also an example of a foundation that operates its own activities, notably applied research and The Michael Young Prize for excellence in social science. [13]

Case study 2: Vision and commitment
I set up our private foundation seven years ago at the suggestion of my accountant. We had always made annual donations from our family business, and Ralph

---

12   See Bornstein, Daniel, *How to Change the World: Social Entrepreneurs and the Power of New Ideas* (2007) Oxford University Press (revised edition).
13   http://www.youngfoundation.org.uk/

suggested one year that it would be good to have a foundation for tax reasons. The lawyers did their work and the foundation was established, and we put C$400,000 into it. It was invested in mutual funds with my broker and soon forgotten. We still gave significant amounts annually to charity from the company, but the foundation wasn't part of the picture. We never bothered to have board meetings, as it just didn't make sense to be wasting valuable time over such an insignificant amount of money. Not surprisingly, after a while I began to wonder why it existed. To make matters worse, one year we forgot to complete the regulatory filings and almost lost our charitable status, which in retrospect might have been a good thing. Recently, we have been revising our wills and our lawyer asked if we wanted to "create a legacy" with our foundation. While this is a vaguely attractive idea, we think our legacy is our children and grandchildren – and the business, of course. It strikes me as ridiculous to have some big vision for our family foundation when it is only one of many corporate vehicles that we own. The local hospital is having a capital campaign and we're being hit up for a big gift – maybe we should clean out the foundation once and for all.

In a more classic model, private foundations excel as structures for long-term philanthropy, focusing on certain issues and causes to effect change over time. An excellent example of a 'legacy' foundation that has been effective in long-term giving is The JP Bickell Foundation in Toronto, Canada. Founded in 1953 by Toronto businessman John Paris Bickell, the Foundation started with C$13 million in capital from a bequest. It has a defined granting mandate with a 60% focus on medical research. This seems conservative after 55 years, but you have to imagine the state of medical research in the early 1950s. Medical research was embryonic in Canada, and the need of local hospitals in the post-war period was capital for new buildings. Bickell made a strategic bet on research, not bricks and mortar. The primary beneficiary has been Toronto's Hospital for Sick Children, which has received ongoing Bickell Foundation support and has gone on to become the largest medical science research institute in Canada and world renown in field such as genetics and immunology. As of 2007, the foundation has granted C$118 million to charities, and the capital has grown to C$115 million. And the legacy continues with annual distributions of C$4 million. Bickell could have made outright gifts to charities (although most of the beneficiaries to date were not in existence when he died), and if he did the capital would probably have been well spent within five to 10 years. Instead, he chose to create a perpetual, dynamic legacy that meets the ongoing needs of society. Models like the Bickell Foundation are very attractive to certain philanthropists, especially entrepreneurs who see their family business and community engagement as a source of legacy.

4. The private foundation readiness checklist

We have explored in our practices how the professional designation of the advisor affects the planning process. For example, to the family accountant, a private foundation is often primarily an exercise in tax minimisation (depending upon the jurisdiction) and ongoing compliance. At the other end of the professional spectrum, a family business advisor/philanthropic consultant views the challenge in terms of strategic philanthropy for the family or public benefit. Returning to our focus on the business owner at the moment of transition to serious philanthropy, what does he/she need to consider?

The following checklist was developed as a quick assessment tool for professional advisors to determine whether a private foundation is an appropriate philanthropic structure for a client.[14] It examines what we believe are the key attributes or characteristics of a successful private or family foundation, and the readiness of your client to embark upon one.

The checklist is purposefully simplistic and agnostic and may be used by advisors from a variety of backgrounds. The questions are of the "yes/no" variety, and the scoring is straightforward. In our view, a score of seven or more "yes" answers out of 10 questions indicates that a private foundation is a suitable structure for the individual or family. A score of six or fewer "yes" answers suggests that a further discussion of philanthropic options is required. For example, you may wish to suggest that a direct gift to charity might be more appropriate, or a donor-advised fund. Alternately, if tax is a potent motivator, it may make sense to explore tax planning strategies that have nothing to do with charity.

While many successful private foundations have been founded by individuals and families who would have scored low on this assessment exercise, the comprehensiveness of the questions is intended to provide clues about appropriateness and fit.

The checklist questions are designed to call attention to key emerging themes that can be explored in greater detail at a future meeting where a more open-ended and collaborative examination style is beneficial.

Underlying each inquiry is a commentary for illustrative purposes, which should help the advisor start a dialogue with the client. These themes and topics are not intended to be rigid rules that will restrict what foundations can do, as we happily acknowledge that the greatest philanthropists have a talent for shattering traditional models in pursuit of public good. Rather, the information presented is intended to provide indications as the whether the clients – and their end purposes – would be better served by another approach to philanthropy.

Case study 3: Family dynamics and leadership

We were asked to assist in the leadership transition for an established family foundation. When we interviewed the foundation members, it appeared that the outgoing 85-year-old founding autocratic leader was characterised by the saying, "he has his tongue to speak and his words to hide his thoughts." This culture of deceit was reinforced through oppressive family interactions. "He's the master of the double bind – we can never win with him. And, he doesn't understand that his criticisms and put-downs or complaints censor us and separate us. He thinks he is

---

14   Although the checklist is for the use of wealth advisors with clients, we recommend providing the questions to clients ahead of time – especially husbands and wives – and suggesting that they meditate on the possible responses as preparation for the meeting.

helping us grow and become strong, competent foundation members." Rather than address the presenting problem, and possibly hurt the founder, we decided to focus on the desired outcome and develop a respectful resolution.

We explored the family history using a genogram and unearthed many positive origins of collaboration, respect, trust and philanthropy. We built on these bonds of connection and mutuality and developed a constitution and governance system that clarified the vision, mission, commitment, culture, values, communication, dispute-resolution mechanism, decision-making style, grant-making process and methods to keep the peace. As the team emerged, the family became more cohesive and emotionally connected. And, you guessed it, the founder became more comfortable and trusting of the new approach, and the next leader was someone who demonstrated empathy and sensitivity and valued positive relationships in all areas, and also had a passion for community service. It doesn't happen often but, in this situation, we were pleasantly surprised that a positive foundation experience was the catalyst to repair a damaged family experience.

The 10 questions in the private foundation readiness checklist are intended to help the would-be philanthropist and the advisor to be mindful about the philanthropic choices.

Private foundation readiness checklist

Question	Yes	No
1. Do you have an existing or intended charitable purpose?	☐	☐
2. Do you donate 5% or more of your net annual income?	☐	☐
3. Do you want to be in the business of philanthropy?	☐	☐
4. Will your foundation ultimately have $4 million in capital?	☐	☐
5. Do you want to be directly involved and collaborate with the causes you support?	☐	☐
6. Do you plan to involve/include family members?	☐	☐
7. Will your foundation be active in 25 years?	☐	☐
8. Do you have the skills, talent and appetite to operate a philanthropic business?	☐	☐
9. Do you enjoy being in control?	☐	☐
10. Do you think charities should be accountable to funders?	☐	☐
Total	☐	☐

If the client has answered "yes" to at least seven questions, a private foundation may be the structure to consider.

4.1 The private foundation checklist: background information and assumptions

1. *Do you have an existing or intended charitable purpose?*

    This question assesses whether your client has given any thought to charitable objects or mission. Private foundations are charities, not just another personal trust or holding company, and there should be some glimmer of charitable intent at inception. Especially in jurisdictions where tax incentives are significant, there is a danger that the private foundation will be sold as just another tax-exempt investment account. A foundation without charitable intent is like a yacht without a rudder.

    The charitable vision does not need to be grandiose or well articulated. There is an inherent danger in defining the purpose of the foundation too narrowly at the time of inception. Ideally, private foundations should be dynamic entities that respond to the world around them. Foundations that are defined before they are tested often end up being at odds with the evolving interests of the founding generation, as well as the vastly different perspective of future generations of family directors. When coaching your client, it is often better to encourage him/her to have broad objects that can be refined and adjusted over time. For example, the foundation might consider being able both to conduct its own charitable programmes and grant to other registered charities. Or the objects may be restricted to 'big-tent' purposes, such as international development, education or the environment. We prefer that the legal structure of the foundation should provide the framework for philanthropy but never inhibit the activities. If the foundation is funded by will, it should honour the legacy of the founders, but not be so inflexible that progress is stalled. Put another way, it is better to be guided by board policy – informed by family values and social need – than limited by law and a compliance mindset.

2. *Do you donate more than 5% of your net annual income?*

    This topic identifies existing philanthropic behaviour. It is based on the assumption that a foundation is an outgrowth of established personal priorities and actions. The best indicator of future behaviour is typically past behaviour. The 5% figure is the average amount of net income donated annually by affluent US and Canadian individuals.[15] The 5% benchmark is low for philanthropic individuals and families, especially those raised in religious traditions that tithe at the 10% level. It is also a low level for many high-net-worth individuals. Canadian tax data shows this higher rate of participation. In 2006, 24% of all tax filers claimed a donation, compared with 61% of individuals earning C$100,000 to C$150,000 and 74.5% of those earning more than C$250,000.

    Sometimes higher rates of giving among the affluent are because of personal engagement in social-sector issues, but for others it is reflection of their social circle. The wealthy are constantly being solicited and are often pressured into attending, or at least supporting, galas and, therefore, some give more out of social expectation than genuine commitment. That being said, 5% of net annual income is a significant enough level to indicate that charitable giving is a priority. The annual practice of

---

15 "Charities – An Emerging Opportunity", *Investor Economics*, p 29, Summer 2008.

making donations helps to provide the engaged individual with a sense of how charities operate, the causes, and best practices. Even a limited experience with charitable giving provides helpful preparation for the more intensive experience of a private foundation. Often, regular giving inspires individuals to contribute in a more fulfilling and engaged fashion than they have in the past; hence the choice of a private foundation.

Paradoxically, there is a group of clients who embrace private foundations without a history of giving. Some of these individuals are philanthropists by accident[16] or personal circumstances. For example, the individual or couple without children may bequeath their entire estate to a private foundation without having a history of giving during their lifetime. The challenge can be particularly great with clients who are essentially deeply frugal at heart. Although they may be attracted by the idea of legacy and ensuring that their money does not go to family or government, they are reluctant to give their money to individual charities during life. In cases like these a private foundation provides a conceptual solution for an estate plan and enables the client to put their affairs in order – but the actual good work of the foundation cannot begin until the donor has actually died.

3. *Do you want to be in the business of philanthropy?*

Private foundations are in the business of philanthropy. They exist to carry out charitable programmes or to give money to other charities – year in, year out. Once a private foundation is established and funded, your client loses the ability to decide whether he/she wants to give. Although the situation remains personal, it is the foundation that is in the public arena and the assets may no longer be used for personal purposes. The foundation will be solicited by charities, who will find it through online resources like Guidestar. The foundation will be solicited by friends and business colleagues. Conversely, the foundation structure and grant-making process can also regulate solicitations by putting policies, clear guidelines and an application system in place. The foundation may adopt a pseudonymous name and operate with a low profile, but there is no avoiding the core business. Does your client have the philanthropic maturity and seriousness to commit to a new business venture? If not, consider another giving option.

To some extent, this question is meant to be provocative. There is a popular perception – some might call it a myth – that private foundations are fashion accessories for rich people. Making a foundation analogous to a business is meant to raise the tone of the undertaking, especially for people who have run businesses. The question ideally separates the dilettantes from the engaged. Many private foundations are established at the time a family business is sold or an executive retires; often the foundation is seen as a replacement activity. Think of the high-profile example of Bill Gates, who was challenged by Warren Buffett to turn his attention full time to The Bill and Melinda Gates Foundation and relinquish his day job at Microsoft.

---

16   Look for an article to be published in STEP in Summer 2009 entitled "The Accidental Philanthropist" by Burrows and Pervin.

4. *Will your foundation ultimately have at least $4 million in capital?*

Minimum funding amounts are one of the most frequently debated aspects of private foundation planning. Why $4 million and not $10 or $20 million? The minimum value cut-off can seem very arbitrary. The question is intended to test for personal commitment and self-sufficiency of the foundation after it is established. This question is often linked to question 1, namely existing or intended purpose.

The question of personal commitment is the harder of the two dialogues to explore and especially to pin down. On the emotional side, we tend to listen for passion as well as compassion, as an individual relates his/her views on altruism, social activism and sustainable directions. These people often discuss leadership and continuity at the onset, as they can often visualise the outcome with great clarity. On the physical side, wealth varies greatly, and there is no ideal amount a family should dedicate to its foundation. There will be clients who devote all their wealth to a foundation and others who dedicate 10%. To a wealthy family, $4 million can be a rounding error – pocket change not worth mentioning and easy to leave behind without a thought. The point of the question is to examine whether the amount being considering is material. With these guidelines in mind, do not hesitate to translate this figure into your local currency or to adapt the figure to the appropriate threshold for individual clients. The amount should be significant enough to inspire the client to be focused and engaged, and to get them to think beyond a single transaction. A benchmark figure helps the client to commit to a personal goal.

The second concern relates to the self-sufficiency of the foundation, which is an issue for entities that either by design or accident often outlive the founder. Does the foundation have enough money to do some real good as a standalone entity? Is the capital base (and/or the annual contributions) significant enough both to pay for professional support and maximise charitable benefit? A small capital base will drive up costs in relative terms to a point where it becomes an ethical issue: too much is being spent on administration and too little on charitable purpose. Perhaps in these situations a donor-advised fund that is cost-effective may be more appropriate. These questions should be considered, especially if the intent is perpetual. The most efficient way of creating a neglected and ineffective foundation is to provide negligible one-off funding.

5. *Do you want to be directly involved and collaborate with causes you support?*

In most cases, the existence of a foundation will change the way the founder engages with charities and the community. The foundation is more likely to have a well-articulated mission and to initiate strategic grants in areas of interest, whether this is formally documented or not. The foundation has the ability to operate its own charitable activities. The foundation can choose to engage in granting partnerships. While some foundations continue to give in the same way as the founder did before, charities almost always interact differently with foundations than with individual donors. The expectation is that a foundation will be a knowledgeable funder, not just a trusting donor. This is reflected in the greater responsibilities foundations have in law and to charity regulators.

Being a charity rather than an individual opens up opportunities for engagement with other charities and with the social sector as a whole. Private foundations provide a platform for a heightened, more formal interaction with charities. Clients should be aware that having a healthy private foundation prompts greater social responsibility and market awareness in the area of grant making and, therefore, greater interaction with society, not less. This question tests for that appetite and awareness. It also filters out the hermits.

6.   *Do you plan to involve/include family members?*
"Feelings of worth can flourish only in an atmosphere where individual differences are appreciated, mistakes are tolerated, communication is open, and rules are flexible – the kind of atmosphere that is found in a nurturing family." (Virginia Satir)

Private foundations are synonymous with family. This question raises the issue of family engagement, while helping the founder consider just who will be involved and when the involvement will begin. Especially in the context of family business, private foundations often provide a way to engage family members not involved in the business, as well as those who are. In an ideal sense, private foundations provide a vessel (with a rudder) through which a family can act on its values and transmit those values as a legacy to future generations. Private foundations are attractive to some business families as a type of pedagogical trust where the next generation can learn about business practices, as well as philanthropy, through hands-on practice. For example, a founder may want to enable his/her children to gain experience with governance, organising community projects, strategic decision making, managing wealth, examining risk/benefit characteristics, interacting with professional advisors, and community profile. Many founders – especially those who have been so busy with business that family has taken a back seat – aspire to ignite a 'kitchen table' style of family discussion about priorities and community engagement. A private foundation is a living structure that requires active and often passionate engagement. It requires a different style of competency, and for many family members it has fewer emotional and physical risks than the family enterprise.

Case study 4: Competence and participation
It might have been my cousin's outburst 20 years ago, "How hard can giving away money be?" that made me concerned about giving equal access to every family member. Growing up, I always perceived him to be less competent and somewhat entitled – not a taker, but definitely not that dedicated to collaboration. At the same time, my thoughts raced to my grandfather's tendency towards inclusion and informal participation in order to embrace the broadest range of grant making. My grandparents were both dead, and my dad and his two siblings were trying to continue the family foundation tradition, and things were not going well. My aunt never learned how to read financial statements or comprehend investment strategies. This added tension to some of the meetings and caused tears at times. To her credit, she had passion and compassion but often lacked objectivity; she was great with people but appeared to miss many of the details and nuances, which contribute to teamwork, relationship building and collaboration; she became

confused at times over the need for results and direct action rather than facilitation; and, she seldom performed any individual research into any of the organisations we supported. It's now our turn and there isn't room for 18 cousins and siblings around the table. We started to make sense of the situation and came up with the notion that it's a privilege to serve on the foundation board; it's not a birthright! At the same time we decided that there should be a minimum level of learning attained to participate. We're getting better at this and can rely on each other in new and wonderful ways. We decided that understanding change is the core competency and that the key for change is effective communication. It looks like family unity and our giving legacy will be preserved.

The caveat about family is that there is no standard model; each family is different. Despite the romantic myth of private foundations being a place to share and reconnect around core values, it can just as often be a place where family members are shunned and excluded. In our experience, foundations often begin with the founder retaining legal and/or effective control of the foundation. The intended and sometimes mumbled plan is to include the next generation at a "later date", which is perhaps defined as when they get through the teenage years, are "old enough", or in all to many cases, after the founder is dead.

Experience confirms that reluctance to consider the role of family is often a good indicator that a private foundation might not be an appropriate structure. Please also note that this is not the only, or the most definitive, clue. But we strongly suggest that it should cause you to pause and explore the situation in greater detail with your client, as a private foundation may make perfect sense once a better understanding of family is reached.

7.   ***Will your foundation be active in 25 years?***
As previously discussed, a classic characteristic of private foundations is longevity. Foundations frequently aspire to be perpetual. Perpetuity is an untested concept, as few foundations or endowments have survived for more than a hundred years, but it is promoted by charities and popular with donors. (In discussions with clients about the concept of perpetuity, consider defining perpetuity as 'at least 100 years'. It is more concrete.) Alternatively, foundations can be time-limited by design. Some have best-before dates of 25 or 50 years, which may reflect a desire to maximise the foundation's resources for public benefit and/or wisdom on the part of the founder about the natural life cycle of human entities. For example, The RS McLaughlin Foundation in Canada had a 50-year time limit imposed by the original donor. It functioned as a granting foundation for the prescribed period, and in the early 2000s the directors went through an intensive period of granting out C$100 million for strategic purposes.

The private foundation is a structure for long-term philanthropy. As a normally tax-exempt holding entity, it can build an endowment efficiently over time through investments. It can take on multi-year causes, changing strategy as it goes. It is also a long-term planning structure able to receive money over a number of years – during life and through an estate. If your client is going to take the trouble to set one up, he/she should be encouraged to define how long it will be active.

Why then test for a 25-year plan? Our benchmark of 25 years suggests that the foundation will exist for more than a single generation. It challenges the founder to think beyond the circumstances of inception and imagine a future – to consider continuity as a family legacy. Shorter-term goals can probably be better dealt with through direct gifts or a short- or mid-term donor-advised fund.

8.   *Do you have the skills, talent and appetite to operate a philanthropic business?*

As previously discussed, in question 3, private foundations are philanthropic businesses. While it is easy enough to get administrative, professional and investment support to operate them, the directors or trustees still have a fiduciary duty to ensure they operate well. It is no accident that private foundations are typically the philanthropic choice of business owners or executives. People who have created and operated businesses typically have the skills to run a private foundation. They are more likely to be able to conduct a board meeting, read a balance sheet, and make strategic decisions.

The other factor is appetite, which is another word for engagement. Does the founder really want to run another active entity, even one that will be significantly less taxing than the family enterprise?

The final topic is talent, which is harder for the founder to self-assess. Often the talent question applies best to the next generation of family directors or trustees. Private foundations established by people who have neither the skills nor the appetite to run them have limited success.

This topic requires you to use your intuition and provide aware, caring and respectful feedback to your client. In some situations, it is better to use a more passive philanthropic structure, such as a donor-advised fund.

9.   *Do you enjoy being in control?*

The desire for control is considered an antisocial impulse in the charitable world. That being said, control is a key feature for private foundation founders.[17] Charitable giving involves that control is relinquished, as a donation is freely given without consideration. Control is perhaps a provocative way of asking whether the donor wants legal direction – both responsibility and authority – over his/her philanthropy. Many executives, entrepreneurs and business owners have always had a high measure of control over their business lives, and could not imagine entering into a philanthropic structure where this was not the case. Private foundations need directors and trustees who provide vision and energy to fulfil their charitable mission. Excessive need for personal control will, at times, conflict with the charitable purpose of the foundation and the ethos of the charitable sector.

A related psychological dilemma that often accompanies large donations is anxiety. In its worst form, we have encountered entrepreneurs who experience panic attacks at the philanthropic moment, often just prior to the actual transition stage.

---

17   For more information, see "The Many Faces of Control Freaks" by Pervin; visit pervinfamilybusiness.com/library.

Yes, altruism is a deep-rooted impulse and most philanthropists see social value in what they are doing, but there is something inherently counter-intuitive about donating millions of dollars and getting nothing in return. For clients who have spent a life in business, the transition to making major donations can be very difficult. In business succession situations, we have often found that business owners feel the loss of their company. This compounds feelings of anxiety and is often combined with a depressed state due to mourning the loss of the enterprise and the historical lifestyle and prestige.

A private foundation with the founders as directors or trustees provides a philanthropic middle ground – a structure for giving that resembles the family business or the company's advisory board. They are donating their beneficial interest, but retaining legal control. They take comfort in knowing they will control the foundation as they have controlled their business. Especially in business succession scenarios, this knowledge enables owners to make the most significant donation of their life, often giving larger amounts than they would have to any public charity. For better or worse, private foundations sometimes serve as an important transitional step that is essential in getting charitable dollars into society.

Case sudy 5: Philanthropic anxiety or narcissism?

In our first meeting, Bruce meticulously explained his existing community work with detached passion. As only a patriarch can relate, he reported that he would send a note to the charity that read, "Enclosed please find our cheque. We will call in a few weeks and tell you what it's for." He also shared his current entrepreneurial mid-life reappraisal of unfulfilled dreams and shaky career identity in a rather jocular fashion. He described in amazing detail how this current existential crisis required him to find some new situation to conquer and control. He also reported on episodes of anxiety and depression brought on by feelings of vulnerability and loss of control. Bruce was not exceedingly wealthy but he had done quite well. He (and his wife) wanted to start a foundation for a few reasons – he was motivated by tax savings, keeping passive wealth out of the hands of his adult children and an interest in effecting positive change (read: control) in the community, which experience confirms is often a suitable outlet for narcissistic tendencies. Bruce had proudly built his business from nothing to C$25 million on his own and struggled with the fundamental philanthropy concept we presented that states: "The moment the funds are foundation assets, it's not your money any more! It's public money!" To his credit, Bruce eloquently provided a rebuttal and explained how the funds for donations come from one source – business profits. He described how the idea of *putting* his money in the foundation was the same as *giving* his money to the foundation. He explained how he and his family would give up potential dividend income for the sake of a charitable cause – something he may find easier to do if he could preserve ongoing control and oversight. It was clear he needed action in his philanthropic endeavours. People like Bruce often end up working on site with the people and community effort they fund.

10.   *Do you think charities should be accountable to funders?*

Within the charity system, grantors (like private foundations) provide checks and balances. Private foundations are separate funders, often providing significant support, that are typically not tied to a single charity. They can grant on the basis of outcomes or effectiveness. They can increase funding to the exceptional charities and cut off funding to those that are less successful. By contrast, large gifts to public charities often end up being endowed, which creates a perpetual income stream and sometimes little accountability on the part of the internal recipient. (It makes little practical or legal sense for charities to be rigidly accountable to the original donor many years after the donation was made, although large institutions are becoming adept at keeping donors informed and involved.)

> *Case study 6: Clarity of mission creates third-generation dream*
>
> As the last second generation foundation chairman, Harry knew that it was time to discuss grant-making continuity with the clan. He understood that it was critical to allow the original foundation direction to maintain its rightful place in the family legacy while the third-generation foundation members refocus the philanthropic direction. Harry discussed this situation with everyone for months and then presented the meeting theme and some additional questions:
>
> * What is the future of our family's giving? Simply: why are we doing this and why am I participating?
> * How can we better plan our work?
> * How can we improve implementation activities?
> * How can we track progress towards our collaborative goals?

Whether you visualise your philanthropic direction as a dream[18] or establish your private foundation by "beginning with the end in mind",[19] the most skilled, intelligent and sensitive leaders in each generation are able – or quickly learn how– to manage and negotiate both the personalities of the family members and the priorities of the foundation initiatives. The positive family foundation culture and a clear strategic mission serve to unite the family, reinforce its identity and preserve its values.

While it is important to have sustaining support for institutions such as universities, hospitals and museums, some philanthropists are concerned that this institutionalised internal source of funding creates an indolent bureaucracy. There is a school of thought that one of the structural issues with the charitable sector is that certain charities outlive their effectiveness, but because of historical support they do not outlive their support base.

This question tests for the level of trust and confidence a client has in charities. Those individuals who have a high level of trust and do not expect long-term accountability should be encouraged to give direct gifts. A private foundation would

---

18   Kelin Gersick, *Generations of Giving* (2004) Lexington Books.
19   Stephen Covey, Habit #2 in *The Seven Habits of Highly Effective People*, Free Press, 1989.

be a better structure for individuals who wish to reserve the right to change their mind about their favourite charities, or wish to use strategic or venture funding to foster change, or believe that recourse and consequences are important tools in a funding relationship.

5.   Conclusion

Margaret Thatcher was once asked to comment on the most important aspect of communication and her response was "the pause". The private foundation readiness checklist presented here was developed to benefit advisors in their dialogue with clients who have expressed an interest in philanthropy.

For wealthy clients at key life stages, a private foundation is often settled upon as a solution by default. Over the years, we have found that when our client is facing that moment of philanthropic transition, our technical acumen can sometimes get in the way and possibly undermine the intent or message being presented by our client. We offer that "pause" in the form of a framework or a model for understanding more about the needs of the client. We suggest that best practice would have us be less of an expert and more of a listener. In addition, the yes/no script of our 10 questions allows us to suspend our own need to analyse the situation too deeply. It is more useful than using a Socratic approach and open-ended questions at the onset, as it provides the opportunity to have an insightful conversation about suitability. Truly, the outcome is to provide the philanthropic result that matches the values, priorities and dreams of the client and his or her family and to help make this legacy concept of the philanthropic planning process more 'mindful'.

Finally, we are reminded of a statement made by the author Alex Haley: "In every conceivable manner, the family is link to our past, bridge to our future." In our words, we stress that each advisor must manage the intangibles. Do not be fooled into thinking you should only worry about what you can touch and measure. Managing the intangibles is often more important to the success of the philanthropic direction than many of the tangible goals.

This chapter merely provides a brief overview of philanthropy and an indication of the appropriateness of one option – the private foundation. The private foundation readiness checklist is a base from which an advisor may develop his/her own script – one that benefits the particular client and his/her family – and commence the sensitive and 'mindful' dialogue of philanthropic transition. In fact, it is important that the advisor help his/her client ascertain what would be a good fit. Failure to mesh skills, values, priorities and experience with personal requirements, especially in relation to intangibles such as culture, commitment and style, can be counterproductive at best, disastrous at worst.

Establishing and growing the family business

Stephen F Cutts
Rawlinson & Hunter SAM

1. Phases of the business

1.1 Start-up and early phases

Many businesses around the world are started either by individuals who, as the business develops, will bring in other family members, or by two or more family members. But just one in three of these family businesses survives to the next generation.

Family-owned businesses have many advantages, not least in terms of potential skills and finance, which are crucial in the early years of a business. Family members will have known each other for many years and build up a trust of working with one another. Successful family businesses are able to harness this trust and togetherness in a business environment.

There are a number of considerations when a family decides to set up a business.

Any new business is a risky venture and the family should consider whether it should maintain a separate source of income while the business is in its start-up phase. Family members could remain in employment, for example, until the business has become more established.

The business itself must be treated foremost as a business, with the family aspect coming second. There are often difficult business decisions that need to be taken and these should not be allowed to result in conflicts within the family. This will invariably lead to the failure of the business.

Each family member's specific skills should be assessed and applied in the most appropriate areas of the business. It is often difficult in family situations, but there can be no place in the business if the skills of the individual are not fully required for the success of the business.

Each member of the family in the business should be allocated distinct roles and responsibilities dependent upon that individual's particular skills. The positions should then be made clear in a management structure with clear reporting lines. This will both help the family focus on what those relationships will be and avoid any misunderstandings with regard to roles, responsibilities and benefits.

Once the structure is agreed, the family should ensure that there are good communication channels, both formal and informal, to avoid misunderstandings and potential areas of dispute. It is an unfortunate fact that many family businesses fail due in part to poor communication.

The family should also set boundaries between their business and family lives, as tensions between families at home often arise in situations where there is no release from the business. Time away from the daily running of the business can bring a more balanced perspective for the business and provides space where objective and strategic decisions can be taken. Families managing their businesses need to balance these requirements.

1.2 Growth phase

Once the business is established, the family will then consider setting it on a sound base for the growth phase. The principal issue is ensuring that conflicts between the requirements of the business and those of the family are managed. The company has passed through its early stages and is becoming well established, has been operating for some years, is profitable and is growing.

Many of the more informal communication channels that existed previously will become stretched. More formal channels will therefore be required. The family may create a family charter or constitution, which is a document that sets outs the family's culture, ethos and guiding principles. This document represents the start of formalising the separate nature of the family's involvement as shareholders and as managers of the business. It will form a basis for a practical guide to their ownership and management of the business. Issues covered will include strategy, leadership and management structure, rights and responsibilities of both owners and managers, dispute-resolution procedures and whether or how family members may be taken on by the family business.

As it develops, a family business may consider hiring an experienced manager or non-executive director to bring specific expertise and objectivity to the business. This person's role and responsibility needs to be clearly set out, along with their relationship with the family both in their capacity as owners of the business and as fellow managers. Incentives for high-level managers need to be considered carefully, especially if there is no possibility of them sharing in the ownership of the company at any stage.

The company will also be hiring people as it grows. Decisions will need to be taken at this stage as to whether to employ members of the family and, if so, under what circumstances. Members of the family should be treated equally and fairly, commensurate with their skills and responsibilities, both in relation to each other and with employees who are not family members. Family members should not be provided with extra benefits or opportunities simply due to their family status, as this will invariably either lead to conflict or act as a barrier to non-family members entering the firm. Those employees who are not family members should nonetheless be made to feel 'part of the family', and treated fairly in comparison with family members with regard to salary, benefits and opportunities. Moreover, their contribution to the success of the family business should be recognised.

Where other family members wish to join the business, there should only be a place for family members who can offer appropriate skills or experience. Some family businesses take the view that no family members can join the business unless certain criteria have been met, such as five years' experience in another company, or even that no family members can become an employee.

If not considered previously, the family owners will need to consider succession of the ownership and management of the business by this stage. Succession planning is not simply a question of resigning and not going to work any longer. The business is often the cornerstone of the family's wealth and the principal generator of its income. Decisions on who will manage the business going forward, how ownership will be transferred and how the existing family owners extract sufficient value to live in retirement are all questions that the succession plan will need to have considered. The three main aspects of a succession plan are transfer of management, transfer of ownership and taxes. It can, however, become especially complicated because of the relationships and emotions involved. Families going through this process should consider engaging recognised family business advisers at this point, to assist them.

1.3   The next generation

Family businesses that reach maturity after many years now face the moment of truth. The original family member(s) have built a successful company, but the time has come to hand over the reins. Implementation of a well-prepared succession plan is crucial as its success will ensure the passing of a valuable asset to the next generation. The sooner the succession plan is created the better.

By this stage, the family business will probably have been in existence for many years, with the family retaining ownership and the managers being either solely family members or a mixture of family members and non-family members.

The family charter, likely to have been written in the growth phase, will need to be updated to evolve with the business. A more formal code of conduct, written governance rules and formal meetings will be required. The issue of family members who are not managers of the business but who have perhaps inherited shares needs to be considered.

The family always needs to be aware of external factors and the question often arises as to whether the family should stay in the family business or sell and move on.

1.4   The multi-generational family business

The final phase is the multi-generational family business. Family businesses will evolve and grow, being passed on to the next generation of family members to own and manage.

It is estimated that about one-third of family businesses fail after each generation. Essentially, this means that barely 4% survive three generations and the Dutch expression of "clogs to clogs in three generations" has its variations in a number of countries around the world. Those family businesses that survive more than three generations generally have a number of common threads.

The family's values are clear and integrity is high. The business has grown by focusing on the long-term but with an ability to evolve, sometimes quickly, with changing times and generations. Succession is dealt with at an early age; young members of the family are trained to either take up the ownership and/or management roles and the family constitution, whether written or unwritten, is constantly reviewed and updated.

The family has successfully managed to separate its business from the private family affairs, and the relationship between the two is well managed. This is not to say conflicts do not occur, but there are clear rules on how disputes should be settled.

Multi-generational family offices also have an aura of being managed by the current generation for the benefit of future generations.

2. Financing the business

When a family business wishes to expand, one of the important components of success is finding the finance. Lenders and investors look favourably on business leaders who can clearly and concisely communicate the company's vision, demonstrate a solid understanding of its competitive vision and deliver a simple plan for future action. Lenders will also look favourably on companies that understand their risk and articulate how capital will be raised and spent within the context of the overall business plan.

The cost of financing the business will depend on the risks taken by the lender and other factors such as whether other assets are pledged.

2.1 Family financing

At the start-up and in the early years of a family company's existence, the individuals starting the company often look to other family members as well as friends for financing. These loans can be interest bearing, or with no right of interest but a share in the profits instead. This is known as equity financing. Whichever is selected, it is important that the loans are on a proper contractual basis in writing to avoid future conflicts.

Equity financing enables the business to take on loans at a later stage, as the gearing capacity (the ratio of loans to equity) is that much greater.

Where a loan is made, the agreement should be clear as to whether the loan is to the individual family member or to the company. Repayment terms should also be explicit. If the funds are provided as a gift with no expectations, this too should be laid out in the agreement.

With equity financing, the loan agreement should explicitly state under what circumstances the company will pay a dividend to the family investor. It should also make clear what voting or management rights, if any, are available to the family member.

2.2 Internal growth/profits

Family businesses are often managed more conservatively than other businesses. Many will grow through profits being reinvested back into the business rather than by acquisitions. As a result, they will have low debt/equity levels and findings suggest that this is especially so for those with larger market share in their particular markets. This does, however, mean that those companies have lower financial performance than other companies that have a smaller market share.

This conservative policy of family-owned businesses is part of their generally lower overall risk culture and will often go with similarly conservative policies on paying dividends, risk, capitalisation and investment strategies.

Financing through profits is therefore a very important means by which many family-owned businesses grow, due to the risk-averse nature of the shareholders. Theirs is a longer-term view that many quoted companies cannot share.

2.3   Bank loans

Bank loans are a source of finance once the company has outgrown immediate family funding capabilities. Banks generally expect to see a track record of at least three years' financial statements together with forecasts and plans for the future, and they take special interest in how the funds they loan to the company will be used. Often collateral and personal guarantees are required to be provided by the shareholders of the company. In the context of family firms, this is often a defining time as the risks are high, and the family businesses that succeed are those that are able to harness the strengths of the family for the benefit of the business.

Loan finance will either be a short-term loan or long-term loan. A short-term loan takes the form of operating term loans for a maximum of one year, or a credit facility. These finance the operating costs of the business, including payment of wages and salaries and purchase of stock. Long-term loans are arranged when the scheduled repayment and the estimated useful life of the asset being purchased is expected to exceed one year. These are used to finance the purchase of buildings, land, machinery, equipment or another company.

Bank loans are cheaper than equity, although banks are more risk averse as they are less able to cover their losses on any loans written off. For example, if a bank writes off a loan of £1,000 on a portfolio with a 2% spread, it will need to source performing loans of £50,000 to cover the loss. Therefore, although bank loans are cheaper they will be harder to obtain, especially for higher-risk acquisitions such as takeovers. Collateral will, therefore, often be required.

2.4   Bond and mezzanine finance

Family businesses prefer to issue bonds, because these do not dilute the family's ownership. There is also some certainty in both the interest due on the bonds and their repayment dates.

Mezzanine finance is sometimes preferred to equity financing as it does not dilute the ownership as much as equity financing. Lenders receive their return in the form of high-yield interest rates (10%+) together with some equity appreciation, usually in the form of warrants, for a total return of between 15% and 25%.

2.5   Private equity

Family businesses may also wish to raise capital by partnering with a private equity fund. This is a fundamental shift away from the original family business model of private ownership, so it is often linked to the exit of family members who wish to sell their shares in the family business. Private equity has been a relatively recent source of finance for family-owned businesses and the private equity firms believe their investment lends additional credibility to businesses and a solid foundation for their future expansion or sale. There are inevitably financial objectives that the family business will then need to achieve in order for the private equity firm to realise a profit on its investment.

Equity investors have the highest tolerance for risk, as they target returns of between 30% and 50% per annum on their investment. This allows them to accept some investments that are total write-offs and still meet their targets.

Private equity is not for all family-owned businesses, as it needs an aggressive growth model to succeed. It is therefore best considered by family businesses with this aggressive growth strategy. The benefit for established companies of partnering a private equity firm is the provision of a relatively flexible and dependable source of capital. It is also useful where some family members wish to sell their shares, the business wants to professionalise, or it is simply struggling to manage itself.

As well as funds, private equity firms aim to bring financial and operational expertise to improve the long-term performance of the family-owned business. Their time horizon before exiting is often between three and five years, so the family will have its own strategy in mind when engaging with private equity firms. Often, this strategy is ultimately to list on a stock exchange, although it is not unknown for families to buy back the private equity company's holding.

Private equity transactions can take the form of leveraged acquisitions, buyouts or recapitalisations and invariably will require assurances from the family that they and the principal managers will stay with the company to make it grow for the benefit of all shareholders.

In addition to specialist private equity firms, a number of multi-family offices also provide private equity to family businesses.

2.6   Stock exchange listing

A family-owned business may wish to raise finance on a stock exchange to expand its business and release capital for the family. Depending on local stock exchange rules in individual countries, the sale of 25% to 40% of the family-owned business is often deemed sufficient to provide enough of a market in shares without diluting too much control by the family, although there are many family-owned businesses where the family retains a minority stake only.

In addition to raising capital for expansion, some families also list on stock exchanges in order to raise credibility and profile. This also has the benefit of attracting top talent to manage their businesses and provide those non-family members with a chance to acquire equity holdings as part of an incentive package. It will also create a straightforward valuation mechanism for those family members wishing to sell their holdings.

As with engaging with private equity firms, raising the professionalism within the family business is often cited as a reason for floating on a stock exchange. Many family-owned businesses, though, are surprised by the amount of reporting and regulation involved.

More fundamentally, family-owned businesses that have partly floated need to be able to manage the often short-term nature of the markets, which frequently conflicts with the much longer-term view taken by many family businesses.

2.7   Joint ventures

Recently, with the rise of family offices and family-owned businesses that are acknowledged as having their own identity and culture, there has been a growth in the number of joint ventures between family businesses. In particular, there has been an increase in the number of family office clubs, creating both more opportunities for family businesses to collaborate and increasing the number of potential investment opportunities available to them.

It has been argued that the likelihood of success of an international joint venture is increased when the partners are family-owned businesses, as these companies have shared values and objectives enabling them to bridge cultural differences more easily than multinational corporations. There is much to be said for this view.

Joint ventures are attractive to family offices, as they are collaborating on investment opportunities from a base of shared values and culture. It also appeals to the more conservative nature of families who prefer not to load themselves with debt in order to take advantage of opportunities.

Family businesses can collaborate in a number of ways. There is the straightforward joint venture where each will take an equity stake in an underlying company. Alternatively, a leading family will invite a limited number of other families to take equity stakes in a new business opportunity. The leading family will manage the investment on behalf of the other investors and distributions are made in accordance with pre-agreed arrangements.

There are a number of clubs where family offices and family-owned businesses meet with peers and discuss, among other things, such new business ventures. These first became popular in the United States, but they are also increasing in number in Europe, Asia and elsewhere.

3. Priorities of family v the traditional view of growth – what does the family want?

3.1 Traditional view of growth

Investors like to see companies grow because if profits grow, so too do returns to the investors. The important aspect for the investor, however, is that the company increases the returns to shareholders. A company that grows at the expense of shareholder returns is not generally a good investment.

Thus, earnings per share growth, and the ability to keep well ahead of inflation, is a key factor in certain investors' investment strategies. Earnings that are consistently increased are an indication of a quality company, soundly managed, with little or no reliance on commodity-type products. This leads to predictability of future earnings and cash flows.

For a CEO with shareholders to satisfy, growth is secondary to market performance and dividends. Investors are always looking at the return they are making on a particular investment, either by way of capital appreciation or dividends, and this can only be achieved if the company increases turnover or cuts costs. Increasing turnover is the primary driver of increased earnings per share and therefore the objective of most companies. These companies will therefore chase growth in order to achieve higher profits, including through acquisitions or mergers.

However, while longer-term business objectives are drawn up, the CEO must keep one eye firmly on the short-term share price and act to ensure that both long- and short-term objectives are satisfied. Decisions taken to benefit short-term investors may not necessarily be the best way to ensure long-term success.

3.2 Priorities of the family

The priorities of a family-owned company are not dissimilar to those of other companies.

A comparative analysis by the *International Journal of Entrepreneurship and Innovation* looked at a sample of high-growth firms in three groups based on family ownership, namely no family ownership, low family ownership and high family ownership. The study compared these three groups on the variables previously identified as barriers to growth, being growth objectives, growth strategy and incentives to employees. The data revealed no significant differences between the three groups for growth objectives, although the high family ownership group placed more importance on maximising profits and the low family ownership group placed more importance on maximising sales. There were no significant differences between the groups on strategy selected to achieve growth, with all three groups achieving the majority of their sales growth from market penetration and market development strategies. But firms with a high concentration of family ownership were significantly more likely to offer profit sharing.

Family business leaders consistently emphasise that where they believe they have an advantage over companies with non-family shareholders is in their ability to take long-term strategic decisions without the need to look to the needs of short-term investors who keep their eye on share prices.

A priority of the owners of a family business is to ensure that it is managed well and remains in safe hands, where growth, risk, strategy and innovation are combined in a long-term plan that builds wealth for all the family and for the next generation. Short-term measures driven by investors focused on immediate returns detrimental to this long-term strategy are avoided.

Each family will decide what it wants out of the family business. However, although dividends and growth are important, the long-term health of the company comes first.

4. Structure to support growth

4.1 Start-up and early phases

Even at this early stage, choosing the right ownership and legal structure for the family business is one of the most important decisions that a family needs to take. While it does not impact on the daily operations of a business, it can have a big impact on tax, when the company needs to borrow or to protect the non-business assets of the family members. Also, while it is possible to change structures at a later date, this can be a complex and expensive process. The forms of legal structure are detailed elsewhere in this book.

In addition to the legal structure, the family will have to decide on the precise nature of their relationships with one another. Some family members will be working in the business, some owning it and others may be providing finance. Each legal relationship should be set out in a written agreement, and include:

- *Shareholders' agreements* – These should include details of each owner's rights to participate, vote, receive dividend distributions and sell shares, as well as rights of management in the business. The agreement may also include restrictions on non-family members owning shares.

- *Loan agreements* – These should detail the rights of the family investor to repayment, if any; the party to the contract (whether this is the family owners in an individual capacity or the company); rights to interest payments; rights to equity or other assets in the event of a default; any charge over assets.
- *Directors' or management agreements* – This will set out each family member's responsibilities, role and duties as well as their relationship with each other in their capacity as directors of the company. Directors' remuneration and benefits, if any, should be set out clearly to avoid any conflict with family members who are owners but not directors. This agreement should be attached to a management structure. If there are non-family members serving on the board of directors, either in an executive or non-executive capacity, such individuals will require separate agreements detailing all of the above as well as a clear reporting line.
- *Employment agreements* – It will be necessary to provide those family members who are not directors with a contract of employment that sets out their roles, responsibilities and remuneration. It is not inconceivable that such family members could own a part share of the business, so the contract should clearly show the separation of their rights as employees from their rights as owners.
- *Family charter* – It is never too early for the family to consider drawing up a family charter that will serve as a guide to their values and vision, both for the family as owners and for their business. Something quite rudimentary is sufficient at this stage, but it will enable the family to understand why they are in business together.

Once the agreements are in place and a legal structure created, family businesses are often small dynamic workplaces where communication is the key to success. The agreements or structure alone will not lead to success but will provide a sound base on which success can be built. Communication is important for dispute resolution, and personal family relationships will often provide strong bonds that may be difficult to achieve in non-family partnerships.

4.2 Growth phase

After a number of years, the family business has become more successful and has grown. However, the legacy being created is at risk if the owners do not create effective governance procedures.

The family needs more formally to separate ownership and management activities. This is especially so in those family businesses where there is a single owner/director and the younger generation is starting to emerge. The earlier this is recognised and the process started so as to create the right governance models, the more chance there is of success.

As part of the process, the organisation structure requires modification to ensure it remains relevant. But it must be based on the reality of the situation. Many owner/directors of family businesses prefer to retain control by requiring everyone to report to them, rather than delegating authority to a middle manager. This will create problems for the succession.

As part of the governance review process, the succession plan needs to be fleshed out and initiated. Owner/managers who do not make plans now will create problems for their successor in the future.

The primary aim of formal governance procedures will be to separate the family's ownership from its management of the business. At this point, the families may consider setting up a family office in order to manage their private affairs.

4.3   Separation of family and business

A structure that has worked for one generation of the family can very easily lead to conflict for the next. If, for example, a family business is handed over by two founders to their children, and each founder has two children, the existing structure can easily become dysfunctional. There can be deadlock at board and/or shareholder level and a lack of clarity on leadership responsibilities.

The first step is to separate the business from the family's private assets. The family then needs to separate the ownership from the management of the business. Both of these steps can be times of great emotion for the family, so appointing a family business adviser who can bring objectivity, experience and communication is often a sensible course of action.

It is necessary to avoid conflicts at each step. If certain family members receive land and buildings used by the company, and others receive the business that leases the land and buildings from them, it is not too hard to see how this will create conflict in the future.

The family will decide how to allocate private assets and the family business, to ensure both continuity and that the most capable person is in charge of management of the company. The new leader may either be a family member or be brought in from outside for their expertise.

The family will now finalise and implement their family charter, together with the structures leading from the charter that formally separate the business from the family. The charter balances the rights, obligations and expectations of those family members with an ownership interest with the commercial needs of the business. Family members who both own shares and help manage the business will have each role clearly defined. The charter has many advantages: it reinforces the relationships between members of the family, defines a fair and equitable distribution of the profits of the business and ultimately is the best guarantee of the harmony, independence and prosperity of the family.

As part of a restructure, the family may consider creating shareholder committees that the family as owners will attend, family investment committees to oversee management of the family's investments or family philanthropic foundations. Often, members of the family's younger generation will serve on the philanthropic foundation committees as part of their induction into the family's affairs.

4.4 Creation of a family office

A family office structure can be created while the family still owns a family business to ensure that management of the family's private assets and affairs are kept separate from the family business. Alternatively, it might be formed when the family has sold its business and needs to create a private office in order to manage and protect the family's wealth.

The family office may be managed by a family member or non-family member and its location is usually kept separate from any ongoing businesses the family may own.

Families can also outsource to multi-family offices. These are set up either to manage investments, or to coordinate asset structures, accounting and tax matters for the family. Families use this option when either the cost of having a private office cannot be justified, or they do not have the expertise or inclination to set up a private office.

Structuring the family business

Joanna Boatfield
Andrew Parsons
Dixon Wilson

1. Introduction

The structure of any business will prove a key factor in determining its success. For family businesses in particular it is important that structures are established that support the varying objectives of the family members, as well as the needs of the business. If the family business is to thrive, ownership, control and management structures need to reflect family views on who should control the business and how this control should be exercised. Attitudes towards extraction of value from the business and acceptable methods of raising finance, succession planning, asset protection and strategies for growth will all inform the development of an appropriate structure.

The structuring of a family business has a further role to play in attempting to reconcile the often conflicting demands of the different family members. Any family business needs to be structured with an eye to avoiding unproductive dispute where possible and to minimising the impact on the business where dispute does arise. Attitudes and priorities will vary from family member to family member and will change over time as the family grows, individual situations change and the business develops. It is vital that the business structures that are put in place are flexible enough to adapt to these changes.

A successful structure for the family business can only be established after detailed consideration of the key family objectives. This chapter reflects this assertion by looking in turn at each of the areas where business structure will most significantly impact business success and the achievement of family aims.

2. Taxation

Taxation considerations are inevitably central to any discussion on business structure. Having said that, this chapter illustrates the fact that taxation should not be the only consideration when structuring a family business. Indeed, in many cases it may not be the main factor.

The precise taxation consequences of a particular structure will vary from jurisdiction to jurisdiction, and it is not within the remit of this chapter to look at jurisdictional-specific aspects in detail. In general terms the key areas where taxation will impact, and that will need to be considered in most detail, are listed below:

- on transfer of assets into the family business;
- on transfer of ownership, either during the lifetime of the transferring owner or on death;

- taxation of profits of the business; and
- taxation arising on extraction of funds from the business.

An assessment of the tax position of a proposed structure against these four areas will be central to determining how well the structure meets the needs of the family business and the family.

3.   Satisfying family stakeholders

All successful businesses manage and anticipate conflict between different stakeholders. This will include owners and management, employees, customers and suppliers. In a family business the groups of stakeholders will include different members of the family, all of whom are likely to have different aims and priorities. A family business that considers these conflicts and implements a structure that is capable of dealing with and anticipating these differences of opinion is well placed to run successfully.

In the early stages of a family business there are likely to be fewer conflicts as there will be fewer family stakeholders. The business will be driven by the attitudes of one individual or a small group of individuals. Survival of the business, growth and providing a livelihood are likely to be the key considerations. It is unlikely that at this stage a complex structure will be needed to manage differing family views.

As the business and the family grow, careful consideration should be given to those areas where differences of opinion are likely to arise. Individual perspectives will be influenced by factors such as whether or not the family member works in the business (discussed further below and elsewhere in this publication), the internal family relationships, hierarchies, life stage and circumstances. For example, does the participant have children whom they wish to benefit from the business? The source of a family member's equity participation in the family business may also be relevant here: has it been anticipated and planned for, or received unexpectedly, for example as a result of a sudden death?

As early as possible in the development of a family business and normally when the second or third generation become involved, these issues can be addressed by creation of a family charter. This should be a formal document agreed by as many family members as possible, and ideally by all family stakeholders, which sets outs a vision of the family's aims for the business and values. It would normally cover issues such as control of the business, preparing the next generation, extraction of funds, philanthropy, retirement policy and long-term business strategy. All members of the family need to be aware of the aims and ideals contained in the family charter, which provides a framework for discussion where individual aims and priorities conflict.

A family charter typically allows for regular family meetings, which provide a further opportunity for reconciling family members with differing perspectives on the family business. In particular, the family meeting provides an opportunity for those family members who are not involved in the day-to-day running of the business to make their views heard. This opportunity to enfranchise non-active members often proves to be key to preventing family discord.

As the family business grows, the original family charter may not be sufficient to exercise control over the various potential conflicts. The charter can be reviewed and amended to take into account changing circumstances such as growth of the business and/or succession by the next generation.

Shareholders and partnership agreements can also be drafted to cover in more detail some of the areas where conflict is likely to arise. These documents may include detailed provisions relating to issues such as business management, appointment of directors, sources of funding and who can purchase an ownership stake. They may also include details of actions that require the consent of all shareholders or partners, for example sale to an external party or borrowing above a certain level. Either a shareholders' agreement or a partnership agreement should offer ample scope for dealing with such issues.

4.   Who manages the business day to day?

In the early stages of a family business, it is likely that ownership and management will be aligned in the same individual or small group of individuals, typically the business founder(s). It is a truism that families grow faster than their businesses. Many families will find themselves in a position where not all family members work in the business, whilst most or all of the family hold some form of equity stake.

There are two main issues here: how are those who work in the business rewarded for their involvement (discussed below) and how is the business structured so that as the number of family members increases, the integrity of the key strategic decision-making process is not compromised?

In certain families, this could be achieved by use of a family partnership, which might own the main family trading vehicle, probably a limited company. This form of partnership arrangement will include both limited partners and at least one general partner. The partnership might include limited partners who are family (or other) investors whose liability is limited to the extent that they have contributed capital to the partnership. The limited partner(s) is precluded from any involvement in management decisions. The general partner is liable for company creditors and responsible for managing the partnership. The general partner may be formed as a separate limited company whose shareholders are those members of the family who are responsible for key decision making. This structure allows a clear delineation between the strategic control of the business (at the general partner level), the day-to-day running of the business (at the trading entity level) and ownership (at the limited partner level). Using a corporate entity as the general partner will limit the liability of the family members who control this entity. In this way, the family can choose whom they wish to be the key strategic decisions makers, making use of the members' experience of working in the business and (where appropriate) the expertise of members who have not worked in the business.

In a traditional corporate structure, the board of directors will fulfil the role of key strategic decision makers. The composition of the board can again be a mixture of the family members who have worked in the business and, if appropriate, family members who have not worked in the business but who have relevant skills. The family may also want to involve non-family members at board level. If this is acceptable to the family, it is probably to be encouraged as good governance, particularly where there are outside investors.

5. Extraction of funds from the business

The divide between the active and non-active family member often manifests itself in different views on how and to what extent funds should be extracted from the business.

In the early stages of the family business it is common to see a reluctance to extract funds, except in so far as these are required to sustain the day-to-day needs of the founder members. Profits are reinvested to allow the business to grow, in preference to seeking funding from other sources. The owner/founders are typically motivated by business growth and security rather than the desire to amass individual wealth, and there is a reluctance to suffer taxation on extraction of profits. The structure of the business at this stage should be designed to ensure that where funds are withdrawn, the methods of withdrawal are both equitable and tax efficient, but in the main it is likely that the mechanics of how to extract value will not be a significant or problematic area.

Moving forward perhaps one generation from that of the founder members, there are now a greater number of interested family members, only some of whom work in the business. Some will have sources of income outside the business; others will not. It quickly becomes clear that the attitudes of the members of this second generation towards extracting value from the business will often have diverged. It is likely that those who work in the business will have a greater interest in reinvesting profits, whereas external family members may view their interest primarily as an investment, expecting a reasonable rate of return. This will be enhanced if those external to the business have no other source of income and therefore rely on their share of the family business profits to fund their lifestyle.

In a corporate structure, the primary way in which funds will be passed to non-active family members will be via dividend payments. In this case it is possible to structure the share capital of the family company so that different owners hold different classes of shares, some of which carry rights to higher dividends than others. Those who receive low or no dividend shares may expect some compensation for the loss of dividend, perhaps a higher percentage shareholding.

Preference share capital, carrying a right to receive a fixed dividend in priority to ordinary shareholders but with restricted power to influence the business, may be appropriate for those family members for whom their dividend from the family company is their primary source of income. It should be borne in mind that this may prove unpopular with those running the company, given the restrictions it places on use of company funds that they will often consider they have generated. Preference share capital also carries a preferential right over ordinary share capital to company assets on liquidation, which it may not be felt equitable to give to only certain family members. In this case it should be possible to ascribe a preferential right to a fixed rate of dividends to a separate class of ordinary shares that rank equally with other classes of share capital on liquidation.

Partnerships are far less common than corporate structures, but a partnership arrangement may provide a convenient way of addressing a situation where different family members have different attitudes towards extraction of funds from the family business. A partnership profit-sharing arrangement can provide for profits to be split between the partners on the basis of the combined value of their capital and current accounts. This gives the opportunity for the amount of profit extracted from the business by each individual partner to vary, and rewards individual partners financially if they leave profits in the business. It is likely in this case that the partnership agreement would include stipulations as to how and when profit can be withdrawn in order to allow medium- to long-term planning by management. The partnership agreement might also address what impact reinvested profits should have on the proceeds of any future sale or part sale of the business.

If a partnership is to be used as a trading vehicle in this way, there are problems in many jurisdictions where partnerships do not offer limited liability, so that partners remain personally liable for company debts. This has been addressed in the United Kingdom by the introduction of limited liability partnerships, in which partner liabilities are limited to their investment in the business. For many family businesses, the additional administration burden which these partnerships carry, along with the requirement to make accounts and other information publicly available, unlike in a traditional partnership, will make them unattractive. However, in certain professions (finance or the law, for example) they are increasingly popular and may be appropriate for the family business.

6. Rewarding those family members employed in the business

Family members employed in the business can of course expect to receive salaries, and perhaps bonuses. It may also be desirable to provide further performance-related incentives. This is most easily achievable through a corporate structure, where reward can be structured as some form of additional equity stake.

Deferred share capital may be useful here. This type of share offers limited rights as against ordinary share capital. Commonly it carries a reduced right or no right to assets on liquidation. Dividends are payable only after all other classes of shareholder have received their dividend, which means in effect that they will only pay dividends if a predetermined level of profitability is reached. This is highly relevant in the family business, where they can be used to provide an incentive to active family members to increase profits without prejudicing the share of company assets on liquidation held by other family members. The dividend pay-out only when performance reaches a certain level helps to recommend the share incentive to those who do not work in the business and will not benefit from it.

This type of share capital may also have relevance in a situation where there are non-family investors who are seeking reassurance that their dividend expectations will be met. If the family majority hold deferred share capital, with dividends only paid after the external investor, this provides some level of reassurance.

Share-based reward for family members within the business may also be achieved through the issue of growth shares. These shares offer a return contingent on the future performance of the business. This might be a future sale or, perhaps more relevant to the family business, the meeting of a particular target for growth in, say, profitability or company net asset value. Only on meeting this target do the growth shares deliver value to the holder in the form of an additional equity stake in the business, perhaps with an associated dividend payment.

This type of share has particular use in the context of a family business in so far as it offers financial reward, but it allows that reward to remain tied up in the company, as opposed to, for example, the payment of a bonus. Again, this may prove acceptable to family participators who are not actively involved in the business, since the value of the new shares will normally be contingent on an increase in the value of the company and of their own shareholding.

More generally, the business structure needs to ensure that family members working in the business are appropriately remunerated for their time, commitment and expertise, in addition to the return they receive on their ownership stake. It is important that non-active family members feel comfortable with the remuneration of the active members, as this area very often proves to be a source of dispute. Appropriate structures to govern this area might include specifically addressing the setting of salaries, bonuses and benefits in one or more of the ways discussed above: in the shareholders' or partnership agreements, the family charter, or by discussion at family meetings.

7.   Non-family members in the business

Even when the family business is a relatively modest size, it is often desirable to involve non-family members in the business management. These may be loyal and trusted employees who have worked alongside the founder, or individuals who have joined the business later in its lifetime. Some form of equity participation may prove useful as a means of aligning their interests with the interests of the firm and also to reward and incentivise these non-family members.

Equity participation will be most easily achieved via a corporate structure, perhaps through the issue of share options. In the family business, these options are likely to relate to the non-controlling shares of the trading vehicle. This should be relatively straightforward for a listed family company where these non-controlling shares are publicly traded, thereby offering an exit for the employee once the options have been exercised. Where this is not the case, it may be appropriate to establish an employee benefit trust. The employee benefit trust provides an internal market for non-listed shares, which can be sold back to the employee benefit trust at their market value, making ownership more meaningful for the employee. The way in which this market value is determined will need to be established as part of the process of introducing the employee benefit trust.

8.   Maintaining family control

In many cases the single most important concern when structuring the family business is the maintenance of family control. Whilst in some cases the family might be looking to dispose of the business, more commonly the main priority is to allow the business to grow and develop and to pass down the generations. This attitude will vary from individual to individual within the family. Often, the desire of the founding members or of the family majority to maintain control of the business will not be shared by all family members. In these cases it may be desirable that the business structure makes it difficult, if not impossible, for individuals to pass ownership and control to non-family members, or for shares to pass on divorce.

It is possible for the constitutional documents of a corporate body to restrict who shares can be owned by. For example, there may be a clause stating that only direct descendants of one or more named individuals can own shares in the family company. Although it is possible to amend the company articles, this would require approval by at least a majority of voting shareholders and in many jurisdictions a higher proportion. This provides a safeguard against an isolated individual family member who wishes to sell or transfer on death his shares in the family company to a non-family member. It is worth noting that this may effectively preclude the transfer of shares to the spouses of family members as well as to entirely unconnected parties.

Further provisions restricting who shares can be sold to may be included in the shareholders' agreement. This might state that shares must first be offered to existing family members before they can be sold externally. It is common for similar stipulations to be built into a partnership agreement.

Going to all this effort to prevent the transfer of interests in the business outside the immediate family raises problems if it becomes desirable for a particular individual to relinquish his interest. This may arise when a family member has a need to realise substantial amounts of cash, perhaps on divorce, or when it becomes clear that there are differences between an individual and the family majority that cannot be reconciled and that pose a threat to the future performance of the business. The ideal solution may be for existing family members to purchase the interest, but in many cases there will not be sufficient external financial resources to make this possible. In cases where only one family member is in a position to purchase a further share in ownership, other family members may have concerns as to the shift in power and control within the family that will inevitably follow the ownership changes.

If there are sufficient resources available, it may be attractive for the business itself to fund the purchase of the exiting member's ownership share. The opportunities for doing this will depend on the funds available in the business and the structure of the business. It should be straightforward for a partner to be bought out of a partnership arrangement where the funds are available within the partnership. The precise mechanism for this exit will be determined primarily by the partnership agreement.

Where a corporate structure is in place, the opportunities for directly buying back a shareholding will depend on the available profit reserves and the applicable legislation governing these types of share capital rearrangements. In either case this course of action will mean that potentially substantial sums of money are directed away from the business, which will reduce opportunities for investment and growth. This can prove unpopular with certain family members, which is a further example of the value of family charters. It would also be wise to consider the likelihood that other family participators will then expect that they too are offered the same chance to realise their stake in the business.

Perhaps a more watertight method of maintaining control within the family is the establishment of a trust structure to hold the shares in the family company for the benefit of a wide class of family members. This also provides some protection against a situation where a majority of the members of one particular generation share the desire to dilute family control of the business. We consider this in more detail below.

9. Protection of assets

Like all businesses, the family business will face challenges throughout its existence; these may range from changes in macroeconomic conditions to competition from rival products. Unlike other businesses, family firms also potentially face challenges caused by internal family issues. Divorce and succession disputes can result in family members needing to realise significant cash sums from the business or handing over equity stakes to individuals outside the family. Protecting business assets against re-distribution on divorce is fast becoming the single biggest challenge facing family business structures today. In addition, there remains the age-old problem of the 'black sheep' family member who, if invested with too much power, can in one generation run the family business into the ground.

The aim of a carefully structured family business should be to protect against these potential issues damaging the firm, whilst allowing the business to continue to run according to its usual practices. This is commonly achieved by separating the beneficial ownership of the business from the legal title or the controlling stake, in one of a number of ways.

Historically, trusts have been used for this purpose. In a typical structure the family trading vehicle is a limited company, whose shares are owned by a family trust. The trust terms can be drafted in such a way that the beneficiaries enjoy wide-ranging benefits associated with the shares, but ultimately legal ownership and control is vested in the trustees. This has traditionally offered protection on the divorce of one or more beneficiaries: the assets have not been treated as legally owned by that beneficiary and therefore there is no requirement for them to be considered in any divorce settlement.

Increasingly in some jurisdictions this protection is being eroded by the courts. There are a number of examples where trusts have been 'looked through' in a divorce settlement, with the result that trust assets are included in the divorce settlement. As a number of trust structures have failed to give the required level of protection, families in the affected jurisdictions are increasingly looking to alternative structures for the protection that trusts have traditionally offered.

There remain a number of advantages to a trust structure (albeit that protection of assets on divorce may now be less certain). These relate primarily to protection of family assets in other circumstances and the succession of the family business from one generation to the next (considered below).

Trusts can be drafted however the family sees fit. Provisions can be made so that family members only become entitled to income at a certain age, have income available at trustees' discretion, or have rights to income removed. Entitlements to income can change as individuals age or circumstances change, for example limiting the right to income of a minor beneficiary where an entitlement to large amounts of income is likely to be inappropriate. This would not be possible if they were to own shares in the business outright. Businesses can protect against 'black sheep' family members by using a trust structure that restricts an individual's right to sell shares and to extract profits from the business.

Having the control of the business vested in a group of trustees rather than one individual will guard against one person being able to make unwise or high-risk decisions without checks or balances, given that it is normally required that all the trustees agree on decisions made. Having said that, the ability of any trustee effectively to veto a particular course of action may prove impractical. The extent to which this will slow down decision making, and so prove a business disadvantage, must be considered.

Where a family firm is not held in a trust structure, the use of golden shares can restrict the ability of one or more black sheep majority shareholder(s) to make inappropriate investments, or adopt a strategy viewed as high risk or not in accordance with family ambitions for the business. In this case, the company constitution will detail specific decisions or courses of action that require the approval of the member holding the 'golden share'. Commonly these would include decisions relating to sale or merger of the business, but it is possible for them to deal with any area that is of particular significance to the family or to the older generation who are giving way to younger family members.

A similar level of protection can be achieved in a partnership by the establishment of a controlling partner. In this case, the decisions on which this partner's agreement is required will be outlined in the partnership agreement.

10.   Succession

A typical family business is established initially with a view to providing a livelihood for the founder and their immediate family. As the business and family grows, it becomes important that the business not only provides an income for the family but is also preserved for future generations. This gives the family business the incentive to adopt a longer-term view than many non-family businesses are able to take. The ability to look beyond the need for short-term returns to shareholders is often held up as a primary reason for the enduring success of the family business. Having an appropriate structure to allow succession of the business down the generations is key to protecting and encouraging this longer-term perspective.

The structure of the family business should make it possible for succession to occur either on death or during the lifetime of the older generation. The choice of timing will depend on family attitudes and the attitude of the older generation, but it should be noted that lifetime succession can be achieved whilst maintaining some level of involvement by the older generation.

Trusts can sometimes be useful in preventing succession disputes, which may arise where parties feel ill treated by the way in which the older generation of family members have organised their affairs on death. The transfer of family business assets into trust during the lifetime of the older generation allows their decisions and rationale to be effectively communicated to the successor generation at the time.

Trust structures are commonly used to support the ability of the family business to take a longer-term view, with the controlling trustees having to balance the long-term survival and growth of the business with the need to fund the lifestyle of the family. In this way a trust structure will provide a safety net against any particular individual who may want to realise a short-term advantage, to the detriment of the longer-term success of the business. This is useful where the family aim is to preserve the asset for future generations as a legacy.

Additionally, if the controlling shares are held by a trust, whilst the economic benefit can be made available to many individuals, the ownership and voting power vests with one entity. In this way 'voting blocs' can be preserved down the generations rather than being broken up, furthering the ability of the business to see through a long-term strategy.

The use of a trust structure also allows eventual decisions about ownership to be deferred. This is relevant where it is not yet clear who, if anyone, is suitable to succeed to ownership and/or management of the business. The trustees are then able to wait until it is appropriate for the business to be passed to the next generation. This may be important where the older generation has died sooner than expected.

Trustee selection is important. Normally, senior family members are appointed, perhaps along with trusted external individuals. Family advisors can also play a key role here. A further advantage can be the continued involvement of family members from the older generations who are passing on their ownership interests. These individuals will often retain an emotional attachment to the business until death. A role as trustee will offer them continuing involvement with the running of the business at a strategic, rather than a hands-on, level.

11.   Sources of finance

The family business tends to be particularly averse to taking on external finance. Particularly in the founder generation the preference is, where possible, to fund growth organically from reinvested profits. Where further finance proves necessary, the business will first look to loans from individual family members.

If the family business is to continue to grow, non-family finance may become unavoidable. This may be because a family member has had to withdraw funds from the business for external reasons, or due to a desire to increase the scale of operations beyond that which can be sustained by existing family resources. It is at this point that careful structuring of the business will be crucial in reconciling the need for external investment with the desire to retain family control.

Typically, a corporate structure will be most attractive to potential investors – although, assuming that trade is carried out via a corporate body, there should be little concern as to the nature of the ownership structure above the trading company, which may include trusts and/or partnerships. Bank finance will normally be the first stop for raising additional finance. This should not pose any real threat to family control, although as with any business the bank may impose restrictive covenants that limit the directors' actions.

Where greater levels of funding are needed or where family members are particularly averse to high levels of debt finance, private equity or venture capital finance may be available. Whether this is appropriate for the family business will depend on the medium-term aims of the family. Venture capitalists will normally look for a short- to medium-term exit from their investment, usually by sale or flotation of the business. Private equity investors may take a longer-term view but at some point will want to realise their investment. If the intention is eventually to float the business, perhaps using a structure that allows the family to retain control, venture capital finance may be appropriate. If not, then more careful thought is needed as to how the venture capitalist or private equity investor will exit their investment.

It may be that there is an intention eventually to sell part of the business in a trade sale, perhaps in order to raise funds for other parts of the business. In this case venture capital or private equity may be attractive, as the sale proceeds will offer the exit they require. It would be sensible here to structure the business so that the aspect eventually destined for sale is as autonomous as possible, perhaps carried out via a separate company, in order to enhance its appeal to any prospective purchaser.

It is also possible that at some point in the future the family expects to have sufficient resources to buy out the external investor, perhaps on realisation of a business asset or if an individual family member anticipates realising funds from an investment outside the main family business. This depends as well on the ambition of the investor, which is often to sell and may not be compatible with many family businesses. If there is sufficient certainty as to the availability of family funds in the future, it would be worth considering the issue of redeemable shares, which contain an agreement that the shares will be repurchased at a fixed point in the future.

Such investors will sometimes expect to be involved in the day-to-day activities of the business and are likely to demand a presence on the board of directors. This may be viewed as a key advantage of the offering, if they have the requisite experience providing external expertise in the field in which the family business operates and also in corporate finance. In the context of the family business it may, however, be highly unwelcome, viewed as outside interference in family matters. Establishing attitudes towards this will be key in determining whether venture capital is a suitable source of finance.

Many listed companies, among the largest corporate groups in the world, remain in essence family companies. This is achieved primarily by the existence of various, often numerous, classes of share, all of which carry different rights to votes, dividend payments and a share in company assets on liquidation. Most commonly the shares made available to the public and traded on the various national stock markets will carry no, or only limited, voting rights.

As an example, every share in the share classes owned by the family might carry 10 votes whilst every publicly owned share carries one vote. A more straightforward arrangement might be that the classes of share capital owned by the public carry no votes at all, though such shares may prove in some cases difficult to sell to the public and particularly to institutional shareholders.

A structure of this sort allows large-scale investment whilst the family effectively retains control of the business. This can be enhanced by retaining a majority of family members on the board of directors, either via exercise of the family voting rights or by prescription in the company articles.

Having said all this, it would be naïve to believe that a structure of this sort can entirely protect the family from the influence of the external shareholders. The value of the company will depend in part on the value of its traded non-family shares, and the value of these shares in the market will rest on perceptions of the capability of the individuals running the company and decisions made as to the company direction. In order to maintain the value of the company, the family will inevitably need to make concessions to their external investors.

An institutional shareholder with a large shareholding may not be able to influence the company directly by voting power, but the threat of sale of a large shareholding and the likely resulting fall in value of all company shares does give that shareholder power over the directors and the family shareholders. This power may exercise itself in, for example, insisting that non-family directors are elected to the board. More generally, a degree of transparency will be needed from a public company and this may initially be uncomfortable for those family members who have traditionally seen the company as theirs to run as they see fit.

12.   Structures to support growth

We have already demonstrated that the notion of the term 'family business' covers a diverse variety of enterprises, ranging from the small start-up run by its founder to the multinational corporate group. Clearly, the business structures that would be highly suitable for the former business will be by no means adequate for the latter. It is therefore vital that the way in which the family business is structured is regularly reviewed to ensure that it remains appropriate to the scale and nature of the business operations.

One impetus for such a review will be the change of generation. Successor generations may bring renewed desire to grow or change the business; in particular they may seek to move the business in different directions in terms of product or area of operation. It is important that the business structure is sufficiently robust to support planned growth, which may well mean establishing a more complex corporate structure with various layers of ownership and a number of entities to deal with different areas of operation. This may also provide a useful opportunity for the family business to allocate responsibility to different family members for their area of expertise or interest. The opportunity to take responsibility for a defined and autonomous area of the business may prove useful in bringing on the younger family members.

Where expansion is international, it may also prove necessary to establish separate entities in different geographical regions. There will be significant tax considerations here and there may also be issues for certain entities with cross-jurisdictional recognition and legal status. This may be an issue where a partnership structure is adopted, and in particular where that partnership takes the form of a limited partnership or a limited liability partnership. These issues will always need to be considered where there is an international aspect to the family business.

13.   Conclusion

The key decisions to be made when thinking about family business structure fall into three areas:

- What type of entity or entities should the family business trade through?

- What sort of an ownership structure, is needed above those trading vehicles?
- How can we adapt the chosen vehicles to meet family and business needs?

In most cases an existing structure will already be in place and so it may be that not all these areas will be open for debate. Certainly, the last question will always be relevant.

This chapter has returned a number of times to the opportunities offered by corporate structures, and suggestions for ways in which these can be formed. This is no coincidence: companies are by far the most common form of family business, and particularly for the main trading vehicle(s) of the business. They are flexible, recognised internationally and offer many opportunities for ownership and reward structures that can be customised so as to meet family needs.

Partnerships may be useful as a trading vehicle, particularly in certain professions. In jurisdictions where partnerships can be structured so as to limit the liability of their partners to business debts, for example as a limited liability partnership or limited partnership, it is likely that their use will increase. Partnerships have a further role to play, along with trusts, in forming an ownership structure above the trading entities. This will often prove as important as the trading vehicle in determining the success of the business against the family's criteria.

This chapter has outlined some of the ways in which the structures available to the family business can be used to meet family aims. It is our belief that a detailed and ongoing assessment of how business structure can be used effectively in each of the areas outlined above is vital for the continuing success of any family business.

Preparing for transfer of ownership

Ivan Lansberg
Maria Dolores Moreno
Lansberg, Gersick & Associates LLC

1. Introduction

The transfer of ownership is one of the most significant events in the life of a family business. Over the past two decades many business families, especially those who own medium-to-large enterprises, have invested much time and resources preparing an orderly transition of their wealth and their enterprises. Many have adopted family constitutions and formal shareholders' agreements to regulate the relationships among their heirs for generations to come. The Dickensian image of the family meeting at the lawyer's office, to hear for the first time a relative's last will and testament, is increasingly a thing of the past. Today, much emphasis is given to the creation of structures and organisational forms (such as trusts, holding companies, shareholder contracts and family protocols) with the hope that these mechanisms will minimise estate taxation and at the same time preserve family harmony in the future. While it is early to tell on the aggregate whether these instruments have in fact accomplished their intended purpose, our experience over 20 years working with business families is that these tools are certainly no panaceas: despite much effort to avoid inheritance and succession conflicts through formal legal arrangements, many business families still run into serious trouble during generational transitions. While we strongly support the notion that formal agreements and legal structures regulating owners are helpful and, indeed, often necessary for the successful continuity of a family enterprise, experience shows that these tools are certainly not sufficient. For there is no legal agreement or structure that, at the end of the day, does not depend on the good will and commitment of the people whose life it sets out to regulate.

At first brush this may seem like a self-evident, if not obvious, idea. However, in the seemingly 'messy' process of generational transition many business owners and their advisors are often seduced by the tangible nature of the legalities. In these processes trusts, contracts and structures seem like *terra firma* in the sea of vague familial obligations, promises and good intentions.

Consider the case of a prominent business family who retained the services of a top estate lawyer and worked to forge an 'iron-clad' shareholders' agreement. A few years into the transition the oldest of the three brothers died unexpectedly from a heart attack, triggering a wave of conflict that threatened to unravel the family and ultimately their enterprise. Shortly upon her husband's death, his wife learned for the first time that the agreement stipulated that his shares of the family business would pass directly to their children – de facto leaving her out of the bulk of his inheritance. While she was to be the beneficiary of other assets, the fact that her children (rather than she) would now become shareholders in the family business felt as a deep betrayal and estranged her both from her in-laws and her own offspring. More importantly, the sudden unveiling of the shareholders' agreement had repercussions with the surviving brothers' spouses, who were shocked to learn that their husbands too had signed a legally binding document of such consequence without ever consulting them. Only after a prolonged mediation, through which the original shareholders' agreement was renegotiated with 'all the cards on the table' and with the structured involvement of all relevant stakeholders, was the family able to heal the mistrust that ensued and recommit to the continuity of the family enterprise. As this family learned, no matter how strong (or well intended) a shareholders' agreement is, it can serve to undermine continuity if drawn in secrecy and without the informed (and understood) consent of the relevant stakeholders. As one of the brothers indicated: "The irony of this is that had we followed a different process – one that was transparent rather than shrouded in secrecy – we may have gotten to the *same* agreement but with very different outcomes ..." The key is to structure the process so that it enhances trust.

The purpose of this chapter is to offer a guide to family business owners and their advisors about how best to manage the process through which future asset allocations priorities are defined and decisions about ownership transfers are made and formalised. Our fundamental premise is that the way formal agreements are drafted has a very significant impact on their practical enforceability and on either enhancing or undermining the commitment to continuity. While much attention has been paid to the content of ownership decisions – for example, what makes for better or worse shareholders' agreements or trust architectures – few commentators have focused on how the process through which ownership choices are made ultimately influences the outcomes of continuity planning.

Specifically, we will suggest that, ideally, effective ownership transfers ought to follow a four-step process:

- *preparing:* setting the stage for ownership discussions;
- *visioning:* getting current and future owners to articulate their aspirations and negotiate a shared vision across generations;
- *formalising:* getting owners to document the agreements into legally binding contracts; and
- *implementing:* getting the owners to turn agreements on paper into living organisations.

2. Preparing: setting the stage for ownership discussions

Imagine a family with little mountaineering knowledge or experience that was about to embark on a strenuous mountain crossing over the Alps. Imagine, further, that the family's wealth, its emotional well-being, the realisation of its deepest aspirations for the future as well as its stature in the community, all depended on the successful completion of the trek. Wouldn't you advise the family to go out of its way to prepare for the journey? Wouldn't you, at a minimum, give them the basic survival skills necessary to complete the crossing successfully? Of course you would. And yet, when it comes to decisions influencing the future ownership of their joint assets, most business families engage in just such a high-stakes journey with little or no preparation.

The starting point of any ownership transfer should always involve a period of grounding, coaching and preparation. The fundamental task of this initial stage is clarifying expectations about the process itself – Who will be involved? How long will it take? What information will they need? What homework will they need to do to understand the basic issues and choices at hand? What roadblocks and frustrations are they likely to encounter? How might they go about resolving their differences when these occur? Preparing a family for effective ownership transfer requires addressing these and many other process questions upfront.

It is important to 'normalise' and anticipate the generic challenges that business families typically face during these transitions, with the purpose of raising the family's coping capacity. For example, helping a family to view the transfer of ownership not just as a set of rational decisions with associated costs and benefits but also as choices that have emotional underpinnings is often useful. For instance, it is useful to inoculate the family to expect that these conversations are never easy even in the best of families. Indeed, the transfer of ownership can (and often does) trigger a deep sense of loss and affects the senior generation's perceptions of control over their destiny, or even their sense of stature in the family's hierarchy. Likewise, it is common for the junior generation to worry about coming across as greedy or ungrateful when discussing these issues with their parents. Moreover, in many cultures discussing the aftermath of the parents' death is even equated with tempting fate.

The objective in the preparation stage is to frame the process such that it legitimises the expression of ambivalence and emotion most families go through when faced with issues related to a transfer of ownership, and makes those aspects of the process an integral part of the work that, if managed constructively, can help establish a climate of trust among family members. Families need time to acknowledge and resolve their mixed feelings about these complex issues. Creating expectations that the process of ownership transfer will unfold in a tidy linear way often squanders the opportunity that it offers to educate the family and to build their capacity to understand, communicate and solve problems effectively. Naturally, this is not an argument for not structuring the process and providing direction; it is simply an acknowledgement that sometimes in this work the shortest distance between two points is not a straight line – the logical, the *psychological* and the interpersonal work must go hand in hand within the family.

It is often helpful to start the preparation process with an educational workshop that raises the family's awareness of the generic content and process issues associated with ownership transitions and introduces a common language with which to engage in a shared exploration project. These workshops need to be staged carefully and with the active involvement of the family. The aim is to customise the issues to the family's culture of origin, wealth and business portfolio, and stage of development. The workshop also serves as an efficient vehicle to develop a 'psychological contract' for the process to be followed. It clarifies expectations about the time horizon for the transition, the roles that everyone will need to play and the tasks that each individual is expected to perform.

It can be tempting for families to begin discussions about ownership transfers with the most difficult issues they have to resolve. However, rather than tackling the toughest subjects at the front end of the process, it is helpful to organise the agendas backwards so that family members begin with those topics that reinforce their shared identity and their common objectives and gradually build the level of confidence necessary to engage constructively on issues where their individual needs and aspirations might not be in alignment. For example, rather than starting the discussion with issues such as stock allocations between those who work in the business and those who do not, or how much wealth is to be passed on to each individual, it is better to start by discussing the family's history with ownership transfers – what has gone well in the past and what has not; what lessons did family members draw from those experiences and how might they shape their expectations. Also, talking about the family's shared values and how they wish to apply those values to their discussions of ownership in the future can also strengthen the family's commitment to protecting the unity of the group even in families who may wish to ultimately separate their assets.

Another critical element of the preparation stage is gathering accurate information about the current ownership situation. Often, family enterprises grow in opportunistic ways over many years – new ventures are started, minority investments in other people's business are made, joint ventures with partners in foreign jurisdictions are done, and land and buildings are purchased simply because opportunities to do so became available. It is not unusual for highly entrepreneurial families to end up with a complex, diverse and fragmented portfolio of investments and properties that have accumulated over time. Each one of these assets has a particular ownership structure (and a market value) that is frequently unknown to the family at the time when they start thinking about inheritance. In cultures in which conspicuous wealth exposes the family to political or personal risks, asset portfolios are deliberately kept under wraps. Also, past ownership decisions are often obfuscated by elusive memories. In many families the internal structure of ownership that was originally established for a particular entity or property might have been forgotten – a company was set up between a father and a son with the intention of bringing the others in later; a venture between two sisters excluded a third who was still too young; a spouse was kept out from an entity because the marriage at the time was going through a turbulent phase; children then unborn were not taken into account at the time a trust was formed; a friend who was named director of the holding has since died or moved away – are all quite common. Ownership documents are static and frozen at the time they were drafted; the family, its wealth, its enterprises and society at large (as well as the laws guiding ownership) are dynamic and continue to evolve. Families can quickly lose track of what they actually have. Forgotten as the original ownership documents might be *psychologically*, they remain *legally* binding until they are modified.

When it comes to ownership transfers, history matters. Unearthing and reconstructing the family's portfolio of assets and capturing the assumptions that led to the original choices made can be a delicate task at the preparation stage. Often surprises emerge that can unintentionally affect the process. For example, when two sisters in a business family we worked with got to learn that, 15 years before, their father had given stock in the flagship business of the family only to the sons that worked with him in the company, they felt so excluded and betrayed that they were reluctant to participate in the discussions as to how the future ownership transfer would be carried out. Even though much had happened in the ensuing time (one of the brothers had started his own venture under the umbrella of family holding and the other had left the family business altogether), the original choices still stood. The parents, who did not even remember that these choices had been made long ago, quickly moved to explain to their daughters that the original assumptions no longer held true and that the whole purpose of the ownership planning process was to reconfigure the portfolio in a more fair and balanced way that reflected the current situation of the family. Again, ownership decisions and especially the underlying assumptions that drive them are frequently interpreted in emotional ways. Because of the precise and tangible nature of ownership, these issues can become the standard through which comparative assessments about who is loved the most are made. As in Shakespeare's *King Lear*, rivalries among siblings, cousins and their spouses are rapidly fuelled by social comparisons within the family. If past ownership choices are not appropriately contextualised at the front end of the process, if the history is not revisited and reinterpreted in the context of the future, trust can be compromised and the process for resolving asset transfers constructively can derail even before it starts.

Past compensation practices – specifically, how family shareholders, directors and executives are remunerated – are without a doubt among the most difficult issues to uncover during the preparation stage. This is particularly so in transitions from a founder entrepreneur to his or her children. Entrepreneurs are typically 'deal makers' who thrive in making personal agreements with the key stakeholders that help cement their loyalty. In many first-generation family businesses there is a 'secret chequebook', controlled exclusively by the founder, that is used to compensate individuals in a variety of roles. Typically at this stage there is little distinction between salaries, bonuses, dividends and simply paternalistic gifts that the founder may feel like making to specific individuals at any point in time. In one family we worked with, the founder personally paid the salaries of his sons who worked in the business, and a monthly stipend to his daughters who did not work in the company and he was the only one who knew how much each was getting. Because the sons earned considerably more, the father was very hesitant to discuss past 'compensation' during the ownership transfer process, even though he realised that in order to clarify how the family would deal with this issue in the future past practices had to be revealed. However, when this issue was framed in the context of clarifying future privileges, rights, obligations and responsibilities of owners and managers as well as the different roles each would play in the future, the family was able to understand and discuss openly the reasons why different sources of remuneration existed – including the difference between executive salaries and bonuses on the one hand, and shareholder dividends on the other.

A critical task during the preparation stage involves not just documenting what the legal structure of ownership actually is, but also uncovering the gaps that may exist between the de facto structure and the proprietary family's governance practices. Often long-established governance practices are not supported by the legal structure as family members and other stakeholders assume. For example, it is not unusual for a senior group of siblings or cousins to function explicitly as a shareholder assembly or even as a board of directors without actually having the legal right to do so. The discrepancy between the practice and the legal structure can become explicit when the unexpected happens – the founder of the business dies suddenly and the corporate bye-laws are actually read, or the tax authorities suddenly intervene and uncover who the legally liable parties to an alleged violation actually are. Here again, surprises can and do occur – as the heir of a prominent family told us: "Before they all died, my uncles established a board of directors with handpicked cousins from the next generation and empowered it to make all governance decisions. However, we did not discover that group was not a *real* board until we tried to fire an incompetent shareholder from the management of the business. As it turned out, the uncles had not bothered with making the appropriate legal changes to the corporate statutes and, when contested, we discovered that in fact we had little control to shape governance decisions after they were gone. We had to put the matter to a vote of all the shareholders and lost."

In our experience, the upfront investment of time and resources made during the preparation stage needs to be explicitly conveyed to client families as an essential part of the process. Sometimes families, eager to put uncomfortable ownership discussions behind them and conscious of the costs involved in working with outside professionals, get impatient and want to get to the 'real issues' right away. Explaining the critical importance of this stage is very important to set the right tone for the process. As in matters of family health, the critical message here needs to be "an ounce of prevention can spare you a life time of pain ..."

3. **Visioning: getting current and future owners to articulate their aspirations and negotiate a shared vision across generations**
Once a family has been educated about the process of ownership transfer and they have taken stock of what they own, they are ready to engage in the next step of the transition: imagining an ownership structure for the future.

Just as with the preparation phase, the work involved in visualising an alternative ownership structure for the future of a business family is often dismissed and devalued as an unnecessary distraction. Against the backdrop of hard ownership choices – portfolio configuration and returns; inheritance allocations; governance architecture for corporate and trust structures; liquidity needs; and, especially, estate taxes – taking the time to articulate aspirations and dreams seems like an ephemeral and tangential task. And yet, customising ownership solutions so that they resonate with the aspirations of current and future owners is essential for the successful implementation of any plan for the transfer of ownership.

Moreover, when the visioning work is done effectively, it serves to bond the commitment of the owners to their legacy and motivates them to invest in the responsible governance (and management) of their assets. The very fact of inviting the current and future owners to articulate their life aspirations and dreams at the front end of the ownership transition serves to legitimise the idea that continuity is always a choice and that the family's wealth is, in part, a resource to support the lives they aspire to live. Indeed, when the life aspirations of the owners are articulated and used as a backdrop to frame inheritance choices, the design of ownership and governance structures, commitment to the enterprise and its continuity is enhanced.

However, getting the current and future owners to articulate what they want is seldom an easy task – this is particularly so when it comes to the future of their wealth and the ownership and governance structures built to support it. Research and experience suggest that humans in general – and business families in particular – are notoriously poor at defining desirable possibilities for their future lives. The cognitive effort necessary to conceive alternative scenarios for our lives that are unencumbered by our present experience is significant. Most fall prey to what Daniel Gilbert, the notable Harvard psychologist, calls 'presentism' – the tendency to define our aspirations for the future in ways that are simply unimaginative extrapolations of the life we are currently living. The current existence of business owners imprisons their capacity to envisage alternatives: founding entrepreneurs actively seek out the child to succeed them who is most like them because they cannot fathom a system that is not led by a single charismatic leader; sibling owners look to replicate their fraternal ties in a complex network of cousins of widely dispersed ages and interests; families that have owned businesses for generations simply cannot visualise continuity without an operating business; and so forth. Presentism is unquestionably a mental trap that poses a challenge for business families wanting to design a future ownership structure.

Simply asking the owners point blank, "What do you want?" is often not all that helpful, either. Many owners do have vague conceptions of the future they wish for, but rarely do they devote the time and energy necessary to clearly define what it is that they want. While the seniors are typically so caught up in the momentum of their lives that it is hard for them to imagine an alternative, the juniors often do not even feel like they have permission to articulate their own life dreams in the context of the planning process. Some fear that exposing their aspirations to the rest of the family may elicit disapproval and criticism. Others may simply not be developmentally ready to know what they want at the time the planning process takes place. And yet, it is important to recognise that while the developmental planets might never quite be in perfect alignment, the planning process must nonetheless go forth. The fundamental recognition that there are no 'silver bullets' to solve all the nuances and potential complications associated with the transfer of ownership and wealth is important. Every 'solution' engenders a new set of dilemmas and problems that need to be managed and resolved. Hence, the goal is not to find the perfect answer; it is to build the owning family's capacity to understand, communicate and problem-solve effectively. As with gardening, this kind of planning requires a long-term mindset in which stretches of sustained attention and hard work – weeding, fertilising, watering and pruning – are punctuated by moments when the garden blooms. And then the cycle starts all over again as the family continues to develop and the circumstances change. Contrary to the 'engineering' mindset often espoused by the professions, the process of ownership transfer is not just a collection of tangible problems to be solved; it is an unfolding human drama with the potential to bring families together or drive them apart depending on how it is managed.

Its inherent messiness notwithstanding, the visioning process often benefits from being stimulated and structured in a building-block fashion: starting with opportunities for individual reflection, followed by facilitated conversations within and among couples. Cross-generational meetings that bring together the whole family, or particular segments of it, are also helpful and necessary. Sometimes the family's imagination needs to be 'seeded' with questions, examples and case descriptions about the experience of others. Benchmarking visits with other families, who have already implemented ownership scenarios that might be unimaginable at the front end of the process, are often the best window into possible futures. In this work individual or group epiphanies are rare – the vision for the future ownership scenario usually emerges gradually out of a period of sustained reflection and exploration of possibilities.

Visioning is therefore an iterative process that involves a back and forth between individual reflection and collective dialogue over a protracted period of time. There are many reasons why this is so. For some families the process of visioning can be scary because it confronts them with the fact that not everyone may want the same thing. Naturally, working through these discrepancies is important. For other families, the process is hard because defining a new vision forces them to articulate what they want and, in so doing, give rise to fears of disappointment in the event that their aspirations cannot be realised. Sometimes, families may even deliberately keep their aspirations vague as a defence against their fear of failure.

However, the fact that defining the future is difficult is not a reason not to do it. The natural aging process *forces* families to embark on a process of change whether or not they have chosen a destination for their journey. Their choice, in fact, is not whether to go on the journey; it is whether or not they want to *manage* the journey – by choosing a destination and marshalling the strategic and tactical skills, the resources and the energy necessary to get them from where they are to where they want to go.

The visioning process, if done thoughtfully, serves to further educate family members about the fundamental dilemmas and trade-offs associated with family enterprise continuity – for example, the trade-off between economies of scale and risk reduction associated with diversified aggregate wealth on the one hand and the loss of individual autonomy on the other that comes with the delegation of authority to the collective decision-making processes necessary to manage pooled assets. Similarly, the complexities associated with governing and managing aggregated wealth require a level of meritocratic professionalism that may exclude some of the owners from direct involvement in decisions about their wealth. As these trade-offs become evident, individuals enhance their capacity to compromise and to accept the opportunities and risks that the family enterprise in the future might offer. The process itself also serves as a rehearsal of the future the family might be exploring. If, through the process of visioning, the family finds new ways of communicating and collaborating, and if their problem-solving capacity is enhanced through the planning process, then the possibility of a joint future is reinforced. But if the family cannot even bring itself to collaborate around the development of a new vision, then the natural conclusion might well be that separating the assets is in fact the best course of action. Not all business families are meant to be together.

The visioning process also requires assisting individuals in both generations to anticipate personal, financial and career issues. For the seniors, helping them to articulate dreams yet unrealised – things, if you will, that they would lament not having done before their death – and encouraging them to take those aspirations seriously, assisting them with fleshing out the practical steps that might be taken to realise them, is essential. It is common for seniors to underestimate the extent to which skills that they have honed over a lifetime in the family enterprise are applicable in new areas such as philanthropy, education, community institutions and politics. Often, the seniors need considerable coaching in thinking through the evolution of their roles away from day-to-day management and toward governance. As the chairman of a prominent family enterprise put it: "When we started this process I did not really understand what a chairman actually did and thought they were kicking me upstairs ... I was so focused on operational decision-making that I did not realise all the hard work that governance involved ..."

Perhaps the most delicate visioning work with the seniors involves helping them with their financial planning. Getting them to anchor their cost-of-living assumptions on their actual historical pattern of expenditure; assisting them with estimating the income they will need in order to live their later years in the style to which they grown accustomed; helping them to articulate their philanthropic aspirations and the funds necessary to realise them; alerting them to the importance of securing their own financial independence – all are integral parts of the visioning work. If possible, it is also important for them to estimate the discretionary income needed to handle unexpected expenses unencumbered by the inheritance expectations of their heirs. For example, some parents want to help children (or grandchildren) with special needs – a divorced son or daughter who might be going through a rough patch in their lives; a disabled grandchild who requires special medical attention; or a relative who cannot afford adequate housing.

The financial costs associated with the retirement of the seniors and the successful transition to multi-generational enterprises is often underestimated (particularly in privately held enterprises). As the seniors contemplate their departure from the management and governance roles they have occupied, they quickly realise that their (and their family's) lifestyle is often tightly intertwined with the economics of their business. The compensation they have drawn historically through salaries, bonuses and dividends typically does not reflect the income they will need in order to sustain the life to which they have grown accustomed – office space; secretarial assistance; access to professional help (lawyers, accountants and consultants) and staff to look after their personal affairs; a travel and entertainment budget; the protection of security guards; and the use of the corporate plane, to mention a few – are all hidden costs that need to be catalogued and quantified if adequate budgeting for the future is to occur. Similarly, formalising the governance structures and processes necessary to continue a complex multi-generational enterprise will also cost additional money. For example, bringing the family together regularly for meetings and retreats; compensating family members serving on newly formed committees of the emergent governance structure for their time and their travel costs; remunerating independent directors and trustees that may be hired; paying for professionals assisting with the transition (consultants, lawyers, financial planners and so on) need also to be appropriately estimated. Indeed, the viability of continuity often hinges on estimating adequate financing.

Occasionally, some seniors are also called upon to assist the businesses they turned over to their successors. In a family we worked with, the seniors had long retired when one of the sons acting arbitrarily (and in violation of the shareholders' agreement) made decisions that seriously compromised the viability of the family enterprise. The parents were then asked by the banks to reinvest a significant portion of their savings in order to rescue the company and the family's reputation. As the mother explained to us: "You think that once you retire you're done. But you're not. You simply can't stand on the sidelines idly while the business you built for so many years takes a dive. Getting out of the cockpit is one thing; getting off the plane is quite another ..." Also helping the seniors identify financial obligations they may have underwritten (such as collateralised loan guarantees) and working to articulate policies to protect them from downturns in the family's fortune are all critical at this stage. Unless the seniors feel reassured that their interests have been protected, they are likely to resist transferring assets – and especially control over decisions – to the next generation.

Another fundamental task that falls on the seniors during the visioning stage of the ownership transfer process is that of defining the boundaries of the family as they pertain to access to financial information and the inheritance of risks, burdens, opportunities and assets. How these boundaries are drawn also has a profound impact on who is involved in what way with the planning process. Are all future shareholders willing and able to honour the access to financial information in a responsible and confidential manner? Who will be entitled to what share of the wealth and why? Are all children to be shareholders in companies owned by the family? If so, in what proportion will shares and voting right be allocated to whom? How will in-laws be treated? What about adopted and stepchildren? These decisions are not just pertinent to matters of inheritance; they also affect the participation of heirs in future governance roles. Under what conditions should children or in-laws serve as trustees or on business boards? Underlying many of these questions are assumptions about how the composition of the family will drive ownership expectations, rights and responsibilities.

Drawing these 'entitlement' boundaries is particularly thorny with regard to how in-laws will be treated. In some families when the children marry, their spouses are brought into the family as 'full citizens' and are thus treated exactly like blood descendants. So in these families, in-laws are given the same access to financial information and comparable opportunities to participate in the governance (or even the management) of the enterprise as their direct descendant spouses. In other families, in-laws are treated more like 'resident aliens': they are offered 'voice' but not 'vote'; they have access to some (but not all) financial information; and their potential involvement with the family enterprise is more restricted. In these cases, the underlying assumption is that the in-laws can be trusted up to a point but not further. And, finally, there are families in which the in-laws are treated as visitors with 'temporary visas'. In these families, in-laws are explicitly (and often unapologetically) excluded from any conversations regarding ownership and financial matters. The underlying assumption is that giving them access to information about the family's wealth is risky and potentially harmful to both the family and the enterprise. Whereabouts a given family places its in-laws in this 'continuum of trust' is affected by many factors, including: the quality of marital relationships in the first generation; the family's history with contentious divorce; the financial independence of the in-laws, as well as the family's values and its religious and ethnic background. Clarifying these boundaries and reflecting on the consequences of drawing them in one way or another is a critical task during the visioning stage. Ultimately, the family must emerge from the visioning stage with a clear understanding of the implications of their choice, a narrative that explains why they have adopted the inclusion philosophy that they have and a plan to share the information with the relevant stakeholders and assure that legal agreements are drafted consistent with this choice (eg, ownership structures, shareholders' agreements, wills).

The visioning work with the junior generation (most of whom are typically the future owners) also poses its own set of challenges. For them the process of defining the future ownership structure can be both exhilarating and daunting. After many years of apprenticeship and deference, the experience of discussing ownership issues with the seniors can feel like the next stage in an evolving partnership with them. Over the years we have seen many cases in which groups of juniors, who were alienated from the family enterprise, enthusiastically embraced the planning process and invigorated the development of a new vision for the future. The challenge is often how to harness their energy to do this work while still keeping their expectations in alignment with what the seniors want and need from them. It is particularly important to clarify with the seniors how much influence they want to give their heirs to shape the ownership choices during the visioning process. Few things are more discouraging for the junior generation (and more destructive to family harmony) than when they engage in the visioning process thinking they have more authority to shape ownership decisions than their seniors are actually willing to give them. Unfortunately, it is quite common for seniors to squander the goodwill built during the visioning stage by going along with a more inclusive process only to yank authority back from the juniors and impose their own preferences at the crucial moment when decisions have to be formalised legally. Again, taking the time at the front end to clarify expectations about this is critical. There are basically, four ways decisions about the future ownership structure can be made:

- the seniors *retain all the authority* and make the choices all on their own;
- the seniors *retain all decision-making authority* but choose to *consult* with their children – sharing with them the relevant information and inviting their point of view and preferences into the mix of ideas that guide their choices;
- the seniors choose to share their authority with their children and invite

them into a *joint decision* process; and
- the seniors *delegate* all of their authority to the juniors and have them make all the ownership decisions.

Both research on decision making[1] and our experience strongly suggest that either consultation (second bullet) or joint decision making (third bullet) are the most effective processes to use during the ownership transfer. This is particularly so when the family aspires to keep its enterprises and wealth as an interdependent portfolio owned collectively and governed through an integrated structure. There are two basic reasons why this is so. First, the successful implementation of ownership decisions often requires the involvement of those whose lives will be affected by them. If these stakeholders participate in the decision-making process in some constructive way, they are more likely to own, accept and commit to the choices that are made. Secondly, even in close-knit families, the seniors often make the wrong assumptions about what the juniors may want for their future. By involving the juniors in the decision process, the possibility for open and direct communication is enhanced, often leading to choices that are better informed. The one potential drawback of a more participatory process, however, is that it takes *time*. Educating people to understand the issues, creating structured opportunities for them to reach consensus on the choices, helping them learn the interpersonal and communication skills necessary for effective negotiation, can all lengthen the transition period. This is why the sooner a family can motivate itself to engage in planning, the more options it will have for managing the transition process.

Learning how to collaborate effectively with their seniors is not the only challenge the juniors face during the visioning process – they must also learn to collaborate *with each other*. When a group of siblings and/or cousins meet for the first time to discuss their future and that of the family's wealth and its enterprise, they quickly learn that they are quite diverse in their background and perspectives – some are older, others younger; some are daughters others sons; some feel like favourites others not; some have worked in the business for many years while others have pursued their studies and careers away; some are very successful and wealthy in their own right while others may be struggling economically and are still quite dependent of the parents; some have expertise that is relevant to the discussion of ownership issues while for others these issues are quite foreign and even intimidating. These differences notwithstanding, the juniors must learn to deal with each other in new ways. Indeed the visioning process offers the juniors an opportunity to shed biases, roles and stereotypes from childhood that may have lingered in their relationships and rediscover each other in an arena defined by a new set of issues.

There is an inevitable asymmetry of information and understanding about the family enterprise – its strategy and operations, its products, customers and suppliers and, especially, its economics and legalities – that builds over time between those who work more centrally in senior management roles and those who do not. Discussions about inheritance of stock and the future ownership structure make this

---

1   Vroom, V and Yetton, P, *Leadership and Decision-making*. Pittsburgh (1973) University of Pittsburgh Press.

gap evident. How those who have built careers in the family business will be treated in the future, with regard to stock allocations, is often a serious concern among the junior generation that emerges during the visioning process. It is not unusual for those who have devoted their careers to the family company to expect a larger share of stock than their siblings and cousins who have not contributed to building the enterprise. As the oldest son from a prominent Latin American business told us: "In our case my sister and I joined the company when our father was just starting out. We worked by his side since the start like partners, so why should we now be treated as equals to our brothers and sisters who weren't involved at all?" The tendency for people who have worked in building something to overvalue the worth of their contribution, and hence the share of stock they deserve, is so common that Dan Ariely, a renowned behavioural economist from MIT, named it the "IKEA effect" (after the store whose customers must invest considerable effort in building its unassembled furniture products – and which presumably leads them to overvalue their purchases once these are assembled). In contrast, the juniors who were not involved with the company often take the position that those who worked in the family business were using the family's shared equity as capital, that they received ample compensation as executives and that consequently they are not necessarily deserving of larger shares of stock in the future. As we have indicated, these conversations offer wonderful opportunities to contextualise expectations of entitlement and educate family members about the need for a governance architecture that helps regulate and institutionalise the relationship between those in the family, those who will be shareholders and those who are (or aspire to serve) in management roles.

4. Formalising: getting owners to document the agreements into legally binding contracts

Once a family emerges from the visioning work with a clear consensus on what it wants for the future, the next stage of the process requires transitioning from an 'imagined possibility' to a set of formal agreements that will add permanence to their vision. Some of these documents, such as the family constitution or the family business protocol, are *morally* binding, whereas trusts and shareholders' agreements are contractual documents and hence are also *legally* binding.

What documents a given family chooses to legalise varies considerably depending on the family's history, its culture of origin, the nature of the assets that are owned collectively and the jurisdiction in which the family operates. For example, families with a history of litigious shareholder battles (or acrimonious divorces) often draw more elaborate legally binding agreements; whereas families who have enjoyed a more harmonious relationship over generations frequently settle for more informal documents that are mostly morally binding. Similarly, families in common-law cultures tend to prefer agreements that articulate broad principles while being short on policies, whereas families from civil-law cultures tend to prefer elaborate documents that spell out many policies for dealing with a wide array of contingencies.

While our focus on this chapter in on the *process* through which families reach these agreements, it is useful to list kinds of issues that form the *content* of these formal documents. The figure below attempts to organise the types of issues that these agreements cover into the three-circle model depicted.[2]

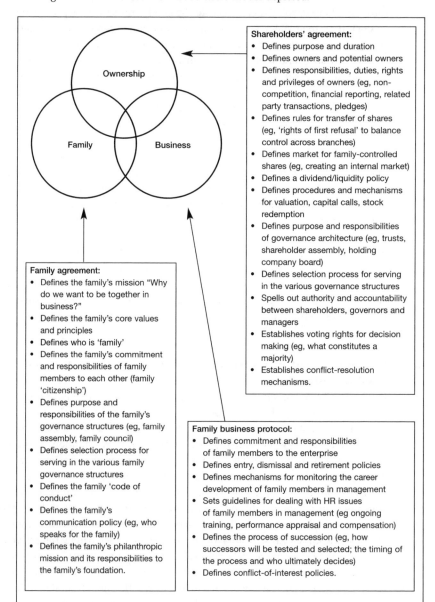

Shareholders' agreement:
- Defines purpose and duration
- Defines owners and potential owners
- Defines responsibilities, duties, rights and privileges of owners (eg, non-competition, financial reporting, related party transactions, pledges)
- Defines rules for transfer of shares (eg, 'rights of first refusal' to balance control across branches)
- Defines market for family-controlled shares (eg, creating an internal market)
- Defines a dividend/liquidity policy
- Defines procedures and mechanisms for valuation, capital calls, stock redemption
- Defines purpose and responsibilities of governance architecture (eg, trusts, shareholder assembly, holding company board)
- Defines selection process for serving in the various governance structures
- Spells out authority and accountability between shareholders, governors and managers
- Establishes voting rights for decision making (eg, what constitutes a majority)
- Establishes conflict-resolution mechanisms.

Family agreement:
- Defines the family's mission "Why do we want to be together in business?"
- Defines the family's core values and principles
- Defines who is 'family'
- Defines the family's commitment and responsibilities of family members to each other (family 'citizenship')
- Defines purpose and responsibilities of the family's governance structures (eg, family assembly, family council)
- Defines selection process for serving in the various family governance structures
- Defines the family 'code of conduct'
- Defines the family's communication policy (eg, who speaks for the family)
- Defines the family's philanthropic mission and its responsibilities to the family's foundation.

Family business protocol:
- Defines commitment and responsibilities of family members to the enterprise
- Defines entry, dismissal and retirement policies
- Defines mechanisms for monitoring the career development of family members in management
- Sets guidelines for dealing with HR issues of family members in management (eg ongoing training, performance appraisal and compensation)
- Defines the process of succession (eg, how successors will be tested and selected; the timing of the process and who ultimately decides)
- Defines conflict-of-interest policies.

---

2   Adapted from Montenegro, D and Ward, JL, *The Family Constitution* (2005) Marietta GA Family Enterprise Publishers.

Not all family agreements cover all of these areas. Typically, the issues that fall under 'ownership' are articulated in a shareholders' agreement and are legally binding. (Sometimes these policies are woven into the articles of incorporation of the business, or built into the trust that holds the family's controlling shares.) Some families in jurisdictions where there are no trusts go off-shore to formalise their agreements or look for local legal arrangements that serve to formalise their commitments. For example, we have worked with families create a legal 'family association' in order to legitimise the norms that they adopt in the family. Indeed, in some jurisdictions, such as Spain, the *protocolo familiar* has been legally sanctioned as a binding agreement among family shareholders that bridges the gap between the traditional wills used for stipulating inheritance and corporate shareholders' agreements.

An essential step in formalising these agreements is picking a good team of advisors. As the list of issues suggests, formalising these agreements requires a multi-disciplinary team, involving at least a lawyer with estate and corporate experience, a financial/wealth management expert, a business strategist and someone well versed in family business governance. While the issues are typically segmented in accordance with disciplinary boundaries, most are in fact interdependent – for example, whether a group of current and future owners want to stay together or not is often a function of the quality of the family relationships they have; financial planning for retirement is driven by the economic performance of the assets; leadership succession depends on business strategy and the family's preferences; and so forth. These issues do not fall neatly into the domain of one or another profession.

As George Bernard Shaw once put it, "all professions are conspiracies against the laity" – they each have their methods, nomenclatures, ethical codes and fee structures. Creating a team of professionals, accustomed to working on their own, to assist a family in formalising its vision is indispensable though seldom simple. This is particularly so with regard to ownership issues, in which professionals may feel more liable and vulnerable to errors of judgement. When the process is well managed, families pay careful attention to picking advisors who understand the interdisciplinary nature of these issues, are interested, and are willing and able to collaborate with colleagues from different backgrounds. Moreover, it is important for families, as the clients, to explicitly request integrated advice that examines the issues from a variety of perspectives. In addition, it is highly recommended to build into the process opportunities for the professionals to meet regularly in order to examine their assumptions, coordinate their strategies and think through the implications of formalising the family's vision across their respective disciplines. Emerging with an integrated approach can greatly expedite the process of formalising a vision.

As families get closer and closer to formalising and, especially, to *legalising* their agreements, it is common for them to grow increasingly anxious about the formal commitments into which they are entering – issues that seemed resolved at an earlier juncture re-emerge even more forcefully, second thoughts and even regrets about concessions made on an issue earlier in the process are quite common, as are recriminations that the give-and-take among the family owners involved in the negotiation has not been fair or even-handed. It is important for the team of advisors to serve as 'midwives' of the formalising process – upholding the values of the family; being empathic and staying open to new solutions that may have not been evident earlier on in the process but still, when appropriate, serve to provide an 'institutional memory' that reminds everyone of the reasons why they chose their original positions; nudging the process along without pushing or imposing their own views on the issues; and, above all, remaining impartial and focused on the interests of all.

This is not an easy mandate to fulfil. Professionals often become the lightning rods that absorb the owners' frustrations with the wear and tear associated with any protracted negotiation. The professionals are at their best when they, as Nelson Mandela put it, "lead from behind" while still managing to give their clients and each other support.

The final signing of ownership agreements constitutes an important milestone in the history of any family business and deserves to be noted and celebrated. When the process is well managed, it concludes the formalising phase with a signing ritual that marks the beginning of a new era in the life of the family.

5. Implementing: getting the owners to turn agreements on paper into living organisations

While the formalising of agreements certainly brings an important phase of the ownership transfer process to a close, it is important to keep in mind that agreements (even legal ones) on paper are often not followed through in practice. For example, many families agree to set up independent boards of directors to oversee their businesses and holdings, but then fail to recruit the external directors to serve on them. Following exhaustive negotiations, some owners agree on elaborate voting policies to manage decision making among shareholders or at the board, but then continue relying on the old guard to decide for them. Others endlessly negotiate policies to regulate the involvement of family members with governance and management roles, but then fail to operationalise them effectively. The truth is that old habits are hard to change: committees designed to oversee the implementation of policies take too much time and can be ultimately neglected; and individuals charged with certain responsibilities do not follow through or resist being held accountable.

Families and the professionals who serve them must be attentive to the fact that translating agreements into functioning organisations is one of the most difficult (and frequently neglected) challenges underlying the orderly transfer of ownership.

It is often useful to pick a transition committee staffed with individuals with the authority and leadership skills necessary to oversee the implementation of the ownership agreement. It is important for this committee to have a clear mandate and be formally given the authority it needs to make decisions on behalf of the owners to implement the agreement. Mapping out the critical tasks, seeking the appropriate professional assistance, budgeting the financial resources necessary, establishing a timetable for implementation, developing a user-friendly version of the agreements to serve the purpose of communicating, educating, and supporting the task of implementing – all are essential. Also, it is important to build into the implementation process quarterly meetings with the owners in which they can be kept abreast of the process and provide oversight to the committee's progress. These meetings are also opportunities to foster transparency and hold those charged with implementing the ownership agreement accountable.

One of the most difficult tasks facing a transition committee during the implementation stage is populating the emergent structure that grows out of the agreements. It is important to recognise that while an open inclusive process is generally more conducive to collaborative problem solving, not everyone needs to be involved with everything. It is, therefore, useful to differentiate the family owners into three basic categories:

- *The make-it-happen group* – composed of the people who absolutely have to be involved with the implementation effort if it is going to work. Because they have both the power to make the critical decisions and access to all the relevant information, these people form the core constituency for the ownership transfer and their support is essential for the plan to be implemented.
- *The let-it-happen group* – these are the people who have the power to derail the process and need to be sufficiently involved as to feel that they understand and can bless the choices and decisions that are being made on their behalf, but they do not need to be the drivers of the process.
- *The watch-it-happen group* – these people need to be kept informed periodically about how the implementation process is unfolding. Their views should be heard and put into the mix of implementation opinions. However, they are more marginal to the process.

Organising the implementation process requires paying careful attention to who gets involved with what elements of the work at particular junctures.

Finally, as suggested at the outset, no ownership agreement lasts for ever, even if flawlessly drafted and implemented. The fundamental driver of change in families is the biological clock – the same individuals will have very different needs, wants and aspirations at different junctures of their lives. Adopting a developmental mindset and recognising that every agreement is but a temporary equilibrium that, with luck, buys the system some years of stability is in our estimation essential. The further in time the ownership agreement gets from the people who forged it, the higher the likelihood that a new agreement will need to be renegotiated. This is so because the psychological ownership that grows from having participated in the forging of the ownership agreement cannot adequately be transferred to subsequent generations. At some point down the line they will need to roll up their sleeves and get their own hands dirty with the process of drafting a new compact to guide their economic and familial interests. As Goethe so eloquently put it: "What you've inherited ... you must earn to possess."

Rewarding and incentivising non-family directors and employees

Paul McGrath
Withers LLP
Jason Ogelman
John Lamb Partnership Ltd

1. Attracting and retaining the best people

As with any business, to be successful a family business needs the right people. Families are apt to look inwards for help and skills. The family's pool of talent can be an excellent resource but if there is no one with the right experience, it would be a mistake to try to muddle through with what there is, rather than searching out the correct individual.

As a business grows and develops, the family may not be able to run all aspects of it themselves. The board will need to ask whether those family members involved in the business have the right skills. This is not just common sense but, in relation to the directors themselves, may also be a legal requirement: in the United Kingdom, for example, Section 174 of the Companies Act 2006 requires a director to act with "… the care, skill and diligence that would be exercised by a reasonably diligent person with … the general knowledge, skill and experience that may reasonably be expected of a person carrying out the functions carried out by the director …". A finance director, for example, will therefore need to have appropriate financial skills.

Examples of where outside talent can be useful at a senior level include:

- where the business is diversifying into areas where there is a shortage of home-grown talent;
- if there are actual or potential conflicts between family members, where an outsider (particularly a non-executive director) can bring a neutral, measured and professional approach; and
- if the family wishes to sell all or part of the business, where an outside manager who has had experience of grooming a business for sale, and the sale process itself, can be a real asset.

When looking to attract and retain a non-family member, it is important to bear in mind that the outsider will not share the same aspirations and values as the family. Care must be taken to ensure on the one hand that the package of salary and benefits on offer is competitive, and on the other hand that there is a sufficient deterrent in place to make leaving unattractive. In other words, it pays to adopt a carrot-and-stick approach.

2. Employment agreements

All employees of the business should have a written statement of the terms and conditions of their employment, which contains all the details required by local employment law. This applies to executive directors too, since they will be both directors and employees. Written particulars should include basic information such as place of work, salary, holiday entitlement and notice requirements.

It is common (and advisable) to provide a more detailed employment agreement, particularly for directors and other senior staff. Other provisions that may be suitable to include in such a contract are an express confidentiality clause, restrictive covenants (discussed at Section 3 below), an assignment in favour of the company of intellectual property created during the course of employment and a right for the company to pay the employee in lieu of giving notice or to put the employee on 'garden leave'.

There are some additional issues to consider when dealing with a director's employment agreement:

- The agreement may first need to be approved by the shareholders (eg, this will be necessary in the United Kingdom if the director's employment agreement is to be for a fixed period of more than two years).
- Whilst an individual can be both director and employee, the two relationships are independent. Thus, if a director is given notice that his employment is to be terminated in accordance with his employment agreement, this will not of itself mean that he ceases to be a director when his employment ends. For this reason, it is common to include a term in a director's employment agreement that he is deemed to have resigned as a director upon ceasing to be an employee. Conversely, the shareholders may have the right (either under the articles or pursuant to general company law) to remove a person as a director notwithstanding anything to the contrary in his employment agreement. That said, if he is removed in this way, he may be entitled to damages for breach of contract or unfair dismissal.
- By acting as a director, an individual exposes himself to potential personal liabilities (both to the company and to third parties). A well-advised director will wish to see that the company has in place directors' and officers' insurance to provide him with some protection. This will sometimes appear as a contractual benefit under a director's employment agreement.

3. Non-competition agreements

One of the key provisions to be included in the employment agreement of a non-family director or key employee will be 'restrictive covenants'. These are agreements on the employee's part not to do certain things that might harm the business, not only during the employment but for a period of time afterwards. The most common restrictive covenants are:

- not to compete with the business;
- not to deal with the business' customers or clients;
- not to entice away from the business its customers or clients; and
- not to poach the business's employees.

To be enforceable, restrictive covenants should go no further than is necessary to protect the company's legitimate business interests, such as its confidential information and know-how, its customer connections and maintaining a stable workforce. It is therefore usual for covenants to be limited in duration and geographical scope and to differ from one employee to another, depending upon their seniority and the extent of their contact with customers. It is hard to generalise about the duration and scope of restrictive covenants, but in many jurisdictions it may be difficult to enforce non-competition covenants of more than six months and non-solicitation and non-dealing covenants (whether of employees or customers) of more than 12 months.

Where a non-family director or employee acquires shares or share options in the company, restrictive covenants can be repeated in the option scheme rules or shareholders' agreement. Covenants in share-related documents are separate from those in the employment agreement and may be enforceable even if those in the employment agreement are found not to be. The consequences of a breach of these covenants can be spelt out in the document: for example, options might lapse and any shares held by the ex-employee could be made the subject of a compulsory transfer notice as if he were a 'bad leaver' (see Section 6.2 below).

4. Equity incentives

As stated above, an outsider will not share the same aspirations and values as the family. One way of getting him to buy into the family's goals is to give him a part of the company's equity, whether directly by the issue or transfer of shares or indirectly by the grant of share options, that is, rights to acquire shares at some point in the future at a specified price. In this way, rather than simply looking to his monthly salary, he should be motivated to work in such a way as to enhance the value of the company overall and hence his shareholding.

Share-based rewards have a number of advantages in addition to the bringing together of aspirations. For example, it is possible to design them so as to lock in the manager for a period of time, say three to five years. If the manager leaves before this period has expired, he could forfeit his shares or options.

Equity can be efficient in terms of cash cost to the company, since awards can be made that involve little or no cash expenditure on the company's behalf and even a net cash gain on receipt of the employee's exercise price or subscription monies. The downside is the cost to the other shareholders, being the dilution of their shareholdings that they may suffer.

Although there is generally little actual cost to the employer itself in providing equity for employees (aside from advisers' fees and some tax charges), accounting standards – such as International Financial Reporting Standard 2 – require companies in most jurisdictions to account for share-based awards. This means that the value of awards made to employees needs to be assessed and recorded as an expense in the company's accounts. Calculating the value of an award can be a complex process when the award is subject to performance conditions.

## 5.	Other approved and unapproved options

The taxation of equity provided to employees is a vast area, a detailed explanation of which is beyond the scope of this work. However, a couple of general comments can be made:

- If structured correctly, it is possible for employees to make substantial gains on equity provided by their employers and for some or all of these gains to be treated as capital rather than employment income. Tax rates vary from one country to another, but it is often beneficial to have a gain taxed as capital rather than income.
- In calculating its own tax, the employer may be able to obtain relief for the cost of providing shares to employees.

When designing any equity incentive arrangement for non-family members, it is important to ensure that the potential benefits are not lost by adverse tax treatment, either for the employee or the company.

Most developed tax systems will seek to levy income tax (or its equivalent) on benefits received by employees from share options and other awards of equity. Social security contributions may also be payable by the employee and/or the employer. The timing of any charge varies from country to country. Some countries will seek to tax a share option when it is granted; others, such as the United Kingdom, will look to the exercise of the option to determine what benefit the employee has received. Anti-avoidance measures are common too, to prevent employees and employers from sidestepping the rules by, for example, having a family member receive an award or by designing the rights attaching to a share such that the share has a low value at the moment a charge arises but subsequently increases disproportionately to the growth in value of the company as a whole.

In many jurisdictions, it is possible to make awards under plans that have been approved generically or individually by the tax authorities, which confer tax advantages over the general treatment. Examples in the United Kingdom are Enterprise Management Incentive (EMI) options and Approved Company Share Option Plans (CSOP), both of which exempt an employee from income tax and national insurance contributions on option exercise if all the conditions are fulfilled.

## 6.	Controlling equity and providing liquidity

Most family businesses will not be willing to give up more than a small minority of their shares to outsiders. At one level then, there is no real loss of control because a minority shareholder cannot of himself control the company. However, an outsider is potentially able to exert a disproportionate influence over the business by siding with one or more other minority shareholders to form a controlling interest, particularly if the other shareholders are deadlocked.

There are several different ways of maintaining the family's control. The company's articles of association and any shareholders' agreement should be reviewed and, if necessary, updated to provide some or all of the following protections for the family.

6.1   Pre-emption rights

In most cases it will be desirable to have pre-emption rights or rights of first refusal so that managers who acquire shares cannot sell them to outsiders before offering them first to the family shareholders. This will prevent shares reaching the hands of competitors or other people of whom the family does not approve.

Leaving aside the question of forced sales (discussed below), there is something of a philosophical argument to be had concerning the price at which shares may be sold under pre-emption rights. One view is that shareholders should be free to set the price at which they wish to sell. If none of the existing shareholders wishes to buy at that price, the seller should be free to offer his shares to the outside world, provided that the price paid is no less than that at which the existing shareholders could have purchased them. In most circumstances this will be sufficient protection, but there may be cases in which an outsider (a competitor, perhaps) is prepared to pay over the odds to acquire a share. To counter this threat, pre-emption rights often specify that the board can intervene if it believes the offer price to be substantially different from market value. It is common for the shares then to be valued to determine a revised offer price. The choice of valuer can be important. The company's accountants can be a convenient option, but may be seen as being too closely allied with the family's interests to give an independent view. A solution may be to provide for an independent expert to be appointed. Either way, share valuations can be expensive and it is worth considering whether the cost is really justified.

Thought should also be given to whether certain share transfers should be excluded from the pre-emption rights. This could be on the basis of the identity of the transferor (different rules could apply for family and non-family shareholders) or the identity of the transferee (it is common to permit transfers in favour of a close relative or family trust, for estate-planning and tax-efficiency purposes).

6.2   Forfeiture/compulsory transfers

If managers leave (and particularly if they leave to join a competitor), the terms of any options they hold should provide that they lapse (ie, cease to be exercisable).

The articles or shareholders' agreement should also force a departing manager to offer to transfer his shares to the other shareholders. Without a compulsory transfer provision such as this the leaver could hang on to his shares indefinitely, not only being a disruptive influence as a shareholder but also benefiting from any growth in value of his shares created by his replacement.

It is common to draw a distinction between those who leave for a 'good' reason (such as ill-health or redundancy) and those who leave for a bad reason (such as being dismissed for poor performance or misconduct). Typically, most families will wish to differentiate between these scenarios by denying a bad leaver the full value of his shares.

Funding the buying back of a departing manager's shares can be an issue. The articles of association or shareholders' agreement can be drafted to provide that the purchase price can be paid over a period of months or even years.

6.3 Drag-along rights

It comes as a surprise to many families that, if they wish to sell the entire share capital of the family business, they may not be able to force a minority shareholder to join in that sale unless some fairly restrictive statutory conditions are satisfied. In the United Kingdom, for example, under Chapter 3, Part 28 of the Companies Act 2006, it is possible for a purchaser who acquires (broadly speaking) at least 90% of a company's shares to force the remaining shareholders to sell to him. However, this will only be the case if the terms of the offer are identical for all shareholders. This is rarely practical for private companies since buyers and sellers will usually seek to negotiate different terms for different sellers, such as the scope of warranties, indemnities and restrictive covenants.

A disgruntled employee shareholder might therefore be able to frustrate a sale of the company because a purchaser will usually insist on acquiring 100% of the shares. For this reason, it is generally desirable to include a so-called 'drag-along right' in the articles or shareholders' agreement. This is a contractual right for the majority to force a minority to sell in these circumstances.

6.4 Non-voting shares

To limit still further the loss of family control, it is possible to make available shares with the same economic rights as the family's shares, but with no voting rights. A separate class of non-voting employee shares can be created for this purpose.

6.5 Vesting

Another approach to the control issue is to impose additional vesting criteria. As mentioned above (see Section 4), a degree of lock-in can be achieved by deferring the moment at which a share option can be exercised (or a share award becomes unconditional). If the family has a clear strategic goal in mind, such as the sale of all or part of the business, and is seeking the manager's help in achieving this, the manager's options could additionally be restricted by their terms so that he cannot exercise them until immediately before the business is sold. In that way, the manager will be focused on the same goal as the family and will share in growth in value of the shares underlying his option, but without being able to vote them (or indeed receive dividends on them) until the exit is achieved.

6.6 Providing liquidity

For employees of an unquoted company, the absence of a market for their shares, and as a result the means to convert the shares into cash, can be a weakness. Outside the family business context, liquidity is often achieved upon a sale or flotation of a private company. Shares in companies controlled by serial entrepreneurs or private equity firms may therefore be more liquid than those in a family company, even though there is no actual market for either.

Some family companies have a history of paying significant, regular dividends. Employees lucky enough to hold shares in these companies will be less concerned about their ability to find a buyer for their shares.

Liquidity can be introduced into a family business by creating an employee share ownership trust. The trust can act as a buyer of shares (perhaps ranking ahead of the other shareholders under the pre-emption rights) and as a source of shares to satisfy options and other awards. Although a large part of the trust's expenditure would need to be funded by the company, if option exercise monies (and dividends on shares held) are paid to the trust, it will to some extent be self-financing. A well-funded trust can increase liquidity in a private company's shares.

7. Non-equity-based incentive schemes – phantom options

An alternative solution to the control issue is the use of 'phantom' or 'shadow' equity or options. This sidesteps the issue by not actually giving the manager real equity at all. Instead, the manager will receive a cash sum at some point in the future, frequently calculated by reference to the growth in value over time of a notional shareholding in the company.

Given that most family businesses have no regular market for their shares, one of the key issues with phantom equity will be valuation. It is vital to have a clear valuation mechanism for the phantom shares. The identity of the valuer should also be carefully considered, as with any valuation of the company's actual shares.

The use of phantom equity can be particularly helpful where a manager is responsible for a division of the company that does not have its own corporate identity. The valuation criteria can be modified so that it is the growth in value of the division itself, not the company, that is measured. In that way, the incentive value of the award will not be affected (positively or negatively) by the performance of other divisions of the company.

The use of phantom equity is the preferred solution for those families who really cannot bear to give up any control at all over the family business. However, it comes at a price: the company will have to find the cash to satisfy the awards and the beneficial tax treatment available in respect of some awards of real shares or share options will not generally be available.

8. Managing pensions

The provision of a pension scheme motivates and retains staff and is generally considered to be a highly valued benefit. Pensions are a tax-efficient way for a company to provide retirement benefits for its directors and key employees as full corporation tax relief is available on contributions the company makes. Schemes for larger companies tend to be occupational pension schemes and generally fall into one of two general types – salary-related or money-purchase schemes.

8.1 Salary-related schemes

In a salary-related scheme, the pension that employees receive at retirement is based on their salary and the number of years they have been in the scheme. Such schemes have become less popular with employers due to a rapid rise in the cost and other factors including demographic trends and substantial regulatory responsibility.

8.2 Money-purchase schemes

With a money-purchase scheme the benefits are based on how much is contributed, how well the money has been invested as well as other factors such as charges and interest rates.

On retirement, the fund accumulated is used to provide a pension, usually by buying an annuity (a regular income for life). The amount an employee receives is dependent upon various factors such as age, gender, health and marital or civil partnership status.

Employer contributions can be made at a set rate – say 5% of salary, or contributions could be scaled according to seniority or length of service. Employers often choose to match employee contributions. This targets the people most interested in the pension as a benefit, hence maximising the company's return on its investment.

A refinement of this type of pension scheme is a self-invested pension plan, which makes employers more attractive to potential and existing staff. This variety of pension plan allows individuals to make their own investment decisions from the full range of permitted investments within an approved pension scheme. They are classed as a particular subset of personal pension plans allowing tax relief on contributions in exchange for limits on accessibility. The rules vary across jurisdictions, but they generally allow for a wider range of investments to be held than personal pension plans, notably investments in private companies and commercial property. Rules for contributions, benefit withdrawal etc are generally the same as for other pension plans.

One possible structure might be for senior staff to be offered the full range of self-invested options; middle management can be offered a limited range of self-invested options; and junior or lower paid staff can have a default selection of fund choices, just like a group personal pension scheme. As employees progress in the company, they can move up towards full self investment.

Of course, this is just one possible structure and schemes can be tailored to match needs.

8.3 Salary sacrifice – improved employee benefits at no cost

If employees make contributions into a pension scheme, these could be by salary sacrifice as the contributions may be offset against some social security taxes which can be used to pay for the administrative running costs. Some employers choose to pass on the employer savings, in full or in part, and include them in the contributions made into each employee's pension account so they receive more pension.

8.4 Compulsory pension savings

In many developed countries, pension contributions are either compulsory or incentivised on the part of the employer, the employee or both. In the United Kingdom, for example, the government has recently reviewed the current pension savings system, resulting in a number of changes from 2012 including the introduction of 'personal accounts'. The review identified that private pension provision was uneven and the state pension had many gaps, especially for women and others who take career breaks. Australia is some years ahead and enforces compulsory savings of 9% on employers, with the United States potentially following suit with initially a 5% compulsory contribution level on individuals.

The introduction of personal accounts in the United Kingdom attempts to fill these gaps by using auto-enrolment and minimum contribution levels by both the employee and the employer. In preparation for these changes, employers may want to investigate the following areas in respect of their existing pension arrangements:

- The profile and needs of employees – is there a spread of moderate or higher-income employees who value more choice and control?
- Will any existing pension scheme provide the employer with an exemption from having to run personal accounts?
- Consider what changes need to be made to gain exemption, or if a qualifying scheme needs to be established.
- Consider gradually increasing existing qualifying scheme membership in the period to 2012. This will help avoid a sudden increase in cost due to auto-enrolment and compulsory contributions.

In summary, pensions are excellent tax-advantaged vehicles to help enhance the appeal of a company and provide real long-term benefits for staff. They are tax efficient for the employee, who receives tax concessions on contributions, virtually tax-free growth within their pension fund and a tax-free lump sum at retirement.

9.   Pension planning

There are two common misconceptions when considering how retirement will be financed. The first is that the state will provide for an individual in retirement and the second is that the employer will adequately provide for the employee, who need do nothing more than work each day until he reaches retirement age.

These beliefs are fundamentally flawed. The cost of provision borne by the state is escalating as a smaller proportion of the population remains in the workplace due to demographic change. The government is committed to enhancing state pension provision in the United Kingdom, but the main target is the lower paid. In the main, there are few company-funded pension schemes that will provide an adequate income in retirement and these rely on an employee accruing a long period of service.

It is therefore up to individuals to ensure they fund adequately for retirement through independent provision. Both private and company pension schemes provide a highly tax efficient means to help bridge the gap between what the state will provide and an individual's desired level of income in retirement.

For individuals, the key tax advantage is tax relief on personal contributions. Tax relief is given at the individual's highest rate of income tax.

Salary sacrifice can be a valuable tool to fund a pension plan. Essentially, the employee sacrifices part of his salary or bonus in return for an employer pension contribution. Doing so grants full tax relief immediately. However, care is needed as entitlement to state benefits could be affected and advice is therefore essential.

As well as attractive tax relief on contribution inputs, the value of the underlying fund grows virtually tax free. All growth accrues within the fund entirely free of capital gains and income taxes and it is only the tax credit on dividend payments paid within the fund that pension funds are no longer able to reclaim.

At the point of retirement, under current pension legislation in the United Kingdom for example, similar to other jurisdictions, 25% of the accumulated fund is available as a tax-free lump-sum payment. The minimum retirement age in the United Kingdom is currently 50, increasing to 55 in 2010. The balance of the fund must be used to provide an income that is taxable at marginal rates.

There are two main options at retirement having taken any tax-free lump sum – either buy an annuity or, if the individual is prepared to take more risk, draw unsecured pension (USP). If choosing unsecured pension, the balance of the pension fund remains invested and can provide a taxable income. Because the pension fund is invested through retirement, USP can carry considerable risk and is therefore only suitable for those who can afford to take this risk. If, on the other hand, an annuity is purchased, the remainder of the pension fund is exchanged for a secure lifetime income payable by an insurance company. USP offers considerable flexibility but is a complex area, not without risk, so advice is essential.

9.1 Limits on pension fund size

Most jurisdictions impose an upper limit on the size of any accrued pension fund. In the United Kingdom, exceeding this limit will lead to substantial tax charges on the surplus.

9.2 Contribution limits

Similarly, there are limits on annual contributions.

With tax relievable contributions at the individual's highest rate of income tax, virtually tax-free growth and a tax-free lump sum at retirement, pensions are highly effective vehicles to provide an income in retirement.

10. Non-executive directors

Whether or not the family business employs non-family directors in an executive capacity, there is much to be said for it having one or more non-executive directors, appointed from outside the family. An outside non-executive director should bring with him experience of the wider business world that can be beneficial in the family context where there may be lower staff turnover (if staff and family are synonymous to any extent) and hence less exposure to novel ideas and processes. There can be a tendency in family businesses to run meetings on a very informal basis or blur the distinctions between directors', shareholders' and family meetings. A non-executive director can introduce or reinforce appropriate standards of corporate governance and process. A non-executive director should not be motivated by reward in the same way as an executive director, so he or she can consider the remuneration of directors and senior employees dispassionately. Neutrality can be also useful in managing conflicts between different family members at the board level.

There is no legal distinction between executive and non-executive directors: all directors owe the same duties to the company as directors. A non-executive director is essentially one without an employment agreement. Executive directors will owe additional duties under their employment agreements.

Whilst a non-executive director will not require an employment agreement, it is good practice to provide a statement of terms. This should clarify the company's expectations. For example, how many board meetings per year does the company usually hold and will he have any particular responsibilities such as fixing directors' remuneration or chairing meetings? It should also deal with expenses entitlements and whether the non-executive director is to benefit from directors' and officers' insurance cover.

members in agreeing a succession plan; for example, discussing the relinqui
of control and ownership can be a very political and personally sensi
Reaching agreement between generations (or even the members
generation) on such matters is likely to involve significant diplo
professional skills on the part of those charged with the task in
achieved, however, the rewards for both the family and the
very significant – management time is saved, effort is c
in the same direction and the family's united front
loyalty both internally and amongst any employe
reached between generations, the family busine
succeed than might otherwise be the case.

Generally speaking and regardless
planning requires the setting of clea
group, good communication (the
itself), agreed governance str
action. It also needs the disc
not instinctively like an
with and resolving a
Ideally, a success
generations i
members o
fiscal, e

broader application and relevance so that they might be helpful in ma
jurisdictions too.

2. Succession planning: the objectives and issues facing families

2.1 Initiating appropriate succession planning

The overriding objective of any family when undertaking succession pl
likely to be the desire to ensure the smooth transition of wealth from one g
to another whilst maintaining family harmony and ensuring that the
survives the transition unscathed. One point that is, in our view, of real in
and should be mentioned at the start is that a succession plan should not
a decree from the senior generation. A plan is far more likely to be succes
borne out of agreement and discussion with those who are to be affe
Adopting an authoritarian approach is unlikely to be fruitful in the long

There are often hurdles to overcome and difficult debates to be had w

shment
tive topic.
of any given
matic, social and
the first place. If it is
related business can be
nsolidated and channelled
provides security and builds
d workforce. If agreement can be
ss is put in a much better position to

of the jurisdictions involved, succession
objectives, agreement within the core family
lack of which is potentially a cause of conflict in
ctures, appropriate recognition of risks and timely
pline to implement planning that some individuals may
, as a result, it should seek to provide a strategy for dealing
y sticking-points or disputes that might arise from discussions.
ion plan should demonstrate willingness on the part of the
volved to recognise what is of importance to particular family
generations and to adapt to changes in family circumstances or the
onomic, succession, matrimonial or jurisdictional environment.

many cases the first issue to address is how to encourage the senior generation
turn its attention to succession planning early on. All too often decisions are
ostponed until it is too late and the family is left to deal with the fallout from the
eath or mental incapacity of someone with a substantial shareholding and/or
perational input. It can be hazardous to wait until the senior generation decides the
me is right for retirement. A hastily cobbled-together and poorly thought-though
ccession plan designed under pressure is also likely to lead to family disharmony
d the resulting resentment of individual family members may, at the very least,
stabilise the business and, in the worst case, cause it serious damage. Obstacles to
ercome for the senior generation include facing up to mortality and potential
capacity and adapting to the loss of power, control and identity when members are
longer the driving force behind the family business.

Once the senior generation does turn its mind to succession, a number of key
ues will emerge. Typically, the following matters will have to be addressed, as
cussed below:

- the future of the business; 2.2
- the sort of economic benefit sought; 2.3
- management versus enjoyment; 2.4
- identifying and preparing successors; and 2.5
- individual satisfaction and social responsibility. 2.6

e future of the business

undamental consideration will be whether the family wants the business to

FB vs. Sold.

continue as a family business indefinitely or whether it might, after or during some identifiable period, be sold. This will often be a difficult and emotional decision and may depend upon a number of other issues. Critically, it should be ascertained whether any of the succeeding generations are interested in taking over the business and, if so, whether they are capable of running the business successfully so that it will flourish for the benefit of the whole family.

If the answer to either of those questions is no, then the family might well consider selling the business sooner rather than later. There is no point in implementing a carefully structured succession plan only for the business to fail under the stewardship of an incompetent or disinterested younger generation. The business is likely to be the principal asset of the family and, if there is nobody willing or able to take over the reins, it is likely to be better for the family as a whole to sell the business whilst it retains its value and to reinvest the proceeds in a manner that can benefit the whole family and future generations.

There are, of course, other intermediate options to consider – it is not only the stark choice of "retain" or "sell". There may be means by which some equity value from the business can be released or distributed in a way that provides income for the retired without compromising family ownership. For example, some of the equity may be held outside the business in a suitably diversified and risk-balanced portfolio. Alternatively, a part sale to investors or a partial flotation might be considered. This option may also hedge against the risk of the family wealth being concentrated solely in the family business. Significant time and thought is, however, required to assess the impact of non-family involvement on the business and on the willingness and desire of any successor generation to work alongside or for non-family members.

2.3 Economic benefit

The senior generation will have to consider appropriate succession models. This is a potentially contentious area. In a traditional dynastic model, seen often in relation to landed estates, one heir and their descendants will automatically be designated the primary beneficiaries (often as a result of long-established family trusts and the historical traditions of the family itself). In another model, typically found in entrepreneurial family trading businesses, only 'working' members of the family succeed to the business. Alternatively, a much wider family group could be provided for and charitable purposes could benefit from the business's profitability too. (This may be particularly appropriate where the family business has been sold and the proceeds are looked after by professional managers and trustees.) If the last option is favoured, the senior generation will need to decide whether it would be acceptable for the next generation to inherit (and potentially spend) all, or whether they are really 'custodians' who should benefit from the income only with the capital retained for future generations.

In considering succession models, the financial security of the older generation should not be overlooked. In return for passing down control and ownership of the business, consideration must be given to the means of income and support for those ceding it. On the other hand, providing for the older generation needs to be affordable to the business. The appropriate balance will vary from family to family and there are a variety of mechanisms available. Whatever route is chosen, it should be reviewed from time to time.

A further vital question is the family policy in relation to spouses and civil partners, in terms of knowledge, involvement with and the enjoyment of the family business and wealth.

2.4　Management versus enjoyment

The big question here is whether those who enjoy the economic fruits of the family wealth or business are also to be entrusted with decision-making powers. For example, should family members working in the business and contributing to its success benefit to a greater extent than others? If additional reward is to be provided to working family members, what form of benefit is appropriate – salary, bonus, share options, pension? These issues are discussed more fully elsewhere, but the issues are pertinent to any succession plan.

The family will also have to consider the nature of the decisions each member and the family as a whole will be making. Will the family have control over broad strategic decisions or will it also participate at an operational level? Will strategic decision making be the preserve of the senior family members only or will all family members be part of the process? Once the younger generations are enfranchised, will each individual have control of his or her proportion of the family wealth, or will they be restricted to the enjoyment of their share with control being entrusted to (or made jointly with) external professionals, trustees or executive directors?

These are important questions as those making the decisions will effectively determine the fate of others in the family. Such issues can have a significant impact on the planned structuring too. For example, different classes of shares in a company might be created to accommodate the family's wishes – some may have voting rights whilst others carry preferential rights to dividends. Many structures now offer great flexibility in this context.

At the forefront of these issues lies the need to consider equity in succession. Different families will have different ideas about what constitutes 'equity', but it does not necessarily amount to equality in financial benefit amongst all members of a given generation (or the family more widely). For some families, equity might be achieved by those who participate more actively being the ones having a greater share in ownership or profit. For other families, equity might be achieved intra-generationally by creating structures whereby members within each generation are treated in a similar fashion. For others again, it may be important to achieve inter-generational equity whereby the interests of successor generations are balanced against the interests of more senior generations. Yet again, equity could be measured in terms of input rather than (or as well as) output. Whichever way the particular family views equity, the succession plan should strive to achieve it. This is essential in avoiding or ameliorating future conflict.

Communication between those in the family who make decisions and those who merely enjoy the benefits of the family wealth is also vital if future conflict is to be avoided. It may, for example, be necessary to ensure that a process is put in place whereby the managers and decision takers can report to and, if appropriate, be held to account by non-decision takers. Following on from this, and in relation to all of the above questions and issues, the family will have to ensure that there are robust structures in place to manage conflict.

In any structure, it is also of paramount importance for family members to understand the nature of their rights and responsibilities. This can involve recognition of the fact that a given family member could be connected with the business in a number of different capacities. For instance, a family member could be a company director, employee, trustee, beneficiary and individual shareholder. Failure to recognise and take account of these different roles can lead to conflicts of interest, and families must remember that some roles require individuals to accept potential personal liability as well as fiduciary obligations to others.

2.5 Identifying and preparing successors

Consideration should be given to which of the next generation is most suited to take over. In this respect successful succession planning often takes place over a long period. The succession plan should put processes in place to educate and inform family members from a young age of the nature and workings of the business and, if appropriate, to integrate them into the business. To this end, the family should ensure that the career development of family members who are keen to participate in the business is a key priority. Younger family members should be given work experience opportunities and be encouraged to participate in family business networks so that they can develop the skills they will need as future successors to the business.

Aside from the obvious benefits of encouraging younger family members to participate in the business from an early age (eg, it may help to foster their enthusiasm), their participation can also provide an excellent opportunity to assess their performance and potential. If any family members who had hoped to take a certain role within the business 'come up short', early recognition may provide time to look at other options.

From the point of view of non-family members working in the business, the work experience may go some way to ensuring that family members participating in the business are not simply perceived as attaining any given position or status as a result of nepotism. Where conflict or resentment is detected, the family may also have more time to avoid and resolve difficulties.

Clearly, the senior generation will also need to consider (possibly, and preferably, having first discussed matters with those who will be affected) when the succeeding generation should become fully informed about the family business and associated wealth and how it will go about giving that generation the required information.

2.6 Individual satisfaction and social responsibility

The family ought to try to evaluate how and the extent to which family members will obtain satisfaction from their different roles. Some family members will be key decision makers or managers who bring particular strengths to either the business itself or the family group and therefore have self-evident roles. Others may be less well suited to or have no real interest in those areas. Consideration could be given to finding them specific roles, perhaps in reaching out to other family businesses, taking charge of the social responsibility agenda for the operating entities or becoming involved with the philanthropy programme for the family as a whole. Encouraging involvement and avoiding isolation is likely to result in a more positive family environment and any succession plan should deal with such issues accordingly.

The family must also consider the needs of any non-family employees of the business and, indeed, the business's overall ethical profile. People do not necessarily feel entirely comfortable or fulfilled by just helping a very wealthy family become even wealthier, so a properly run philanthropic programme can help motivate the workforce and, of course, it can give the business a better profile, resulting in more appeal to its customers and a competitive edge. Whilst it may not seem like it at first glance, this is all connected with succession planning since any successor generations will need (and want) to understand the rationale and justification for historic decisions relating to the family business it is taking over. Such things help to mould the identity of the family business too and can create greater family and non-family loyalty to it.

3. Achieving the smooth transition of family business between generations

3.1 Developing and agreeing a succession plan

One of the vital components to successful succession planning is to encourage the family to prepare for identifiable key events well in advance. Working on a suitably flexible yet enduring succession plan can help to highlight such events and form a basis for discussion about how to cope with them.

The way in which a family approaches its succession planning may vary according to the nature, size and structure of both the family and the family business. For example, where a family is small, all members are adult and the associated family business is both owned and run by the family, then meetings around a table to discuss succession planning may be the most feasible, cost-effective and productive way of proceeding. Where a family is larger, where there are minors or unborns with interests in the family business (eg, as part of a class of beneficiaries of a trust) or where the business is part family and part non-family managed and operated, then more sophisticated means of discussing topics and making progress will need to be devised.

It is one thing to put a succession plan in place and another entirely to ensure it endures. Above all else, belief in and commitment to the succession process and the given family business is required at all levels. A succession plan is more likely to be accepted and the implementation successful if the planning process is transparent and inclusive from the start. As well as involving the family members, any trustees and any senior non-family management team should also be fully signed-up to the process. If they are not involved, this is likely to cause great resentment and the business may well suffer as a result.

Although, ultimately, many of the decisions remain for the family to take, input from third-party professionals and non-family executives (eg, lawyers, accountants, and business advisers) is also vital to help the family keep sight of the whole picture and to ensure that all relevant factors are taken into account as part of the process. Whilst family issues are of great importance, business, legal and tax issues should also be prioritised. The failure of the business would of course stymie even the best laid succession plans! Discussion of these non-family topics also allows for a less emotional and more detached approach in the decision-making process. It may also lend a practical edge and framework to the discussion of 'softer' family issues.

The above demonstrates the need for a family to put an effective governance structure in place. Although governance is not covered until a later chapter, its benefits in the context of a family business (and alongside a carefully thought-through succession plan) cannot be underestimated.

3.2 Structuring the family business

Whilst types of business entity and their suitability to meeting family objectives are discussed elsewhere, the type of entity through which the family business is held can have a huge impact on the way in and extent to which a family's goals and aspirations for the transition of business interests between generations can be achieved. Obviously, one is not always starting with a blank sheet of paper and so existing structures as well as possible future structures fall to be considered. In addition, any international aspects to the family or its business may have a bearing and, if that is the case, suitably qualified advisers in the other jurisdictions will need to be consulted before final decisions are taken.

It is also important to remember that structures are often tiered and involve more than one type of entity. Consequently, the succession planning may involve a review of each tier and the part that component plays in the operation of the overall family 'machine'. For example, a family trust (through which the ultimate family wealth is held and distributed amongst members) may own a family trading company (at which level operational control is exercised and strategic business decisions are taken). There may also be subsidiary operations to consider. Depending on the issue at hand, a particular tier may be more pertinent. In our example, when discussing the future allocation or distribution of profits to beneficiaries (particularly those who do not work in the family business), the administration and operation of the trust may be the most important. However, when discussing the day-to-day management and control of the business and identifying possible successors in the next generation who will take on responsibility for this, the family trading company level is likely to be at the centre of the discussion.

With the above in mind, we would make the comments set out next on particular entities and their relevance to the creation of a succession plan.

 (a) *Trusts*

In terms of benefits for holding family businesses for more than one generation, trusts can:

- facilitate the retention of control of the business by the senior generation (as trustees) while transferring its economic value to the next (as beneficiaries);
- allow individual family beneficiaries to be treated differently whilst at the same time providing some benefit to everybody (eg, a discretionary trust structure provides the flexibility to meet different financial objectives for different beneficiaries);

- help fragment ownership and thereby, potentially, secure valuation discounts for tax purposes (thus assisting in the retention of the business in the longer term);
- can, in contrast to the above point, be used to preserve the power of bloc voting for shares in a family company, whilst sharing beneficial entitlement between family members;
- offer, potentially at least, some protection from creditors and divorce;
- protect the family's privacy (since there is no requirement to publish trust accounts in the same way as there is, in the UK at least, to publish company and LLP accounts);
- last a great deal longer than, for example, partnerships, without being substantively altered in form – changes of beneficial interests within trusts do not necessarily trigger tax charges (depending on type of trust) and this means that generational or individual beneficial interests may be increased or decreased over time in accordance with any succession plan (eg, in order to reflect retirement or greater involvement with and contribution to the family business); and
- from a purely UK perspective (although other jurisdictions may offer equivalent opportunities), be the recipient of transferred benefits from business property relief for inheritance tax purposes, for the benefit of current and future generations, with no 'up front' inheritance tax charge and the ability to hold-over any latent capital gains.

On the flip side, there are also some drawbacks to trusts. To mention a few:

- Beneficiaries' rights are limited and so the choice of suitable and appropriate trustees (both initially and on replacement) to administer the trust is crucial.
- Trustees have fiduciary obligations (and cannot therefore act purely for self-interest) and can be held personally liable for breaches of trust. Taking up the position of trustee should therefore be considered carefully before it is accepted.
- Generally speaking, trustees' decisions need to be taken unanimously and so each trustee has an effective veto on any decision (at least in the short term). In the context of a family business, the need potentially to act quickly in light of prevailing economic circumstances or opportunities should not be overlooked in relation to use of a veto.
- If the trust is not suitably flexible and a change is required, an application to the court may be necessary to achieve the desired result. This can be costly and is not always achievable unless there is demonstrable benefit to all classes of beneficiaries with an interest in the trust (including, if relevant, minors, unborns and charities).

(b) Partnerships

Potential advantages of using a partnership structure in the context of succession planning are:

- the ability to incorporate a wide spectrum of rights and obligations by conferring different entitlements to capital and income, separating the management from the enjoyment of the assets through different classes of partner and including express provisions to govern succession and transfer;

- achieving a measure of limited liability and protection against creditors for family members through LLPs (often called family limited partnerships) or other equivalents in the given jurisdiction;
- helping fragment ownership and thereby, potentially, secure valuation discounts for tax purposes (thus assisting in the retention of the business in the longer term); and
- allowing individual family members to be treated differently whilst at the same time providing some benefit to everybody (for instance, partnership controlling interests can be held separately from those that provide economic benefit).

Again, however, there are some drawbacks:
- Unless, for example, a trust is interposed between the individual family member and the partnership interest, there is only limited protection in the event of divorce.
- Partnerships are tax transparent and so, unless relief from inheritance or estate taxes or capital gains tax is available (eg, through business property relief), individual family owners will need to consider and make provision for the impact of tax on a lifetime or testamentary transfer of the partnership interest from one generation to the next.
- A general partnership does not offer limited liability protection and, whilst an LLP does, a major problem with English LLPs is that, assuming that they hold investments for the family (such as shares in the active trading companies carrying on the business), they will be governed by the Financial Services and Markets Act 2000 (FSMA) and must have a discretionary manager and operator who are duly licensed under the FSMA, adding significant extra cost. These problems may not exist in other jurisdictions, of course.
- Whilst, in theory, partnerships can be of unlimited duration, in practice it is tricky to draft a partnership agreement for longer than 20 or perhaps 30 years owing to the difficulties of anticipating accurately what is to happen on the death of each partner (and from a long-term succession perspective, this may be an important consideration).
- It can be difficult to distribute profits to one partner to the exclusion of another of the same class and so pro-rata payment out of profits is usually the norm. In terms of succession planning, this may be a deterrent, particularly where it is intended that family members who work in the business are intended to receive more than those who do not participate.

(c) Companies
Historically at least, family-run and -owned companies have been extremely popular. They have survived generational changes, and perhaps the most obvious benefits in a succession planning context are:

- the wide flexibility that can be incorporated via different classes of shares carrying different rights to suit different generations (eg, voting control can be separated from entitlement to income or classes of shares can be designed that might, over time, facilitate an efficient transfer of value from one generation to the next);
- the ability to fragment value through minority holdings and/or different classifications of shares, potentially attracting valuation discounts for tax purposes;
- the ability to include pre-emption rights and similar devolution clauses in the articles of association, any shareholders' agreement and/or family charter so as to ensure that the company shares remain within the family and the succession plan is effected as envisaged; and
- the availability of limited liability to shareholders, thus helping to protect the wider family wealth from third parties in the event of a business failure.

In terms of drawbacks, the following should be mentioned:
- Unless, for example, a trust is interposed between the individual family member and the shareholder, there is only limited protection in the event of divorce.
- Directors face personal liability (potentially both civil and criminal) and assume fiduciary duties on the acceptance of office. Taking up the position of director should therefore be considered carefully before it is accepted.
- In the UK, there is a potential double charge to tax (at both company and shareholder level) on the extraction of profits and so, if any succession plan anticipates an eventual sale of the family business, careful consideration should be given to this aspect.

3.3   Documenting and giving effect to a succession plan

As part of the succession planning process, it is likely that documentation will need to be drawn up to record and give effect to the agreed principles and plan. Not all of this will necessarily be legally binding and some of it may remain unwritten or be in a constant state of update. However, committing ideas and, to the extent possible, agreed principles to paper can be an aid in the future in terms of ensuring that all interested parties understand and have a record of what has been agreed. It will also assist with any ancillary planning that individual family members decide to undertake (and thereby, hopefully, help to secure adherence to the succession plan across the family). From time to time, the documentation can be reviewed or updated as necessary.

There are two different categories of documentation to comment upon:
- collective documents (such as family charters, family council constitutions, articles of association and partnership deeds); and
- personal documents (eg, wills, letters of wishes, trusts restricted to particular limbs of the family and pre-nuptial/post-nuptial agreements).

We do not intend to comment in detail here on how documents in the first category above should be drafted or what they might include. This information is provided elsewhere in the publication. Suffice it to say that any succession plan that has been agreed will have an impact on the drafting of such documents (and visa versa). It will therefore be very important to ensure that the principles that have been discussed and agreed as part of the succession planning process are recorded clearly and accurately in those documents and, conversely, that and documented succession plan refers appropriately to those documents. It will also be imperative to ensure that all those who are affected by and intending to subscribe to them (formally or otherwise) are happy with the drafting.

As regards the second category above, we can comment a little more substantively. Whilst each individual member of a senior generation (or indeed any generation) is perfectly entitled to have views about whether and how his or her wealth should be transferred *inter vivos* or devolve on death, it is important for that individual to consider their personal planning in the context of any family succession plan. The two are inextricably linked.

In consequence, whenever a piece of financial, tax or testamentary planning is undertaken, the individual concerned ought to consider his or her personal objectives in conjunction with those that have been agreed at a family level. This may impact upon an individual's will drafting, any pre-nuptial or post-nuptial agreement, personal tax planning and any associated transfer documents in connection with lifetime gifts (including any *inter vivos* settlements established). In addition, and whilst one obviously cannot be entirely prescriptive on these matters, individuals should at least consider the management of their own finances with reference to what they have agreed with other family members. For example, an individual may wish to avoid leveraging their own assets to such an extent that their interest in a family business would be at risk if things went wrong.

Wills are likely to be crucial tools in ensuring the smooth transition of family business interests between generations and in reducing avoidable conflict between family members. A will should make proper provision for the poorer spouse and take account of the provisions of any pre-nuptial agreement. The will should seek to do this in a way that does not breach any agreement reached at family level as regards family business interests and should also look to protect that interest in the event that any dispute does arise over the will. Conversely, from the perspective of the other family members, given testamentary freedom it is important to consider the forms of ownership of family business assets carefully at the outset and avoid any unexpected bequests of family assets outside the family group. It cannot necessarily be taken for granted that a family member will 'do the right thing' and it could be disastrous if the succession plan relied heavily on the terms of a will but the testator changed his or her mind prior to death.

To the extent that the testator holds shares outright in the family business, a will might be used (consistently with a broader family succession plan) to create long-term trusts holding those shares for the next two or three generations. However, as wills deal only with the devolution of personally held assets, surrounding arrangements may need to be considered for family business assets. If a family business is owned through a partnership or a company, the relevant provisions of the partnership agreement or articles of association should be considered. Avoiding contradiction and inconsistency between the relevant documents at personal and family level is of paramount importance.

Family business assets may already be held in trust and sometimes specific beneficiaries are given powers of appointment over assets, which can be exercised in the event of their death, by will. The provisions of family trust documents should be carefully checked as a result and, again, the wider family objectives considered as part of the exercise of any such power of appointment by will.

Lastly, if any of the provisions in a will involve an element of discretion, or in the event that the testator wishes to record the reasons for structuring a will in a particular way (perhaps as a result of an agreed succession plan), then an overarching letter of wishes might be used to explain how the pieces of the jigsaw all fit together. This may help to alleviate or prevent misunderstandings on the part of those left behind on the testator's death.

4. Potential obstacles to a succession plan

As has already been mentioned, a well thought-out succession plan can still be thwarted by events outside the control of the business or the family. Vigilance and forward planning are required to ensure that as much as possible is done to protect the family business from external threats. We mention three in a little more detail below.

4.1 Matrimonial aspects

On the subject of divorce, any succession plan should encourage individual family members to (i) obtain legal advice well before getting married; and (ii) enter into a pre- or post-nuptial agreement. It is essential that anyone involved in the family business does this in order to protect themselves and their descendants and the interests of the wider family. If this is not done, it is far more likely that a family member's share of the business may have to be sold, transferred or divided outside the family on divorce. This may scupper not only the individual's plans for the future, but also those of the wider family.

In devising a succession plan at family level, it is therefore important for a policy to be discussed and established as regards pre- or post-nuptial agreements. If the family business is carried on through a company, the terms of any pre-emption rights in the articles of association or shareholders' agreement may also fall to be discussed. It may be advisable to prohibit the transfers of shares to anyone other than a lineal descendant or 'permitted trust', and the interests of spouses in such shares might be regulated accordingly. The same principle applies in the context of partnerships or trusts established to hold family business interests.

4.2 Tax aspects

In the same way that an untimely or unexpected divorce can have a fundamental and damaging effect on a succession plan, an unanticipated tax event or charge can have similar ramifications. For example, in the United Kingdom it is a mistake to assume that all family business assets will automatically be protected from inheritance tax by business property relief or agricultural property relief – there are several potential pitfalls (eg, in general an individual must have owned any business property for two years before a gift/death to qualify for relief, the business must be a 'qualifying business' and the asset must be 'relevant business property'). Regardless of the jurisdiction or the applicable tax regime(s), regular reviews and professional advice ought to be taken to ensure that family members understand their respective legal and tax positions. This should of course be done both at the time an initial succession plan is discussed and agreed, and from time to time thereafter to ensure that nothing has changed that would affect it.

For assets that do not qualify for any relief, the succession plan might, for tax purposes, consider a process by which gradual shifts in value are achieved over long periods of time (and so without up-front charges to tax). For example, again in the United Kingdom, deferred lease schemes can be highly effective to transfer valuable land. Regular gifts and the use of the normal expenditure out of income exemption for inheritance tax might also be helpful to consider.

More generally, although gift, inheritance and estate taxes are obviously very significant when it comes to succession planning, it is clearly important for the family to try to minimise other forms of taxes payable, such as corporation tax, capital gains tax and income tax. Doing so will assist in maximising family wealth and in running the family business efficiently so that it is preserved for future generations. Once again, money may well need to be invested in obtaining appropriate and suitably detailed professional advice in this context. In the long run, however, this is likely to be money well spent.

4.3 Multi-jurisdictional aspects

Where a family business has cross-border issues to consider, the family's advisers should ensure that any proposed succession plan is structured in a way that is both tax efficient and legally effective in the round (ie, taking account of each jurisdiction's tax and legal regime and the interaction between the regimes of the jurisdictions concerned). Taking expert local advice in different jurisdictions will enable the family business to benefit from acceptable tax planning and mitigation while preventing unintended tax evasion.

If family business assets are sited in different jurisdictions, the ability to own, transfer and devolve assets in any given way must also be considered. Is there a matrimonial regime or are there forced heirship rules to be considered? Are there any restrictions on ownership of assets in the jurisdiction concerned (eg, by non-nationals)? Ignoring the potential application of such rules would be a very dangerous and potentially expensive course to adopt.

5. Conclusion

The consequences of failing to consider and carry out succession planning can be catastrophic, for both the business and the family: the family may be forced to sell the business against its will, trustees who are ill-equipped to run the business may have to intervene and the possible conflicts arising from the surrounding turmoil could destroy relationships within the family. On the other hand, the rewards for undertaking successful succession planning can be immense (both financially and in maintaining a happy family).

Whilst there are naturally occasions where succession planning can be divisive or give rise to acrimony amongst family, these occasions are likely to be rarer when appropriate succession planning takes place. It should also be remembered that undertaking succession planning may help to provide a means by which difficulties that do arise might be resolved at an early stage. Without planning, the means of resolution may be far less attractive, more expensive and protracted.

Succession planning should therefore commence early on and be kept continually under review for all family businesses.

Entrepreneurs within the family: encouraging entrepreneurship and innovation

Mary K Duke
Francine RS Lee
HSBC Private Bank

Family businesses face unique issues, as they involve complex interwoven relationships. For example, how do you separate 'personal' family matters from those of the business? How does the next generation follow in the footsteps of the great entrepreneur who started the business? How do you encourage entrepreneurship in children who have been raised in a protective world of isolation and privilege? How does a family utilise its good fortune to encourage future generations to think 'outside the box', beyond the traditional family business? These issues become more complicated as family businesses grow in size and complexity and become multi-generational.

The first question to be addressed is: Does greatness grow in families? The answer is: Not necessarily. Children of successful families may be in a better position to excel, as they have additional resources, connections and opportunities to succeed, but these advantages do not guarantee success. To help achieve 'greatness', families need to kindle the entrepreneurial spirit in the next generation.

The chapter will strive to examine some of the challenges that families face and provide some suggestions on how to encourage entrepreneurship, innovation and greatness in family members.

1. Does greatness grow in families?

Will the children of Michael Phelps, who captured the attention of the world by winning 16 Olympic medals, become Olympic medal swimmers? Will Nick Faldo or Sergio Garcia produce the next generation of championship golfers? When it comes to passing down athletic ability to future generations, it is a toss of the genetic dice.

Michael Jordon, the NBA basketball legend, has two sons who are currently gaining respect on the basketball court. While their careers look promising, it is too soon to tell whether they will follow in their dad's footsteps. Michael does not want his sons to follow in his shoes; he wants them to be themselves: "If you play basketball, you're a doctor, you're a lawyer, whatever, I'm gonna support you with the love and every effort, every inch of my body."[1]

In determining whether greatness grows in families of championship athletes, it is more than physical ability that is important. Proper training, passion, drive, family connections, parental support and encouragement are all tools required for the next generation to be successful.

What about the beauty queen and the scientist? When the beauty queen suggested that she and the scientist produce offspring, proposing that her looks and his brains would produce a powerful combination, the scientist responded: "Well, my dear, suppose the children have my looks and your brains?"

Is the gene lottery different when it comes to the children of entrepreneurs? Does greatness grow in successful businesses families?

You may be familiar with the saying "shirtsleeves to shirtsleeves in three generations". The first generation works hard to create the wealth, the second generation maintains the status quo and the third generation lives in luxury, doing little or no work, spending their fortune. This challenge is not limited to geographical boundaries, as demonstrated by the phrases below:

- "Shirtsleeves to shirtsleeves in three generations" – United States;
- "Peasant shoes to peasant shoes in three generations" – China;
- "Father-merchant, son-playboy, grandson-beggar" – Mexico;
- "First generation creates, second inherits, third destroys" – Germany; and
- "From the stable to the stars and back again" – Italy.

Unfortunately, there are many stories of great family businesses where the entrepreneurial torch died and the family business was destroyed by family wars: Mondavi (wine); Lur-Saluces (Chateau D'Yquem); and Gucci (fashion).[2] Fortunately, there are also many examples where the entrepreneurship that began with the founder has been passed down to future generations.

Leonardo Del Vecchio, one of Italy's richest men and ranked number 77 on the Forbes List of Billionaires, is the founder and chairman of Luxottica Group, manufacturer and retailer of high-quality eyeglass frames.[3] Leonardo was sent to an orphanage when he was seven years old because his mother could not afford to raise five children. What he started as a small eyewear parts business is now a public company with more than 6,000 retail stores. From the age of 14, his son Claudio Del Vecchio spent each summer working in his father's eyeglass factory. He left the day-to-day operations at Luxottica to branch out on his own by purchasing from his father a mid-market women's clothing chain, Casual Corner (which he subsequently liquidated). Next he bought Brooks Brothers in 2001, a business that was established in 1881, which he is working to reinvigorate back to the store, "once synonymous with button-down elegance".[4] Here is an example of the entrepreneurial torch being passed down from one generation to the next.

1   Mike Celizic, "Michael Jordan to Son: Don't be like Mike", Todayshow.com, Nov 9 2007, www.msnbc.msn.com/id/21692348/; See also, Mike Dodd, "Sons Carry on Jordan Legacy on the Hardwood", *USA Today*, updated Feb 1 2007, www.usatoday.com/sports/preps/basketball/2007-01-31-jordans-focus_x.htm.
2   See Grant Gordon and Nigel Nicholson, *Family Wars*, 1st edition (2008) London and Philadelphia: Kogan Page Limited.
3   Forbes.com/lists/2008/10/billionaires08_Leonardo-Del-Vecchio_P765.html.

While greatness does not necessarily grow in families, encouraging the entrepreneurial spirit in the younger family members plays a key role.

2. Steps that families can take to encourage entrepreneurship

One of the challenges faced in a family business is how to develop the entrepreneurial spirit in the next generation. Like the founder of the business who possessed the creativity, vision and drive, new family members must develop their passion to succeed. They may find their passion working in the family business, or they may find their calling following a different path. It is important for families to understand that there is no 'one size fits all'.

It is also important for families to recognise that the assets of a family are the family members themselves; and each family member is different. According to Jay Hughes, in his seminal work *Family Wealth – Keeping It in the Family*,[5] the wealth of each family is the human and intellectual capital of its members. A family should use its capital as a tool to support the growth of the intellectual and human capital of its family members. Entrepreneurship and innovation will occur by allowing each family member to pursue their individual quest for happiness.

Set out next are suggestions that families can use to encourage entrepreneurship and innovation in the next generation.

2.1 Should family members be required to join the family business?

"If you know one family – you know one family."

Some families believe it is the responsibility of the next generation to follow in the family footsteps and assume their responsibility in the family business – and have successfully employed this strategy. There is another train of thought that suggests that children who are not interested in joining the family business should be encouraged to pursue their passion, wherever it may lead.

What would have happened if the entrepreneurs who created the family business were not given the opportunity to pursue their dreams? Where would the world be today without the likes of great entrepreneurs such as:

- Henry Ford, who at a young age developed an interest in engineering which his mother encouraged by letting him use her darning needles to make screwdrivers for fixing timepieces;[6]
- Bill Gates, the son of a lawyer and school teacher, who left his studies at Harvard University in his junior year to start Microsoft with his childhood friend, Paul Allen;[7] or
- Richard Branson, founder of the Virgin brand, who started by publishing a

---

4   Lynnley Browning, "Private Sector; Crown Jewel for a Fashion Heir?", *The New York Times*, Nov 14 2008. See also, Richard Northedge, "Del Vecchio Tailors Brook Brothers for UK", telegraph.co.uk, April 30 2008, http://www.telegraph.co.uk/finance/newsbysector/retailandconsumer/2789122/Del-Vecchio-tailors-Brook-Brothers-for-UK.html; Barbara Kiviat, "The Man Who Brought Back the Golden Fleece", *Time*, Nov 13 2007, time.com/time/magazine/article/0,9171,1664349,00.html.
5   James E Hughes, Jr, *Family Wealth – Keeping It in the Family: How family members and their advisers preserve human, intellectual, and financial assets for generations*, revised and expanded edition (2004) New York: Bloomberg Press.
6   Gordon and Nicholson, *Family Wars*, p 100.
7   Miscrosoft.com/presspass/exec/billg/default.aspx?tab=biography.

student magazine at age 16 and was knighted Sir Richard Branson in 1999 for his contribution to entrepreneurship.[8]

Entrepreneurship, creativity and drive are characteristics that need to be nurtured and developed. While these attributes can be developed within the parameters of the family operating business, children who feel forced to continue the family tradition and run the business might not realise their true potential.

Venturing into a business separate from the family operating business may prove a valuable tool that can take both the individual and the family in a new direction. A great example of a successful shift away from the traditional family business occurred with the Rockefeller family.

John D Rockefeller Sr had one son, John D Rockefeller Jr ("Junior"). Junior chose not to follow his father's career path and instead devoted his life to philanthropy and family governance. He helped set up a family office, which is still in existence today, to manage the needs of the family and established the practice of having family meetings to forge family unity. Junior had five sons, each of whom he encouraged to pursue their own careers and operate independently. The Rockefeller family has made diverse and significant contributions to society, especially in the areas of philanthropy (eg, the restoration of the Chateau du Fontainebleau and the Palace of Versailles – France; Colonial Williamsburg – Virginia; The Museum of Modern Art – New York; Lincoln Center – New York), land conservation, finance and politics (Nelson Rockefeller – vice president of the United States, Jay Rockefeller – US senator and Nelson, Jay and Winthrop Rockefeller – state governors). The Rockefeller family was able to turn its good fortune into a family tradition that nurtures each generation and provides a positive vision for the family that extends beyond the family business.[9]

2.2   Entrepreneurial culture

A family's entrepreneurial culture is important in encouraging entrepreneurship in the next generation. Children learn by example. They look to their parents and grandparents as role models. Entrepreneurs should endeavour to spend as much time with their families as possible. "The kids will learn from watching the entrepreneurs go through pressure, see the sacrifices they have to make and appreciate the business more."[10] "Unless successors of family-run firms possess the same values and drive as their founders, the operation is likely to end up 'stuck in time' due to entrepreneurial malaise."[11]

A family culture that encourages independence and competitiveness helps build entrepreneurship. Rich Products, ranked number 163 in the 2008 Forbes List of

---

8   Woopidoo.com/biography/Richard_branson.htm.

9   See, Wikipedia.org/wiki/Rockefeller_family; Hughes, *Family Wealth*, pp 34 to 35; The Rockefeller Archive Center – JDR Biographical Sketch, www.rockarch.org/bio/jdrjr.php; Wikipedia.org/wiki/John_ D._Rockeferrer,_Jr; Dennis Jaffe, "Lessons from Nineteenth Century Wealth Creators", *Families in Business*, March/April 2004.

10   Dr Sanjay Goel, as quoted in Francis Chan, "Keeping and Growing the Family Fortune", *The Straits Times*, p B22, August 20 2008.

11   *Ibid.*

Largest Private Companies in the United States,[12] is an international food products corporation founded in 1945 by Robert Rich Sr, whose initial product was a non-dairy whipped product topping. According to Ted W Rich, one of the founder's grandsons and President of the Foodservice Division, the founder's aggressive genes run in the family: "it would be impossible to grow up in this family and not feel the importance of competition".[13]

Competition needs to be "positive" and it can impact each family member differently. The founder of Rich Products, Robert Rich Sr, promoted competition between his two sons Robert Jr and David. The father would rouse Robert Jr and David out of bed at 5:00am and make them do push-ups until their arms burned. At their summer house, Robert Sr made the boys run sunrise sprints "until they dropped from exhaustion". He also made them compete against each other in football, tennis and squash. Robert Jr was a natural athlete and thrived under these conditions; David was not and he chose to become an Anglican priest rather than join the family business. Robert Jr joined the family business and succeeded his father as chairman.[14] The Rich family demonstrates that the entrepreneurial culture of the family will influence the next generation; however; the impact it will have will vary for each family member.

2.3   Setting values

A lifestyle that is too comfortable and easy can lead to a lack of interest and motivation. Children of successful business families may sometime grow up in luxury, having their every needed taken care of, spending without limits, growing up in isolation from the rest of the real world and living in a world of fantasy. One challenge is how to motivate privileged children to develop a desire to achieve on their own.

Many children of wealthy parents say one of the best things their parents did to motivate them was not make their life too easy. Parents should set limits for their children and lead by example. Children should be required to get a good education that is suited to their individuality (not necessarily a traditional education focused on academic achievement). They should be involved in the community and society. The next generation must find a passion other than spending their fortune: "Successful families want their heirs to want to 'work', even if this does not mean necessarily working for money."[15]

Bill Gates and Warren Buffett have each stated publicly that they intend to give the bulk of their wealth away to good causes during their lifetime. They believe that "unearned wealth corrupts by depriving them of the dignity of work and interferes with the creative life choices later generations would make if they were not burdened by the wealth they didn't create".[16] Andrew Carnegie also shared this view, believing

---

12   http://www.forbes.com/business/lists/2008/21/privates08_Rich-Products_WOW5.html.
13   Ted W Rich as quoted in Monte Burke, The Forbes 400, "Blame the Milkman", Oct 9 2006, www.forbes.com/forbes/2006/1009/076.html.
14   See, Burke, "Blame the Milkman".
15   Dennis Jaffe, "The Burdens of Wealth", *Families in Business*, June 2003.
16   Hughes, *Family Wealth*, p 63.

that money should be used for public good during the wealth creator's lifetime. Billionaire money manager and author Ken Fisher has stated that "his gift to his descendants will be inspiration."[17] "The main thing you want your grandchildren to realise is that if you can become rich and successful, so can they."[18]

Sir Tom Hunter, who was knighted in 2005 for services to philanthropy and entrepreneurship in Scotland, has also decided to give his fortune away during his lifetime. Stating that he did not want to burden his children with his great wealth, he quoted Warren Buffett's saying: "He would leave his kids enough that they can do something but not too much that they will do nothing".[19]

While some agree with the philosophy that the wealth creator should give away their fortune during their lifetime instead of leaving it to the next generation, this viewpoint is not without controversy.

2.4   Family loans

Another strategy for encouraging entrepreneurship is to provide seed capital and loans to young family members to start their own business. Providing access to capital that may not otherwise be available by traditional banking means or that is available at lower interest rates or on more flexible terms will give family members the opportunity to follow their dreams. To receive the assistance, the borrower should have a clearly defined business plan. The family should work with the borrower to help develop and reach milestones before additional capital is received. Limit the amount loaned to the amount of loss the family is willing to bear in the event that the venture does not work out as planned. Make it clear that the advance is a loan that must be paid back. Providing a loan, instead of a gift, creates a sense of ownership and responsibility for the family member-borrower.

Do not punish the borrower if the new venture fails, even after the borrower has put in the required time and effort. In addition to providing the financial capital, families should help mentor and provide access to both family and non-family mentors for younger members who are branching out on their own. If budding entrepreneurs are afraid to take risks, they will never have the courage to develop new ideas and businesses.

2.5   Philanthropy

Philanthropy can kindle the entrepreneurial spirit of family members at any age. Bill Gates is an excellent example. At age 50, he left his day-to-day job at Microsoft to focus full time on his global health and education work at the Bill and Melinda Gates Foundation.[20]

Entrepreneurs can strive to achieve their philanthropic vision by dedicating their time and resources to charitable causes they believe in. Ted Turner, for example,

---

17   Matthew Bishop and Michael Green, *Philanthrocapitalism*, 1st edition (2008) New York: Bloomsbury Press, 36.
18   Ken Fisher as quoted in Bishop and Green, Philanthrocapitalism, 36.
19   Sir Tom Hunter as quoted in Chris Hope, "Sir Tom Hunter makes record 1 bn donation", July 18 2007, http://www.telegraph.co.uk/news/uknews/1557662/Sir-Tom-Hunter-makes-record-1bn-donation.html.
20   www.microsoft.com/presspass/exec/billg/default.aspx?tab=biography.

pledged $1 billion to the United Nations; Sudanese telecommunications tycoon Mo Ibrahim is using philanthropy to try to transform African politics; and Sir John Templeton, established a foundation whose mission is to be a "catalyst for scientific discovery on what scientists and philosophers call the 'Big Questions'".[21] These individuals are philanthropic entrepreneurs, using their wealth to pursue "high-risk, high-return strategies"[22] in causes that they believe in.

Engaging in philanthropy can provide a meaningful employment alternative for family members who choose not to join the family business. "Giving, done well, is extraordinarily difficult work."[23] Venturing into philanthropy is a natural next step in the development of many wealthy families, as some believe that they have earned enough wealth during their lifetimes and it is now their responsibility to give back to society.

In addition to accomplishing social good, philanthropy can also be used as an educational tool for younger family members. Through philanthropy, the next generation can learn valuable life and business skills. They can also learn to develop their passions and find fulfilment in working for something they believe in.

One suggestion for engaging the next generation in philanthropy is to team up grandchildren and grandparents to engage in philanthropic work. Grandchildren and grandparents are natural allies because they are the enemies of the parents.[24] The exact structure will depend on the ages of the grandchildren. Basically, money can be set aside and earmarked for charity. The group will decide on what causes are important to them (such as health, education, animals and so on) and how many charities they want to support. With oversight from the grandparents, the grandchildren can form an investment committee to determine how to invest the funds and a grant committee to evaluate potential charitable recipients. When the group makes the donation, they can follow the progress of the charity to see how their contribution helped make a difference.[25]

Another suggestion, where there are older teenage and/or college-age family members, is to set an annual budget that is directly entrusted to the group with the direction to distribute the funds among a set numbers of charities. The group will work as a team to determine how they will accomplish this mission (who decides on the recipients of the contribution and amount of the donation; what type of background research is required for each charity; what criteria the charity must meet to be acceptable to the group; whether the contribution will be a general donation or used for a specific purpose; and so on). Once the criteria are agreed upon, the group will donate the funds and follow up on the progress the charity has made.

Engaging young family members in organised family philanthropy passes on core values, instils a sense of fiscal responsibility and encourages teamwork. It also builds analytical and decision-making skills while building closer family relationships. It sets the stage for the family members to develop a passion for

---

21   Bishop and Green, *Philanthrocapitalism*, p 105; see generally pp 98 to 109.
22   *Ibid*, p 114.
23   Hughes, *Family Wealth*, p 127.
24   *Ibid*, p 74.
25   See, Hughes, *Family Wealth*, pp 75 to 76.

helping others. All of these lessons will be valuable for the personal and professional development of the next generation.

2.6 Employment outside the family business

Families can also encourage entrepreneurship and innovation by requiring family members to have outside employment before joining the family business. Gaining valuable work experience away from the family can help develop motivation and self esteem. This is especially helpful for children who may have been raised in a world of isolation and privilege. It teaches the next generation to stand on their own and have their performance evaluated in an environment devoid of family influence. Younger family members may be more open to constructive criticism and career coaching when it is communicated by a non-family member. This is not to suggest throwing the younger generation to the wolves. The family still can, and should, play an active role by providing the next generation with guidance, emotional support and mentoring. Some families establish a formal/personalised mentoring team for each young family member, whom he or she can reach out to for personal development and career advice.

Some family businesses require the younger members to be promoted to a certain level in outside employment before they can join the family business. When they do join the family business, they will have gained a sense of legitimacy on their own, having accomplished certain achievements and gained experience outside the family. (This could of course have the opposite effect if the child fails at outside employment, then joins the family business in a position that the child is not otherwise qualified for.) By gaining valuable work experience before joining the family company, the new employee may become more confident, gaining the respect of co-workers and becoming more innovative and willing to take chances.

Having the younger generation work in a business that is different from the family business may expose younger workers to new concepts and ideas. Where the younger family member gains employment in the same industry, this may provide insight into competitive practices. Working abroad may develop the international skills that are increasingly required in today's global world. When family members decide that they want to join the family business after their required outside work experience, they are more likely to be motivated to join for the right reasons and be ready to make a valuable contribution.

By requiring the next generation to work outside the family umbrella first, they can learn how other companies operate and what it takes to succeed in the business world. They will have the opportunity to grow both personally and professionally. This experience may provide the younger family members with the innovation to grow the business if they choose to join it, or encourage them to pursue their passion in another desired field.

2.7 Gaining training and skills in the family business

This is not to say that the same results cannot be achieved if the next generation of family members begin their career in the family business. In fact, many young family members get their first work experience having vacation jobs in the family company.

What is important is that family members gain the proper training and skills so that they can move the business forward.

Young family members starting out should begin in positions that are commensurate with their level of experience. If they start in a position that is too senior, they are likely to fail and will never rebuild their sense of self-esteem. The next generation should be given a broad range of assignments designed to round out their education and learn the business from the bottom up. The positions should try to develop different business skills and encourage them to work with a variety of people in the company.

Developing the requisite skills is critical for developing entrepreneurship. The next generation must stay current and adapt to changes in today's global world. If the young family members cannot think creatively, and instead continue to run the business in the same old way, the business is at risk of stagnating.

Holding positions in different divisions and even different locations away from the home office is also recommended. By being separated from the home office, the next generation will learn how to develop new working relationships and interpersonal skills away from the nest. Establishing some distance and separation may encourage younger family members to take chances, as they may feel less constrained by the daily presence of family members.

It is important for the next generation to be provided with real jobs having real accountability. "Unfortunately, incumbents in family businesses often try to shelter heirs, sometimes by giving them ambiguous positions such as 'assistant to the CEO'. This erodes young leaders' attempts to earn credibility and robs them of the opportunity to demonstrate what they have to offer."[26]

Family members should have a detailed job description that outlines what is expected. The requirements for position, compensation and promotion should be fair and clearly understood. Their success should be measured by achieving quantitative goals (such as sales targets, projects completed and so on). Establishing a clear path to success will help build the skills and self-confidence necessary for personal and professional growth.

The Bechtel family is an example of a successful business family that has passed the entrepreneurial torch down to the fourth generation. Bechtel Corp is ranked number seven in the 2008 Forbes List of America's Largest Private Companies.[27] It is an engineering giant that started as a small road-grading business, built the Hoover Dam and recently completed the United Kingdom's first high-speed rail line. Riley Bechtel is the fourth-generation head of Bechtel Corp and on the 2008 Forbes list of the 400 richest people in the United States. "Riley Bechtel still has his first paycheck ($18.49 for a week's labor), which his father had framed as a memento."[28] Growing up, Riley did various jobs at Bechtel, including a mechanic's helper, oiler, labourer and front-end loader operator. After law school he briefly practised law, then rejoined Bechtel and took on various strategic assignments, determined to work 'from the

---

26   Ivan Lansberg, "The Tests of a Prince", *Harvard Business Review*, September 2007.
27   www.forbes.com/lists/2008/21/privates08_Bechtel_800U.html.
28   "Bechtel Home: A history of family leadership": Riley P Bechtel, www.bechtel.com/BAC-Riley-P-Bechtel.html.

bottom up' to fill in the gaps in his knowledge. This included an assignment in Indonesia as area superintendent for a liquefied natural gas plant; New Zealand, as a general field superintendent; and London, as a business development representative. As he successfully completed each assignment, he moved up the ranks of Bechtel and eventually earned the position of CEO.[29] Today, members of the fifth Bechtel generation are "at work in the company learning the basics, earning their pay and building their following".[30]

Regardless of whether the next generation get their training inside or outside the family business, it is important that the criteria for employment/advancement are consistently applied. It is recommended that families work through these issues in advance, to avoid having to change the rules when the next generation is already working in, or about to join, the family business.

2.8 Getting out from the shadow of the founder

It is difficult to follow in the footsteps of a great entrepreneur. "Like celebrity children, would-be leaders of family enterprises are in the public eye literally from the time they are born."[31] How does the next generation step into the shoes of Bill Gates or Carlos Slim Helu? Entrepreneurs should take the time to mentor and train the next generation. Young family members should be assigned real responsibility and be placed in areas of the business where they receive visibility commensurate with their role. Senior family members should show respect, patience and interest in the next generation and not see them as competitors or threats. They need to encourage open communication and foster an environment where the younger family members have the confidence to share new ideas.

For children "of towering figures the best advice is, get out from under the shadow: which means, take an independent path and find your own way to make a mark".[32] Edsel Ford was the only child of Henry Ford, the legendary founder of the Ford Motor Company. Henry was an overbearing father who frequently criticised his son both in public and private. In response to the growth of GM's Chevrolet brand, Edsel commissioned a redesign of the Model T car. Henry was strongly opposed to the introduction of another model. "In awe of Henry's fearsome wrath, Edsel backed off, putting on hold any more initiatives to modernize."[33] "Edsel lived in the shadow of his father so much that very little is known about him today."[34] Although Edsel became President of Ford at age 25, he made very few decisions because his father never relinquished control of the company. Edsel died at the age of 49 from cancer.[35]

Living in the shadow of a great entrepreneur is not a problem limited to the second generation. Children of third and subsequent generations may also feel that they exist under this shadow. A strong family business culture can be a positive influence on the family where there is a clear articulation of the firm's values.

---

29   See, www.bechtel.com.
30   "Bechtel Home: A history of family leadership": Riley P Bechtel.
31   Ivan Landsberg, "Test of a Prince".
32   Gordon and Nicholson, *Family Wars*, p 101.
33   *Ibid.*
34   Ron Osborn, "Edsel B Ford", www.edsel.com/pages/edslford.htm.
35   *Ibid*; Edsel Ford, en.wikipedia.org/wiki/Edsel_Ford; Gordon and Nicholson, *Family Wars*, pp 101 to 102.

"However, it can also hamper the subsequent generations in attempts to make the company their own, constraining them in ways that may hurt the company's performance."[36]

Children of great entrepreneurs need to gain legitimacy on their own and gain the respect of their peers and shareholders. The next generation needs to earn the right to be in their position. It is only with the support of the family and others in the business, that the next generation can have the freedom to develop new ideas and implement change.

2.9 Governance

A strong governance system and open communication can also help encourage entrepreneurship. As family businesses grow in size and become multi-generational, the ownership of the businesses may be shared by many family members residing in diverse geographical locations. When the ownership of a business transfers down several generations, some family member owners may not work in the business. These non-working family owners may have a lack of interest in the long-term growth and development of the business, instead viewing the company only as a source of cash revenue. As a result, the ownership may be split among family factions who have different goals for the business, causing family strife and conflict.

Family conflicts divert time and energy away from running a business. Making management decisions focused on creating the greatest short-term financial returns for the family owners may make them more risk adverse, preventing them from embarking on creative ideas to grow the business. Conflict and distrust can lead to poor business decisions. Trust among family members is paramount. Frequent and open lines of communication are necessary to build trust. When there is trust, leaders can have the freedom to pursue the best opportunities for the company and achieve their objectives. Having a good system of governance and open communications will help build family trust, which will in turn set free the family's entrepreneurial spirit.

2.10 Accepting exit strategies

The freedom to pursue an exit strategy from all or part of a family business may encourage entrepreneurship. In many family businesses there is a strong emotional attachment to the business that was built by their family members. The founder and future generations may view the business as part of their identity and see it as their responsibility to continue in perpetuity. They have invested their emotions, time and wealth in the company, which may lead to 'commitment entrapment'.[37] As a result, family members may be unable to respond to change and unable to accept when a business or business unit is no longer profitable, or when it is time to divest themselves and move into new opportunities.[38]

---

36 Dwight Cass, "The Third-Generation Bounce", *Worth*, January 2006.
37 See, Francesco Shirco, "Improving the Long-run Survival of Family Firms: Knowledge management and resource-shedding processes" (submitted for the degree of PhD in Economics, University of Lugano, Switzerland), February 2007.
38 *Ibid.*

Perpetuating the family business, when it is time to let go, may stagnate entrepreneurship. Exiting a business may free up family capital, creating new opportunities and allowing the family to regenerate itself in new industries. Where appropriate, an exit strategy should be considered, as it may produce a better outcome for the next generation.

3. Conclusion

Successful business families face many unique challenges, as the line between the business and the family may at times become blurred due to complex and interwoven relationships. Greatness is not a gene that is automatically passed down to the next generation; it is a trait that must be nurtured and developed. One key to helping develop greatness in the next generation is to encourage entrepreneurship. The formula for encouraging entrepreneurship will differ among families and may need to be adjusted to fit the needs of individual family members. It is important for families to recognise some of the unique issues they face and to think in advance of the steps they can take to address these challenges. Hopefully, some of the suggestions we have made can help inspire entrepreneurship in the next generation.

Preparing the successor generation

Louise Fisher
Family Business Solutions Limited

1. Identifying successors

Although the majority of family business owners hope that the next generation of the family will take over ownership and leadership of the family business, successor development is low on the list of priorities in most business families. However, if the business is to continue to thrive, it is essential that the next business leaders are equipped with the skills, knowledge and experience to face the challenges of running the family business in the future.

In order to ensure that successor selection and development is successful, it is essential to have a clear process. The process adopted by the senior generation is often emotionally driven and based on the seniors' expectations, family history and the tradition that next-generation family members will take over the business (ie, "following in your parents' footsteps is how it has always been done in this family"). Therefore, identifying the next family owners and leaders may have more to do with family relationships than objective selection criteria. In this emotion-driven process the next-generation members may feel obliged to take over – their career in the family business has always been assumed – and consequently they will have no opportunity to question whether or not a role in the family business will fulfil their ambitions for their own careers.

As the family business becomes more complex, the family grows up and gets bigger over time, the business grows and diversifies, and ownership dilutes and fragments, an emotional process for selection and development of successors is no longer feasible. Structure must be introduced to the selection process at this stage to ensure that the next generation has the business and management skills necessary to help the business succeed and a commitment to preserving and extending the family's legacy of ownership and leadership. Important features of a more structured process for developing and selecting successors are: education; the opportunity for young people to gain experience outside of the family business; and transparent selection criteria.

1.1 Education

Important attitudes towards work and the family business are formed during childhood. Children become conscious of their parents' habits, attitudes to the business and the family's values long before formal successor development begins.

As children get older, learning about the family's history and attitude towards wealth, as well as developing knowledge about the structures in the family business, such as the board of directors and how owners make decisions, helps young people foster a connection with the family business. In small families these discussions can occur spontaneously, often over dinner, at weekends or on holiday. However, as both the family and the business grow, educating the family requires more planning and formality. Many families choose to create a family assembly.

As well as delivering next-generation education programmes, the family assembly can also perform social and formal functions. As a family gets bigger, the assembly can generate social interaction that helps to create and sustain the 'glue' that binds family members to one another and to their shared investment in the family business. If this glue is not maintained and begins to dilute, there will come a point when it is no longer strong enough to hold the family and its business together.

The formal role of a family assembly can include creating policies that govern areas where the distinct interests of family members and the enterprise overlap and that can often be the source of conflict. For example, the family may create a policy on employment and remuneration that clarifies how family members can get a job in the family enterprise, how their careers will develop and how they will be paid.

An important part of creating a family assembly is deciding who will perform the different roles. Family governance structures, like the family assembly, can create opportunities for family members to have meaningful roles in governing and overseeing their enterprise without necessarily having to work in the business.

The next, more formal, education stage will be different for every successor. For some business families an MBA, degree or diploma may be an essential minimum requirement for young people looking to enter the business. Further education gives the young person an opportunity to experience the outside world, develop important skills and learn new disciplines such as finance or marketing, all of which will be of benefit to the family business in the future.

Other families consider that developing the successor's management and other skills and knowledge of the business is paramount and consequently the successor's education will continue within the family business. The danger when successors do not have an opportunity to experience life outside the family business is that they may not feel that they have choices about their future career, or have the ability to compete in the outside world.

1.2 Outside work experience

Time spent working in the family business during school and university holidays can give next-generation family members valuable work experience and an insight into its culture and relationships. However, before entering the family business in a permanent role, successors should be encouraged to undertake a period of work experience outside the business. This period gives successors an opportunity to, among other things, get honest feedback from their employers, to be judged on their own merits, and to learn valuable management skills and different ways of running a business.

Many next-generation members feel apprehensive about work in the outside world, particularly if their only previous employment has been in the family business. However, this experience can engender a feeling of self-worth and confidence in their own ability to compete in the marketplace, which is often lacking when the successor takes on what is often perceived as the easy option of taking over the family business without having worked anywhere else first. It also gives young people an opportunity to reflect on whether or not a role in the family business is the right thing for their career and their other ambitions for their own lives.

As well as being beneficial for the young person involved, such a period also benefits the family business as the young person can make mistakes in someone else's business (where he or she is just another employee) and then come back to the family business having gained experience, new skills and maturity as well as having had the opportunity to develop relationships with business leaders and senior management in other businesses, with professional and trade associations and with other next-generation members of family businesses.

If outside work experience is not possible or desired, it is important that the successor is encouraged to develop his or her own leadership style and to identify with other employees and managers to ensure that he or she is not always in the parents' shadow. It is also important for the successor to develop external relationships and to continue some form of outside education in order to ensure that he or she is perceived as an individual who is capable of taking over from the seniors by the family, by the employees and managers and by the marketplace (including suppliers, customers and competitors).

1.3   Selection process

Many families choose to set policies to shape successors' expectations of when, how and under what conditions they will be offered a job in the family business. If the selection process, pay and performance standards are communicated clearly, the minimum expectations for selection are set for the young people and the seniors.

Transparent selection criteria also allow the successor to begin to emerge from the seniors' shadow, as he or she will have been measured against clear and objective criteria and will have earned the job because of qualifications, skills and experience and not because of the family name. This clarity also allows the next-generation family members to earn respect from managers and other employees, as there will no longer be any doubt about the successor's competence; and therefore it is less likely that other employees will be resentful of the young family member.

Some criteria that often appear in family policies on employment and remuneration of family members are set out next.

(a)   Minimum level of further education

As discussed above, successors may be asked to complete an MBA, degree or diploma course before they are considered for a role in the family business. Some families feel that further education gives young family members an opportunity to experience the outside world, develop important skills and learn new disciplines, as well as time to mature and reflect on whether or not a role in the family business will fulfil their ambitions for their careers.

(b) *Outside work experience*

Some business families decide that next-generation family members must undertake a period of work experience outside the family business before they will be considered for a role in it. This period gives the young person an opportunity to learn new skills, work with new people and gain experience in the working world. In general, family business advisers recommend a period of not less than two years.

(c) *Filling a legitimate vacancy*

To maintain fairness within the family and among the employees, the policy may state that no jobs will be created for family members. There must be a legitimate vacancy before the family member's request to enter the family business is considered. The family member will then be assessed on the same objective criteria as other applicants.

(d) *Selection*

A family member will not be chosen to fill a vacancy simply because he or she is a family member. He or she will be assessed objectively and will only be considered if his or her skills, qualifications and experience are appropriate for the job. If the process is to be transparent, the young person's parents will not be on the interview panel or be part of the selection team. Objective selection means that the successor, the family and the employees will know that the individual has been chosen on merit and not because of the family name. This will reduce the likelihood of resentment among the employees and give the successor an opportunity to be seen as an individual who has the capability to run the business in the future.

(e) *Training and promotion*

These are also important elements in the family policy as the successor's performance can be measured against objective criteria and any training needs or skills gaps can be addressed. Successors can also be confident that their career is planned and that they are not under pressure to acquire this knowledge and skills by osmosis or by association with the seniors.

Preparatory training and promotion of successors is discussed more fully in Section 3 below.

The decision to enter the business is an important one for the successor. Before he or she goes hurtling down a career development path with a clearly defined training programme and set of performance criteria, it is important that the young person is allowed the time and space to explore whether joining and leading the family business in the future will fulfil his or her own career ambitions.

2. **What does the next generation want?**

As discussed above, choosing a successor in a family business is often emotionally driven and based on the seniors' expectations that one (or more) of their offspring will be the next owner and leader of the family business. The seniors' needs and expectations are important factors, but it is equally important to ensure that the decision to enter the business is a good one for the young person.

A useful framework to help us explore the needs and motivations of young adults is the work of developmental psychologist Daniel Levinson. Levinson's model for adult development outlines the distinct tasks that must be attended to during each of the three eras in the adult lives of men and women: young adulthood (age 17 to 40); middle adulthood (age 40 to 55); and late adulthood (age 55+).

People in the young adulthood stage have the task of gathering experience, gaining competences and experimenting with choices that build a 'life structure': who you choose to spend your life with, your career choice and your social connections. Therefore, we can predict that people deciding whether or not to enter the business as they enter young adulthood (early twenties) are likely to regard the decision to join as a means of gaining experience of the working world, rather than making a commitment to a particular career path for life. If the family business is seen through the eyes of the next generation, it will be looked upon as a place to gain work experience and the decision to join will be straightforward: it suits both the individual and the system – meaning the family business system which incorporates the family, the owners and the business – as it is a feasible choice for the young person to start on the career ladder and it is possible for the system to create openings or offer existing openings to young family members.

As well as experimenting with potential career options, people in their early twenties will factor other peoples' needs into their decisions and go with the flow, rather than put their own needs to the fore in an assertive, logical way or negotiate a proper career path and career development plan. This is in stark contrast with the seniors' expectation that the young person's decision to join the business is the beginning of a lifelong career that will allow the seniors to realise their ambitions of continuity of ownership and leadership of the family business, whilst also giving them the stability they need to think about retirement as they head towards late adulthood.

Consequently, it is important for the senior generation to appreciate that young people may not yet have acquired enough knowledge in the business world to be able to carve out a career that will guarantee success; and seniors need to know how to steer this course, without introducing personal, family and business needs that will affect how the young person navigates his or her career journey.

Many senior members of business families recognise the developmental pressures that individuals in the early stage of young adulthood face. Consequently, many families encourage next-generation family members to spread their wings and gain work experience outside the family business, as discussed above. But beware – a recurring theme in family businesses is that despite the seniors' encouragement of the next generation to gain outside experience, young people are often pulled back to the family business prematurely when there is a business or family crisis or when the seniors feel ready to retire, and consequently someone else's needs begin to dominate the developmental agenda.

These mixed messages are often given out when the senior and next generation's developmental paths are not synchronised, meaning that either the seniors are ready to retire but the next generation have not completed the developmental tasks of early adulthood and are therefore not ready to take over or, conversely, the next generation want to and are ready to take over the family business but the seniors have not completed the work of middle adulthood and are consequently not ready to enter late adulthood and let go.

Levinson's adult development lifecycle model was applied to parent and offspring relationships in 1982 when Professor John A Davis mapped the life stages of 89 fathers with the life stage of their sons.[1] The research concluded that when the phases of stability and transition in the unfolding life stages of each generation were congruent or synchronised, both parties enjoy a more respectful and productive working relationship. This is of practical value to advisers working with business families in which there are strained or conflicted relationships between parent and offspring, as the adviser can plot the ages of all the key people and assess the implications of being in sync or out of sync based on the intersections that show up in the analysis.

Based on his findings, Davis was able to model periods of time during which father and son can expect to experience varying levels of quality in their working relationships. Three labels, 'poor', 'mixed' and 'good', are used to describe the father and son relationships. In 'poor' relationships there was a high-level anxiety between father and son; this anxiety level reduced in 'mixed' relationships and was at a workable level in 'good' relationships. Each relationship affects the other, as was expected from Levinson's and others' life-stage models, and therefore leads to a predictable generating and shifting of anxiety between the parties.

The period when a father is in his fifties and his son is between his mid-twenties to mid-thirties is a relatively good one, and compatibility seems to be due to the father's willingness to teach, support, and promote his son and to the son's eagerness to grow and not threaten his father at this time.

In contrast, when a father is in his sixties and his son is in his mid-to-late thirties, some tension between them can be expected, because the two cannot have what they are likely to want from the relationship. The son wants to continue to grow, and as he nears 40 his need to be on his own and achieve his personal goals becomes very pressing. But by this time in his career, in the typical smaller business, he cannot satisfy his need for independence with his father still in charge. If the father did not have his own need to demonstrate his vitality in this period, some mutual accommodation might be found. Instead, what often ensues is a struggle for control of the family business.

The findings are summarised in Figure 1 overleaf.

The usefulness of Davis' research in working with business families is that advisers can help families plan for these predictable challenges. In Davis' words:[2]

the more the father and son realise that their needs will change over time, and that their expectations in the relationship must also change, the less they will blame each other personally for incompatibilities.

As Figure 1 shows, Davis found that fathers and sons experienced good-quality

---

1   Davis, JA, "The influences of life stages on father-son working relationships in family companies", unpublished DBA dissertation, Harvard Business School, 1982.
2   *Id*, p 181.

working relationships when fathers were in their fifties and sons in their late twenties to mid-thirties. A contributory factor in the success of these working relationships seems to be that by the time successors enter their thirties and start to face middle adulthood, decision making is managed in a very different way.

Figure 1: Fathers' and sons' quality of work relationship by age (Davis 1982)

| Period | Quality | | Developmental periods |
	Sons	Fathers	
A			
S: 15–27	Mixed		Entering early adulthood
F: 45–53		Poor	Entering middle adulthood
B			
S: 25–36	Good		Early adulthood transition
F: 47–62		Good	Mid-end of middle adulthood
C			
S: 30–40	Poor		Settling down – mid-life transition
F: 58–75		Poor	Entering late adulthood
D			
S: 38–55	Good		Mid-life transition – middle adulthood
F: 66–80		Good	Late adult transition
E			
S: 43–54	Poor		Entering middle adulthood
F: 71–79		Poor	Late adulthood

People at this stage are more able to be 'selfish' in the sense of putting their own needs first, especially as these relate to their own new nuclear family, spouse or partner, and social needs. If these 'selfish' decisions include a decision to enter or continue in the family business, the successor is more likely to be committing to a long-term career path than any such decision in their early twenties.

However, these personal needs can be difficult to state and defend when facing a parent who is accustomed to the parents and/or the business taking priority in career matters. Some of the people in this study could not face this challenge, and they settled for a less than satisfactory career in the family business.

Being more 'selfish' is not a bad thing: if a person is more aware at this time in life of their own dreams, aspirations and desires, and at the same time has a practical sense of what it is still feasible to achieve, then it is more likely that a decision will be made that is good for the self and good for the business – whichever way that decision goes. Again, at this stage of successor development it is important that the seniors allow each next-generation family member the time and space to explore their own needs and ambitions without introducing the seniors' needs or expectations or those of the family business that may influence the successor's decision.

It is important for seniors and the business family to be aware of the type of the decisions that next-generation family members are capable of making at particular times to ensure that their expectations and advice are appropriate. In early adulthood a job in the family business will be an opportunity for a young person to get on the career ladder while they work out what they really want to make of their career, or simply to see what working in the family business is like. By the time the potential successor reaches age 30, he or she will be in a developmental position to make a more informed career choice, at which stage he or she may be reassessing their role if they joined the business in early adulthood; or if he or she decides to enter the business at this stage, it will be a thoughtful decision that may take time but it is more likely to prove to be a foundation for a stable, satisfying career in the family business which is good for the individual and for the business.

3. Training of family members

If a next-generation family member is chosen to take over ownership and leadership of the family business and the young person wants this role, it is important that his or her training needs are addressed to ensure that the successor is well placed to succeed.

As mentioned above, the education and training process often begins long before the young person decides to enter the business. Attitudes towards work and the family business are formed during childhood; and learning about the family's history, its values and attitude towards wealth, as well as developing knowledge about the business and how to be a responsible owner, is a good way to begin the successor's formal family business training.

When successors attain the minimum qualifications and/or outside experience that allow them to enter the business (if the business family sets these criteria), policies on employment and remuneration of family members will clarify the career path that successors will be able to follow. In addition to these entry criteria, family employment and remuneration policies will contain performance measurement criteria, identify training needs and enunciate the promotion pathway. Some important elements of successor education and training are outlined below.

3.1 Role and job description

There may be a number of diverse roles and jobs that the successor must perform to fulfil his or her ambition of leading the business in the future (eg, warehouse manager to sales executive, and administration assistant to finance director). Alternatively, the successor may have entered the business to perform a specific mid- to top-tier management role. Either way, if the successor's job description is clear, both the next-generation family member and the seniors can be comfortable with their respective roles. Such a transparent remit for decision making as part of the young person's role will limit the possibility of the successor being undermined by the seniors whilst carrying out their job.

Clarity of the successor's role also allows managers and non-family employees to recognise the functions that the next-generation family member will carry out, and should help them to get used to authority being exercised by that member rather than the seniors. In turn, this should increase respect for the successor for the role they play and its importance in the running of the family business.

3.2 Performance indicators

The setting of performance indicators helps seniors and management to assess the successor's progress and allows the successor to feel satisfaction in his or her continuing development, giving criteria against which he or she can ensure that long-term goals remain in sight.

It is important that performance indicators build on and develop the successor's attributes, as well as setting achievable management and leadership goals and targets for development of new practical skills. Goals should be specific and measurable (eg, "attend two management seminars in the next year", "learn the company's most profitable manufacturing process in the first quarter"). This ensures that the successor's progress is monitored against objective criteria, not based on a manager's or senior's subjective judgement.

3.3 Skills development

To ensure that the successor is able to build his or her skills and expertise within the family business without being compared constantly with the seniors, more particularly a parent, it is important when thinking about the successor's performance indicators that the young person's development is focused on areas where the parent is not so strong or where there is a gap in the current management or board, provided that such focus is a good use of the successor's talents and fits with the young person's aspirations for their own career. This will secure a career path for the successor, independent of a parent, and it will help to ensure that the seniors are supportive of the young person's development.

If the parent and child developmental paths are out of sync, the relationship may become tense and unsatisfactory. This is particularly so if the parent is not in a developmental position to teach and coach the young person, or if the senior feels threatened by the successor. This potential threat can be minimised by the successor developing complementary skills, which will allow parent and child to have a healthier, more respectful working relationship.

3.4 Management and leadership training

When the successor has developed the skills and experience needed to fulfil the tasks in his or her job profile and met his or her performance indicators, then providing his or her aspirations continue to be to lead the family business in the future, the next stage of development is to enhance his or her management and leadership skills.

Two important goals of this stage of the successor's development are to secure the commitment of all of the stakeholders in the family business system and to be seen as the legitimate next-generation leader within the business.

As the future leader of the family business, the successor must understand that he or she is responsible for looking after all of the varied interests inherent in the family business system. He or she is looking after the shareholders' investment; is responsible for continuing the family's legacy of ownership and leadership of the family business; and must ensure that the business is able to respond to changes in a fast-moving, uncertain business environment. This is a huge amount of responsibility and a successor must be certain that this role is congruent with his or her career ambitions.

If the successor is committed to this career, an incremental increase in responsibility allows them to gain the shareholders' and wider family's trust and to gain legitimacy within the business. Legitimacy is about being seen as having the power to make decisions and run the business without being compared to "how it used to be when the seniors were in charge". Gaining legitimacy takes time in any family business, regardless of the successor's talents.

The successor must demonstrate an awareness of his or her responsibility for his or her own career, and must also develop his or her skills to manage a team. Perhaps the next stage would be to manage business finance and to begin to develop a relationship with the shareholders. If promotions are based on completion of objective performance criteria, the successor's credibility will grow within the business, and the shareholders will recognise that their investment and the family's legacy will continue into the next generation.

When the successor's leadership development is completed, the seniors will feel confident about the transfer of ownership and leadership of the family business, as they will know that their life's work is in safe hands.

3.5 Mentoring/coaching

Working with a mentor can be invaluable in helping a successor achieve his or her potential. The mentor will help the successor grow into an executive and leadership role by providing coaching on how to exercise good business judgement, take acceptable risks and relate to other managers and employees and to the marketplace in which the family business must compete. The mentor may also help the successor develop business skills and achieve the performance indicators set.

It is essential that the mentor relationship is confidential and built on trust and personal rapport; but the mentor should not be the successor's parent. The successor must feel comfortable enough to ask the stupid or difficult questions and not feel intimidated or foolish. The mentor must have the successor's best interests at heart and not be put in a position where the relationship is used to acquire information about the successor on behalf of the seniors.

4. Other roles

The focus of this chapter has been on preparing a next-generation successor to take over management and leadership of the business when the seniors decide to retire. Recycling this owner-management model of business has been used successfully by family businesses over generations. The inherent assumption in this model is that if a next-generation family member decides that he or she does not want to work in the family business, then he or she will not be involved in the business at all.

However, we discussed the importance of next-generation education earlier in this chapter, as it helps engender in the next generation feelings of legacy, history and values in relation to the family and the family business. Is there a way that these feelings of connectedness that have been built up throughout childhood can be harnessed and utilised to allow family members to remain involved with the family business, even if they choose to pursue their careers elsewhere?

This could be done by offering family members the opportunity to have roles as non-working owners who actively oversee and monitor how the board and management are running the business (their managers may be their siblings or cousins), and therefore have a positive role in looking after the family's collective investment.

Some families strongly believe that owners must work in the business. The perceived attraction of working owners is that it will help to avoid conflict between working and non-working owners, and especially resentment among the working owners that their efforts are profiting those who chose not to help the business by the sweat of their brows.

However, a rule restricting shares to working owners can have unintended consequences. Family members who decide to pursue other careers and are cut out of ownership may feel they are also being cut off from the family, especially if the family business represents a significant portion of the family's overall wealth. Alternatively, they might decide to take a career in the family business in order to qualify for ownership but feel they are being bound by 'golden handcuffs' and they might therefore resent the fact that they were forced to give up on their career aspirations in order to become a shareholder in the family business.

Working and non-working owners can collaborate successfully, provided the rules are clear – for example by having a dividend policy for all owners and a remuneration policy for working owners that together make clear who gets what from the family business. Separating ownership and management roles allows the wider family to remain connected with the family and its business as the business grows and the family grows up and grows apart.

Governance and management

Ken McCracken
Family Business Solutions Limited
Charlie Tee
Matthew Woods
Withers LLP

1. Introduction

Successful family businesses have one thing in common: they are well governed and
well managed. Broadly speaking, a family's governance structure is the family's rules
and systems under which the family's business and wealth are held and preserved
and under which a family and all of its members, fiduciaries and advisers can work
together to give the family its own articulated creed and vision. Guidelines will be
established for all family members to follow. A good governance structure will look
to achieve organised accountability and a clear balance of power among the various
interests and bodies that comprise a family and its business. These will include family
members, shareholders and directors of the company, fiduciaries, such as trustees of
family trusts, family advisers, and possibly the family office.

Management, in this context, is the way in which a family business is run by its
directors on a day-to-day basis and on a strategic level (more along the lines of
corporate governance). A good governance and management system will be
integrated as one system and will be interlinked at all levels to ensure that all aspects
of the family business and family exist harmoniously together.

When a business is first established, the founder or controlling owners could be
considered the 'governance structure', since they are likely to be responsible for most
aspects of governance and management of their business. Formal structures tend to be
absent in favour of informality and highly personalised structures. In future
generations, it may become increasingly difficult to replicate this arrangement and
more formal governance is likely to be required. In order successfully to govern a family
business, including the involvement of the family members, the transition from one
generation to the next and managing the expectations of all the family members (both
those involved in the business and those who are not), it is crucial to have a formal
codified system of governance to provide a unique, articulated vision for the family
and how it will interact with the family business and its management.

It is important that any system of governance is given the time and space to
develop naturally out of family discussions and be driven by a family's vision and
ethos. This will help to ensure that it is tailored to the individual needs of each
family. Equally, and so as to ensure the success of any system of governance, it is key
that all of the family members agree with, and are supportive of, the proposed
governance structure, because without this family approval no system can be
expected to work. Whilst there is not a single form of governance that fits every
family business, there are a number of different building blocks that can be utilised,

to a lesser or greater degree, in most systems of governance. Some of these are conventional to the corporate way of thinking whilst others are less common.

The length of this chapter and the sheer scale and number of issues involved mean that the chapter cannot be more than an overview of some of the principal aspects of governance that are available to families, of whatever size or complexity. However, the theory of governance remains the same no matter what the size of the family or type of family business; it will just be incorporated on a different scale and with lesser or greater formality.[1]

2. The family creed or family constitution

The single most important building block for any system of family governance is the family creed or family constitution. This is a formal document that sits on top of all of the other aspects of the governance system. This clearly sets out the family's guiding principles and defines the roles of the family business, the family members and any fiduciaries for all family members to follow.

The importance of this document being a formal written document cannot be underestimated. The process of getting some initial thoughts down on paper, discussing those thoughts between the family members, articulating the main principles for the family and, most crucially, getting buy-in from the whole family is very important for every family. The process enables all relevant issues to come to the surface and to be discussed, which helps ensure that the system of governance grows organically rather than being imposed on a family. An external and neutral facilitator can play a key role in these discussions and give the family the time and space to develop their governance structure. It is well established that a system of governance will only function properly if it is developed, understood and accepted by all major stakeholders in the business, and the process of preparing a family creed will normally serve to fulfil this.

Once established, a family creed or constitution will usually:

- set out the core values that all family members should follow;
- establish a forum and process for decision making;
- clearly set out what each family member can expect to receive, both in terms of shares held in and salary and other benefits from the family business;
- provide a mechanism to introduce younger family members to the family business and its governance structures;
- provide a dispute resolution procedure that avoids family members having to resort to expensive litigation; and
- articulate any philanthropic ambitions of the family.

The family creed is a framework for all aspects of a family's governance system and will have an impact on all of the other building blocks in the structure, which are considered below.

---

1   It is notoriously difficult to fix on an agreed definition of a family business. This chapter aims to provide a general overview of structures that can be applied to most types of family business, particularly those that are family owned and not family run. Where a family business is owner-managed, the governance issues are often less pronounced.

The question may arise about whether or not a family creed is legally binding on family members. Some creeds are intended to have moral rather than legal force, but it may be possible to condense all aspects of governance (family, ownership and management) into one document with the intention that this will be legally enforceable. A single governance document has the advantage of ensuring that the family creed and its contents are taken into account when construing the intention of the parties in relation to formal aspects of governance. A single document will also help ensure that there are no gaps in the structure and is more likely to be accessible to, and understood by, a family member than if there are a number of different governance documents.

3. Family meetings and family councils

The family creed will usually include a formalised system of family meetings. These may be held, say, annually so that all family members can come together to discuss issues, consider how the business is doing and be involved in the family venture.

As a family becomes larger, with increasing numbers of family branches and members, the number of family members involved in the business on a day-to-day basis is likely to decrease. A family meeting, which all members are encouraged to attend, provides an excellent forum for discussing strategy. Whilst it is important that every member of the family has the chance to make their views known and have their say on any issue, this should not be mistaken for running the business. There must be a clearly defined corporate chain of command in relation to the business, namely the directors, for it to be run successfully. The family meeting is a useful forum for the dissemination of information concerning the business, and it gives family members an opportunity to discuss all matters pertaining to the family and to resolve any disputes.

The family meeting will usually be the body charged with reviewing the family creed to ensure that it is brought up to date and adapts to ever changing circumstances. All successful family creeds include an obligation on the family to review the creed periodically – say every five years – to ensure that it remains relevant. As with the initial preparation of the family creed, it is important that the whole family has a role in reviewing and amending it. The family meeting is an appropriate forum for making such changes. Whilst it is important for a system of governance to be formalised, so that everyone knows exactly where they stand and so that the interaction between the various bodies is clearly set out, it is crucial that there is also flexibility to adapt the family creed. If the family creed is overly rigid, all of the efforts put into creating both it and the systems of governance could be wasted as the systems may become obsolete.

The forum of the family meeting is also an excellent first opportunity to get younger family members involved in the family business. Many families encourage children to start attending such meetings when they reach the age of 18 (sometimes even younger) and some families go further and require all children attending such a meeting for the first time to make a presentation to the meeting. The younger generations will be exposed first hand to the governance of the family (and will often be required to sign the family creed), and it can also provide a useful training ground for them to organise and run aspects of the family wealth and business.

Sometimes, in addition to a family meeting, there will be a family council, made up of just a few family members (with different branches and different generations being represented if this is important to the family). The family council can provide executive leadership to the family, formulate the issues for discussion at family meetings and generally ensure that there are lines of communication and information flow between the family and its business. A family council will usually meet on a regular, informal basis and will be the driving force behind calling and running family meetings in accordance with the family creed.

A single family meeting will often suffice where there is only a small number of family members involved. When a family becomes more numerous, it may become necessary to supplement the family meeting with another common form or institution of governance, namely a shareholders' assembly. The shareholders' assembly would exercise the ownership powers over the family business and would be separate from the family meeting. The family meeting would in turn have a more educational or social function, whilst still retaining certain powers, such as control over the remuneration of family members in the family business.

4.   The family business – shareholders

One of the most important aspects of any system of governance is the way it controls the relationships and interaction between the family and what is often the most important component of any family's wealth, the family business.

A well thought-out and implemented governance system will incorporate the usual methods of corporate governance, such as a shareholders' agreement and the articles of association of the companies that comprise the family business. It is important that the theory and good practice set out in any family creed concerning the holding of annual general meetings (AGMs) and extraordinary general meetings (EGMs), the transmission of shares, pre-emption rights, voting rights and dividend rights are all replicated in the legal documents that control the company, creating a wholly unified structure.

4.1   Shareholders' agreements

A shareholders' agreement or voting agreement (which will also be tied into the articles of association) will direct how shareholders in a family business will act in relation to the business. The shareholders' agreement will also ensure shareholders exercise their votes appropriately. Such agreements could also include restrictions on the transfer of shares (by gift, sale or will) and pre-emption rights, to ensure that the shareholding in the business remains within the family. A family will need to consider who can hold the shares – should it be restricted to bloodline descendants only, or can spouses also be involved?

The role of proxies must be considered in such an agreement. Although this would not feature high up on a list of issues with which a family is initially concerned, as the ownership of the family business becomes more fragmented, the choice and exercise of any proxy vote can sometimes be very important. Matters to be decided upon include whether there should be restrictions on who can be a proxy (the chairman of the meeting, another shareholder, another family member, a spouse or an advisor), whether such a proxy should be an open or a closed proxy (ie, whether there is discretion as to how to vote) and directions as to where and when proxies should be lodged in advance of any meeting.

4.2   Ownership of shares

As noted above, it is common for shareholdings in a family business to be tightly controlled. This is an area that the family will have to consider very carefully. Thus:

- Is it best for the shares to be held in a trust structure and, if so, who should be the trustees and other fiduciaries?
- Would it be better for shares to be held individually, which might lead to dissipation of the family's shareholdings and may also be less tax-efficient?
- Should there be different classes of shares depending on whether or not a particular family member is involved with the business or depending on which generation is in the ascendancy at that time? Family members who are actively involved in the business, at least at a senior level, may want to have control over a sufficient number of shares that would reflect their role in the business and that should motivate them to do the best they can. Equally, other family members who are not employed by the family business may want to retain an interest in the family business, forming as it does part of their family's identity and common inheritance.

If it is decided to hold the shares in the family business in trust, then it is important that the family chooses the right trustees. A case can be made for family members to be trustees, given that they likely to have a full understanding of the business and the way it is run and are also likely to be sympathetic to the family values. However, other families might prefer to have independent trustees to provide objectivity and balance to the business. There is always the risk of a conflict of interest if a family member is a trustee. For example, their fiduciary role as a trustee may conflict with their interest in the family business as a family member, or as a member of a particular family branch, or possibly as a beneficiary. The trustees should be chosen carefully to ensure there is a suitable balance of professional skills and personal knowledge of the family, together with the objectivity required to enable them to carry out their fiduciary duties properly.

When non-family trustees are involved, a protector or committee of protectors (consisting of family members or trusted advisers) could be appointed. This would allow the family to oversee the trustees. If such a path is followed, it is necessary to consider what powers can be given to the protector or committee of protectors without them potentially being considered quasi-trustees.

If trustees are to hold the shares in the family business, then any AGM or EGM could become more of a formality as there may only be a small number of shareholders to attend such meetings. This needs to be recognised by the system of governance, and structures may need to be put into place where the trustees have the opportunity to consult with the beneficiaries as to their wishes so that any trustee decisions are fully informed. It may be that the family meeting is the appropriate forum for such discussions, or alternatively there could be another forum for such shareholder discussions, such as the shareholders' assembly mentioned above.

4.3 Management incentives

Another issue is whether non-family employees of the business should be given an opportunity to own shares as a reward or incentive. From a traditional governance perspective, share-based incentives are primarily intended as an effective way of aligning the interests of the directors and the owners. Otherwise it is assumed that directors could act in their own interests and to the detriment of the owners. If the directors are owners or have an opportunity to become owners, they may be less likely to act in a way that might reduce the value of the business

A number of points arise when this model is applied to a family business. In some family businesses with non-working owners, it is assumed that managers will behave and that the family's trust will not be abused and so for these businesses share incentives are not needed to keep the managers in line. However, such owners may still decide that share-based incentives are a good idea for a number of other reasons. If they do, they should ensure they articulate these reasons before introducing an incentive scheme, as only then will it be possible to assess whether the incentive scheme has been successful.

Some family businesses use shares as rewards to tie in key people because this technique preserves cash flow when cash is needed to fund the business. It should be remembered that the short-term benefits of preserving cash flow have to be paid for when the key person leaves the business or retires, at which point their shares will need to be bought back. It is essential to have a clear and well-funded mechanism for these shareholdings to be acquired by the family after employment with the company has ended. If there is not, and if the employee is free to leave the shares to whomever he wishes, this could cause further dilution and fragmentation of the ownership of the family business.

As an alternative, a family business may prefer cash rather than share-based incentives. These can be linked to the increase in value of the business and even be partially deferred to give a longer-term incentive to management to build sustainable value, rather than taking short-term decisions to maximise the value of the current bonus.

4.4 Distribution policy

One of the key areas for any family governance structure to consider (and which impacts on the different classes of shares mentioned above) is the dividend distribution policy. Members of a family who are employed in the family business will draw a salary and receive other benefits. For them there may be less of an imperative towards the company making, and shareholders receiving, dividend distributions. Their position should be contrasted with that of 'passive' family members who, although they are not working for the family business, still have a financial stake on which they should receive a return. A distribution policy can avoid tensions among family shareholders and set a transparent return based on investment targets that the company will need to achieve.

5. **The family business – corporate governance**

The commercial running and management of a family business appears to be much more in keeping with traditional corporate governance. Certainly, conventional UK corporate governance forms a useful backdrop to understanding boardroom governance of a family business. However, it is equally important to grasp that a number of assumptions on which the traditional UK governance guidelines are based do not apply to family businesses. These key assumptions are set out below.

Conventional corporate governance	Family business
Listed public companies	Mainly private companies
Dispersed ownership	Concentrated family shareholders
Predominant role of the financial institutions	Predominant role of the owning family
Shareholder value is paramount	Family value returns on investment that are not entirely economic, such as preserving and extending a legacy, control over one's own life and the availability of careers for family members, might be acceptable
Short-term investor commitment	Long-term family commitment
Short-term performance measurement	Long-term investment horizon
High financial leverage and creative accounting	Low financial leverage and cautious accounting

The source of the potential mismatch between the traditional version of corporate governance and the needs of a family business goes deeper than the obvious difference between privately owned and closely-held companies on the one hand and publicly listed companies that are dominated by institutional investors on the other. Conventional governance is largely based on the external investor's distrust of management and seeks to control the self-interest of managers and to protect the shareholders.

Various corporate scandals have no doubt contributed to the view that there is a need for more rules and guidelines, but unfortunately this usually leads to greater regulatory costs. For this reason, amongst others, conventional corporate governance does not always suit business families.

The more traditional approach to corporate governance risks the pitfalls of management by rulebook and short-term performance measurement. This type of governance does not appeal to many closely held family businesses, which prefer structures and practices that reflect relationships of loyalty and trust and which encourage teamwork. The contrasting styles are summarised next.

Conventional corporate governance	Family business
Elaborate rules and control mechanisms	More autonomy; even a willingness to waive 'rules' in exceptional circumstances
Hierarchical, bureaucratic, top-down relationships	Horizontal relationships/teamwork
Judgement based on acts or consequences (Do it the right way)	Judgement based on intentions; giving the benefit of any doubt (Do the right thing)

Since the natural state that every family business strives to achieve is a balance among different and often competing interests of the owners, the wider family and the business, a balanced outcome will usually involve rules and guidelines combined with trust, loyalty and good judgement. Each family needs to explore where its interests are best served, but it is not safe to assume that the traditional version of corporate governance will work. Traditional corporate governance would not apply to a business where the owners and the managers are the same people. Where there are owners who are not involved in the business, the level of trust between them and the other owners (often their relatives) and managers will have a significant impact on the extent to which rules and guidelines are needed.

6. The family business – the board of directors

A major issue that needs to be decided is which family members should be on the board of directors and how many, if any, non-family members should also be directors. The role of executive and non-executive directors needs to be considered, although having non-executive directors will not be enough to ensure a system of good and effective family governance.

Best practice would be to ensure that no family member has an expectation that they will be guaranteed a place on the board of the family business. Only those who are sufficiently qualified and have proved themselves should be considered for appointment as a director. Without a meritocracy, the future of the family business may be jeopardised.

As well as ensuring objectivity in any appointments to the board, there should also be a clearly defined route into the family business for the next generation (provided they are sufficiently qualified). This should include a clearly defined statement of what those employed by and running the family business can expect by way of remuneration and benefits. The policy may provide family members with an opportunity to work in the business, at a level appropriate to their qualifications and experience (be it at executive level or as a trainee) and prove themselves suitable (or not) to be a custodian of the family's heritage. Often family members will be encouraged to gain experience in other fields or businesses before joining the family business, as well as gaining further education and training. Such requirements should all be included in the family creed and should be adhered to so that there is no possibility of favouritism. This will give all the family members the same opportunity. More importantly, each family member will know exactly where they stand in relation to the business. Only a few members of the family can ever rise to the top of the business, but this is the way that a meritocracy does and should work. A system of meritocracy is arguably of even greater importance in a family business where there are all the other underlying tensions, emotions and intra-family relationships to be considered as well.

Issues to be considered when looking to appoint an outside director to the board (apart from their executive talent) include the prospective candidate's experience, if any, of working with a family business, how far they identify with the family's values and identity, how far they can be relied upon to protect and enhance the family's values and whether they will stand up to the different interests in the family. They will need to act with uncompromising independence when needed to do so in order to balance the best interests of everyone with a stake in the family business. Unfortunately, it is by no means guaranteed that every experienced candidate will have these additional characteristics and attributes.

6.1 Executive and non-executive directors

Traditionally, UK companies have a unitary board structure that combines the distinct functions of executive decision making and governance in the same forum. The distinction between these functions may be reflected in the composition of the board, with executive directors having responsibility for day-to-day management and non-executives primarily having a governance role.

In this respect, it may be important to separate the roles of chairman of the board and chief executive. Normally, the chairman would be a non-executive director and would attend board meetings on, say, a monthly basis. The chief executive would be in charge of the day-to-day running of the company. If a family member is qualified for the role of chief executive, then they should be given the role; however, if there is no suitable family member, it is usually in the best interests of the family and the business to appoint an outsider. The chairman will usually be a more senior member of the family or trusted outsider who is known to the family. If there are several family branches, it may be appropriate for each branch to be represented by, say, one non-executive director, so as to have a greater say and input in the way the company is run.

Aside from the chairman, further non-executive directors can add value to a family business in several ways. They bring outside experience and independent judgement to bear on major matters requiring board decisions. They can also act as a link between the board and the shareholders, provide the benefit of their personal contacts and help to ensure that the overall governance of the family business operates effectively.

In recent years, the role of non-executive directors as a control mechanism to protect shareholders' interests in the governance of public companies listed on a stock exchange has increased in prominence. This is in response to concerns of investors about excessive executive remuneration, board appointments, evaluation of board performance and the relationship between the board and the company's auditors. In order to strengthen the autonomy of these non-executive directors, the corporate governance guidelines for such companies advocate that they should be independent and free from any commercial or personal ties that could impair their ability to probe and challenge the board.

In a privately owned family business, these requirements can be difficult to apply since the choice of non-executive director is often influenced by prior relationships between the controlling family and the candidate. This does not mean, however, that non-executive directors of a family business should not be independent; it just emphasises that non-executive directors should be the type of independently minded people who will base decision making on the merits, rather than on considerations such as relationships with family members or personal financial gain. In addition to this, the more understanding a non-executive director has of the family's values and ownership dynamics, the greater the benefit such a director will bring to the family business. This again highlights the importance of ensuring that there is a well thought-out process in place for selecting all board members.

6.2   Directors' agreements

It is important that there is a clearly defined corporate chain of command and that the responsibility for making decisions in relation to the family business rests with the directors and not the family. The family will have the opportunity to discuss the strategy of the business at the family meetings or shareholders' assembly, but the final decision must lie with the board or nothing will ever be achieved. Care will need to be taken to ensure that a family member does not act in a way that could lead the taxation or governance authorities to treat them as a shadow director.

Directors and non-working owners in a family business will want reassurance that certain important decisions must be taken by the entire board and cannot be delegated to an individual director. This could include decisions that may have an adverse impact on the reputation of the family, such as marketing campaigns involving the family name. For this reason the board of a family business may create a policy that identifies certain decisions that are reserved for the full board and provide for other decisions to be made by a special majority.

The way in which a board conducts itself and the internal governance of the board, rather than the governance of the relationship between the family owners and the board, are also issues to consider. The board, if necessary with consent from the family owners, may create a formal code of conduct or directors' agreement. This might specify when and where meetings will be held, deal with circulation of documents and minutes, and set out the right of directors to obtain professional advice at the company's expense. Such a code may improve the collective performance of the board and avoid the board falling under the control of one person, or separate meetings being used to undermine the overall power of the board. It can also be a means by which all of the directors agree to consider certain factors (such as the underlying ethos and values of the family and the family business) before making any decisions.

6.3 Board committees

In addition to the composition of the board of directors and the reservation of certain key decisions to the full board, there is usually power for the board to appoint committees for specific purposes, either on a temporary or a permanent basis. These committees can be a very useful and flexible means of achieving certain goals and aims and they also offer the opportunity to appoint non-directors with relevant skills or experience to serve on a committee.

The appointment of committees does not in any way depart from the principle of the board and all directors being equally responsible for the affairs of the family business. Any disagreement between a committee's members and the board should always be resolved by the full board.

In UK public companies the governance functions of audit, executive pay and the nomination of directors are referred to permanent board committees in which the majority, and sometimes all, of the members are independent non-executive directors. This committee structure reflects the assumptions underlying the conventional approach to corporate governance that is necessary in order to protect the shareholders from the board itself controlling these areas.

The same concerns may or may not apply in a family business. This may depend on whether some or all of the shareholders are on the board, or the level of trust between non-working family members and the board. There may well be other good reasons for using committees for these functions, such as a sense of fairness and the reduced anxiety resulting from having a remuneration committee set executive remuneration for a group of working family shareholders who do not do the same jobs or contribute equally to the business.

More generally, committees can perform a very useful control function in the governance of family businesses. There could, for example, be a governance committee to keep the effectiveness of the overall governance system under continual review. Wherever a committee is used, the board should make a number of factors very clear:

- the committee's terms of reference;
- the powers delegated to the committee – for example, the power to review, report or make decisions on behalf of the board;
- membership of the committee; and
- the committee's obligation to report to the board, the owners or the wider family and the circulation of committee papers and minutes.

6.4 Other types of board

As well as board committees, family businesses often struggle with the distinction between governance and executive management and in many cases the board tends to have a bias towards day-to-day management. There are different types of board remit that might help to address this natural bias.

(a) Strategic board

A strategic board can help a family business create value by focusing on 'the big picture'. This can involve devising strategies for the business that will achieve the family's main aims, whilst critically evaluating business plans and performance in terms of delivering these strategic goals. The strategic board could also be responsible for ensuring that resources are allocated to best effect.

In a group of companies the board of the group or holding company might perform this type of role. Where there is a single company, however, the board may struggle to find the time or may not have the skills and other resources required to create an overall strategy and so would perhaps find it very helpful to have input on strategy at a senior level.

(b)   *Supervisory board*

A supervisory board in a family business comes into its own when there are non-working owners. If the family business is 100% owner-managed, there is no need for a separate board to supervise management. And even where there are non-working owners, a family business might choose to bring non-executives onto the board to supervise the executive directors and reassure non-working owners that their business is being well managed. In some cases, however, the non-executive model does not provide a satisfactory solution.

For example, if the model of ownership is a branch structure and each branch wishes to appoint its own non-executive director, the number of executive directors and non-executives on the board could get out of balance. The answer might be to create a supervisory board, with the requisite balance of family or owner representation. The primary role of the supervisory board would be to oversee and monitor the executive board without interfering in the commercial affairs of the company.

(c)   *Advisory board*

An advisory board can be a valuable source of ongoing independent advice to a family business. It can be selected for any purpose – for example, to create and implement a succession plan. Such a plan could include helping the senior family members pass their experience on to the next generation, who in turn might welcome the help of an advisory board to embed new governance structures and practices.

Each of these types of board is flexible, and, of course, a mixture of different functions can be constituted in the same board. For example, the same board could perform distinct strategic and supervisory roles. The members of these boards need not be directors in the strict legal sense, which means they do not have tenure, and they can avoid becoming ensnared by legal, compliance and regulatory issues (and should therefore not engage in day-to-day decision making or they will be considered shadow directors). Such boards can also be easily disbanded and changed to suit the changing needs of a family business.

In family business governance and management, the range of functions a board needs to perform may require going beyond the standard model of the unitary board and entail creating one or more of these separate forums. Establishing separate governance boards should in fact help the executive board to achieve its primary responsibility to drive forward the commercial success of the family business.

7. Conclusion

As can be seen from the above discussion, there are a number of mechanisms and structures, both legal and non-legal, that can be utilised by a family seeking to implement a governance and management structure to encompass both the wider family and the family business. The more formal a structure and the more clearly it sets out the roles and responsibilities of the various entities that comprise a family unit, the more effective it will be in preserving the family wealth (including the family business) and building on this generation by generation.

Without the legitimate expectation that such a system of governance imposes and without there being a structure in place for disseminating information between family members and the family business and identifying and resolving disputes as and when they arise, there is an increased likelihood that some family members will be dissatisfied. This can lead to a greater risk to the family assets and a shared legacy being squandered and dissipated through expensive litigation and disputes.

Extracting wealth from the family business

Richard R Brass
Schroders Private Banking

1. Introduction

Consider the scenario where the owners of a well run family business wish to extract wealth from their business without losing control of it. In this chapter we discuss the background to this desire to create liquidity and some ways in which this might be achieved for the benefit of all owners.

Extracting wealth in this way can be an emotional and drawn-out process. If, as is often the case, the owners are made up of a group of individuals perhaps spanning many generations, it is likely that they will each have different wealth requirements and varying degrees of involvement with the family business. Having a 'liquidity strategy' in place – an agreed means by which income and capital are distributed to the owners – will remove uncertainty over future income.

Yet the desire to extract wealth cannot be considered in isolation from the fundamental needs of the business itself. A successful liquidity strategy aligns the interests of the business with those of the owners. Several important questions follow from this. What are the owners' wealth objectives (emotional investment versus financial return)? How will a liquidity strategy affect the business's prospects and values? What are the viable sources of finance? Is outsider influence wanted or needed? How do we address the owners' wealth-planning requirements? This chapter therefore discusses the following topics:

- balancing owner objectives with the business's ongoing capital needs;
- internal and external sources of finance;
- working with private equity;
- using public equity markets;
- alternative sources of finance; and
- wealth planning.

When putting any liquidity strategy in context, there are two key considerations to bear in mind:

- *business succession and planning:* the impact of the chosen liquidity strategy on the long-term prospects of the business; and
- *wealth preservation:* the ability of the chosen liquidity strategy to maximise value for the owners.

More specifically, some questions may be posed to assess how a liquidity strategy may be optimised:

- *How* will a liquidity strategy affect the ongoing health of the business and its stakeholders?
- *What* level of outside involvement is acceptable to incumbent owners and business management?
- *Why* is wealth required, and is the chosen method of extraction tax efficient?

Posing these "how, what and why" questions can help a family navigate their journey through the business issues, opportunities and challenges that inevitably arise. It follows that this chapter should be read as a high-level guide, as any decision-making process should take into account the broader economic environment as well as the specific needs of the family business and its owners.

2. Balancing owner objectives with the business's ongoing capital needs

2.1 The need for a liquidity strategy

A family-controlled, closely held business has the ability to make strategic decisions with a long-term perspective and to be answerable to a small community of owners with (hopefully) the same ultimate objectives. This is a distinct competitive advantage.

However, as the business grows, so can the number of owners and at the same time their level of involvement with the business may vary. A sustainable liquidity strategy is designed to meet owners' future income and capital needs. Having one in place can help avoid confusion and disharmony among key shareholders that in turn will ensure that the family business continues to make objective strategic decisions.

A liquidity strategy will also enable owners to assess their wealth and consider the need to diversify their investments. Owners who become more distanced from day-to-day business affairs may feel less comfortable with having all their wealth tied up in the business and may wish to invest in other asset classes. This uncertainty can affect the business; indeed, studies have shown that if a family's wealth is tied up in the business, then the absence of a means to remove it can increase the owners' required return on any future business investment.[1] Of course, appropriate advice and care needs to be taken as the best investment decisions are made once an investor really understands the relative risk-and-return profile. Suffice to say that any wealth diversification strategy needs to be properly considered.

2.2 Measuring and communicating the business's financial requirements

How is a well thought-out strategic vision of the business clearly communicated to and discussed with all the owners in order to agree both the company's long-term objectives and a sustainable wealth-extraction strategy? What if you need to prepare a valuation of the business? Preparing a business or strategy plan is a helpful discipline, whether it is merely jotting down ideas or preparing a detailed analysis in a more formal manner.

---

1   Paper entitled "The Cost of Capital for the Family Controlled Firm" presented by Daniel L McConaughy at the Family Firm Institute's Annual Conference, Thriving in a Competitive World – Leveraging financial, social and human capital in family enterprises, London, October 29 to 31 2008.

The form and content of a business or strategic plan will be determined by factors such as the number of owners to communicate with and the size and nature of any fundraising requirements. Set out below are some of the elements that it could be appropriate to include in such a plan:

- the current status of the business, including:
  - annual sales figures/turnover;
  - key product lines or services;
  - analysis of the competitive environment and marketing/distribution strategy;
  - number of employees;
  - location of facilities; and
  - details of the corporate structure;
- some history of the family business, including the founding date, major successes and any strategically valuable learning experiences, together with an assessment of the strengths and weaknesses of the incumbent management team and the effectiveness of the board members and key owners;
- a strategic assessment of the business's prospects and the risks it faces. What are the key markets and growth opportunities and how does that impact on likely capital expenditure, increased operational costs and potential strategic transactions (such as acquisitions)?
- the financial plan, addressing:
  - current financing status (current owners, existing loans and liabilities including their terms and obligations);
  - funding needs (linked to the strategic assessment outlined above);
  - financial forecasts (see bullet point below); and
  - a valuation; and
- financial forecasts, comprising a balance sheet, income statement and cash-flow statement. In the context of long-term planning for the family business, it is desirable that projections are for a number of years (a minimum of five to seven) and if possible should be capable of being broken into annual and quarterly versions. Graphs of key metrics can be helpful: gross revenue, profit after tax, etc.

A business or strategic plan will enable owners to assess their potential investment return from different funding strategies and hence form the basis (or at least a starting point) for discussions amongst the owners. This may present a major commitment in terms of time and resource, but it should prove a worthwhile investment over time.

3.   Internal sources of finance
This section considers how owners may receive wealth from the existing operations of the family business.

3.1   Salary, bonuses, pensions and employee share schemes
Salary, bonuses, pensions and participation in employee share-ownership schemes

are all often part of a standard employment package. Terms are relatively flexible and can easily be adjusted to satisfy an owner/employee's liquidity requirements now and in the future. However, this option is normally only applicable to owners who are (and remain) actively involved with the business. Furthermore, the management of employment packages becomes less flexible as the business grows. Share schemes are attractive to employers as there is often little cost up front. As a result, corporation tax deductions are often deferred until such time as the shares are awarded to or share options exercised by employees and not when the shares or share options are initially earmarked for allocation or granted to employees.

3.2 Dividends

A dividend is the distribution of after-tax profits to owners, paid pro rata to equity interest in the business. Dividends tend to be paid once or twice a year and can be an excellent means of providing a regular level of liquidity, particularly where some owners are not working for the business. Dividends are also aligned to the fortunes of the business; they are determined by the board of directors and cannot be paid if there are insufficient reserves.[2] Whilst discretionary in nature, a generous dividend programme can constrain the business's cash flow and cause conflict between those owners requiring income and those wanting to see capital reinvested.

3.3 Improving the working capital cycle

Cash may be generated in the business by improving the working capital cycle. The shortening of debtor periods and stockholding periods can be managed internally (eg, through improved customer relationships and a more rigorous stock management system, respectively). Lengthening creditor periods also brings financial efficiencies. The use of external arrangements with parties such as debt factoring agencies may also be considered (eg, selling trade debts at a discount on a recourse or non-recourse basis). Improving the working capital cycle is, however, a one-off form of finance and the cash savings generated still need to be paid out of the business.

3.4 Internal equity trading

An internal marketplace through which owners can buy and sell shares creates liquidity and crystallises valuation. The company sets a market framework and can introduce additional features such as borrowing facilities for owners looking to buy shares and committing to purchase shares from owners looking to sell. These arrangements can be referred to as 'share redemption and/or repurchase plans', 'company loan programmes' and 'share buy-backs'.

An internal marketplace can be a neat solution with multiple owners where some wish to continue to reinvest in the business and others choose to reduce their holding or exit entirely. However, the longer the timeframe over which the internal marketplace is intended to operate, the more complex the process of valuing shares and setting appropriate governance parameters to control the influence of exiting owners.

---

2   Dividends are restricted to be paid out of the company's profits and reserves available for the purpose of paying dividends and in accordance with relevant company law.

3.5   How, what and why?

(a)   *How will a liquidity strategy affect the ongoing health of the business and its stakeholders?*
Internal sources of finance are flexible and relatively simple to arrange, but they shrink available business capital. It can be difficult to distribute capital fairly between owners with varying levels of involvement in the business. Any internal financing needs to consider the impact on a business's capacity to raise external finance and it may be demotivating to staff and trading partners.

(b)   *What level of outside involvement is acceptable to incumbent owners and business management?*
There is no external influence brought to bear on the owners. An independent valuation will assist the finalisation of any internal equity-trading arrangement.

(c)   *Why is wealth required, and is the chosen method of extraction tax efficient?*
Internal sources of finance meet short-term liquidity needs and can defer a capital windfall. Any wealth distribution is likely to be via income (rather than capital), which usually carries the highest tax charge. Employee share schemes and internal equity trading are probably the more tax-efficient routes, so long as their main purpose is not to turn income into capital. In many jurisdictions, comprehensive anti-avoidance legislation counteracts any perceived abuse of such schemes. The terms of these schemes should therefore be considered carefully and, where possible, tailored to fit those of one of the approved schemes available in the affected jurisdictions in order to obtain the most favourable tax treatment for both owner/employee and the business.

4.   External sources of finance

External finance may be sourced in the form of debt or equity, or a hybrid of the two. From a family business and an investor/lender perspective, it is possible to differentiate between these sources of capital by considering cost, and flexibility and governance:

- *cost:* the annual running costs, eventual return on investment, risk of non-payment and security of finance; and
- *flexibility and governance:* the purpose of the finance, financial stability of the company and the involvement of outsiders in the business.

The figures overleaf map how these factors fit with the external capital types. In general, the more flexible the finance, the higher the cost of capital and the greater the likelihood of outside involvement in the day-to-day running of the business.

External capital may be received directly by the owner or channelled via the business. This chapter focuses on how the business may be used to raise finance and this additional liquidity may, subject to terms, be used by owners to remove some wealth. The type and amount of finance that can be raised will be determined by the value of the underlying assets, the stability of the cash flow and the growth prospects of the business. As a general rule, debt tends to be used for specific capital expenditure while equity finance has a more strategic outlook.

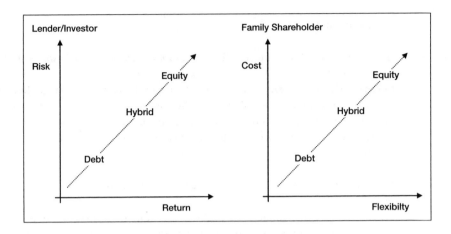

4.1   Equity markets

Equity finance comprises the injection of funds in return for an ownership interest in the business. Funds are raised by placing a current valuation of the business and the issuance of common/ordinary or preferred/preference shares.

Equity finance carries a higher cost of capital as it is unsecured. Perhaps more significantly from a closely controlled business's perspective, it results in third-party involvement in the ongoing strategy and governance of the business. Furthermore any infusion of equity capital from an external source is unlikely to be an isolated transaction. A subsequent liquidity event (eg, sale of the business, as considered in the next chapter) will often be planned at the same time.

The methods of raising equity finance may be divided into two categories: private and public. Taking each in turn:

- Private equity is medium- to long-term finance invested in return for an equity stake. Private equity has its roots in the late eighteenth century and grew into an industry in the late 1970s and early 1980s.[3] It is now a recognised asset class and is mostly provided by venture capital and private equity firms. This investment approach is also used by companies looking to invest in strategic and trading partners.

- Public equity involves selling a percentage of the business into a stock market. A stock market is also known as an equity market. It provides businesses with access to capital and investors with an opportunity to own a share of a business's gains based on its anticipated future performance.

The merits of private and public finance are discussed further in Sections 5 and 6 respectively. Any discussions with potential equity investors will be structured around a robust assessment of the business's financial position and strategic objectives. Preparation for this can be along the lines of the business or strategic plan suggested in Section 2, naturally with a view to it being shared externally.

---

3   British Venture Capital Association (BVCA), "A Guide to Private Equity", BVCA and PricewaterhouseCoopers, 2004.

4.2   Debt financing

Debt finance may take the form of an overdraft facility, a senior secured loan, or subordinated forms of debt. It may be secured against the owner's shares or the assets of the business. The final pricing of any debt will depend on the duration and security of the finance available, as well as the broader economic environment. There will be a fixed repayment schedule requiring interest (generally corporate tax deductible) and capital payments, as well as financial or operational covenants agreed as part of the terms of the debt facility.

Debt can be sourced from banks with a local, retail focus (overdrafts and short- to medium-term loans) to those with an international capital market operation (larger amounts, medium- to long-term in duration). It is an established means of financing business projects that might otherwise absorb funds that could be used as part of a liquidity strategy. More broadly, debt can be used as a general financing tool that can help reduce the business's cost of capital.

4.3   Hybrid facilities

The term 'hybrid' encompasses a range of financial instruments designed to provide a middle ground between debt and equity. These financial products can be differentiated by features such as flexibility on the timing and size of capital repayments. Hybrid capital can carry a second charge after any debt financing. Its higher cost than debt is a result of minority equity participation, usually an equity option or warrant exercisable at the lender or investor's discretion.

Hybrid capital is available from investment banks as well as specialist financial firms and sophisticated private investors. Examples of hybrid debt/equity financial instruments include convertible debt and mezzanine loans with warrants or options. Their detailed structures will be tailored to each situation.

Hybrid capital can provide a convenient solution that delivers the incumbent owners' with more ongoing control than equity and retains a more flexible financing structure than using debt. This type of capital offers more equity participation for existing owners than equity finance and, if the business performs well, makes it easier for those existing owners to buy out the hybrid investor in the future. On the downside, hybrid capital is not much more flexible than debt obligations if the business does not perform to expectations.

An example of where all three capital types have interacted is as follows.

Case study 1: Fragrance and flavours manufacturer
- Purpose – The family wanted to take the company private from the public markets because of the cost of maintaining a listing and in order to secure the long-term future of the business.
- Action – Hybrid capital, debt and the family's own private funds combined to buy the company, with the family reinvesting a significant minority stake in the listed company so as to gain control of the privatised company.
- Result – The family secured long-term control with a supportive investor. The business remained profitable, sold a non-core division to repay a large

portion of the debt and an exit was achieved for the hybrid capital via a sale to the family management at a pre-agreed valuation.

4.4 How, what and why?

(a) *How will a liquidity strategy affect the ongoing health of the business and its stakeholders?*

External financing crystallises a valuation of the business (some perspectives on valuation issues are discussed in the next chapter). It does not draw down the internal capital, and finance not extracted can be used for business growth. The publicity can be used to demonstrate the business's financial strength and prospects. It can also provide a means by which staff can take an equity interest in the business and benefit from future business growth. Debt, of course, increases the company's liabilities so it is critical that such external finance is matched to the business's needs.

(b) *What level of outside involvement is acceptable to incumbent owners and business management?*

External financing brings external investors with relevant industry experience and know how, and professional management skills and experience, with an increasing level of involvement from debt through to equity. It brings a sharper concentration on financial plans and increases administration efficiency and accountability. The broader implications of such outsider involvement are discussed in Sections 5 and 6.

(c) *Why is wealth required, and is the chosen method of extraction tax efficient?*

A focus on strategic objectives, particularly from private equity, can enhance the business's valuation and hence the owners' long-term wealth. Short-term liquidity may also be created by distributing part of the external finance raised. Any wealth distribution that follows from a sale of shares is likely to be taxed as a capital gain. If debt is raised by the business, there will likely need to be another taxable event before the owners can receive wealth.

5. Working with private equity

Private equity is medium-term equity finance in a potentially high-growth private company that is not listed on a stock exchange. It is traditionally deployed alongside debt, where cash flow is used to pay interest/debt finance and a sale of the equity investment delivers a capital return to the investor.

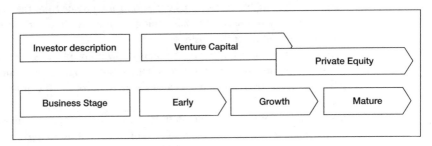

The term 'private equity' is quite generic and in common parlance may include investment firms which fall into the early, growth and mature private equity categories.

The diagram on the previous page endeavours to overlay the appropriate type of investment firm with the stage of a business's development. Each business stage has different financing requirements, as the table below broadly illustrates.

Stage	Funding requirements
Early stage	Research and development Working capital for initial expansion
Growth stage	Growth financing Pre-flotation, pre-IPO capital
Mature stage	Acquisition capital Change of control

Family businesses seeking to extract wealth but retain control should probably focus their time on getting to know private equity firms who specialise in the 'growth' stage. Ideally, capital raised in this growth stage may be seen as a partnership between the family owners and the private equity house, with the following characteristics:

- the business has come to a strategic crossroads, which requires fresh thinking as well as an infusion of capital;
- the private equity firm and family agree specific targets to be achieved for the business; and
- the family remains in control of the business.

5.1   Approach and collaboration

Some heralded contributions that private equity may bring to their investee companies include strategic clarity and focus, more efficient capital structures, additional finance (an 'acquisition currency'), improved and transparent corporate governance, access to overseas markets, clear management practices and appropriate succession planning.

For a family business the infusion of capital may also lead to a solution to other, perhaps less strategic, challenges including:

- existing owners wishing to release equity;
- a fragmented owner base including owners looking to exit;
- professional managers wanting to see new equity being raised to provide them with an opportunity to share in the company's future growth; and
- existing owners and/or non-executive directors wishing to see increased professionalisation.

Case study 2: Printing business
- Purpose – To raise finance to secure large, long-term outsourcing contracts as well as the potential opportunity to acquire its US joint venture partner.
- Action – Growth capital provided for strategic and acquisition finance as well as liquidity for family owners wishing to exit and an equity participation programme for management.
- Result – The business was sold two years later to a trade buyer, having grown its turnover by more than 150% in the space of two years.

Private equity will target an investment return over the medium term. This means that it looks for unrealised strategic value – the ability to grow revenue and profit over a reasonably defined time period. Rules and targets will vary, but perhaps a good rule of thumb is that these investors aim for a return of two times cash invested over three years and three times cash over five years. Another target expressed is an annual internal rate of return (IRR)[4] of 20% through the investment cycle, although this calculation is becoming less used.

At the end of growth capital involvement, it might even be that the family buys back the equity it originally sold.

Case study 3: Food products business
- Purpose – A fourth-generation owner of a food products business sold a 25% equity interest to private equity to secure a strategic investor.
- Action – The business doubled in size, during which time two overseas acquisitions were executed with financing sourced from the investor.
- Result – The private equity house sold its minority stake back to the family four years after its initial investment.

5.2 Governance controls

The terms and conditions upon which private equity is invested will comprise a series of safeguards to ensure the business remains on a pre-agreed strategic path. This is particularly important to the private equity investor in the context of minority interests, where it does not have control over the company. In return, the investor will seek to bring the added value discussed in Section 5.1.

Some minority protections that a private equity investor may seek include are:
- the right to appoint and remove board representatives and/or the chairman, generally in circumstances where the business is significantly underperforming;
- 'good leaver'/'bad leaver' provisions, which dictate whether a member of management who leaves the business is allowed to keep or sell (rather than forfeit) their equity stake and, if so, what proportion and at what value;
- the ability to force a sale of the business (through a 'drag-along' right, which

---

4   The IRR is the annualised effective compounded return rate that can be earned on the invested capital (ie, the yield on the investment). Put another way, the internal rate of return for an investment is the discount rate that makes the net present value of the investment's income stream total to zero.

ensures that if the private equity investor sells its stake, the other owners are forced to join the deal); and

- approval rights over major items of capital expenditure, payment of dividends, entry into litigation proceedings, acceptance of debt finance and other significant corporate actions.

5.3 Finding the right finance provider

Identifying the right party to invest in the business is critical. As such it is important to get as many references as possible on the organisation and the people. Some technical questions to consider as part of the assessment are as follows:

- What stage of development is the business at (as discussed above)?
- How much capital is required? Different private equity firms have different preferences as to their target investment size.
- What industry is the business in? Firms vary as to their industry specialities.
- Where is the relevant geography, now and prospectively?

Most private equity firms set out their investment criteria on their websites.[5] Some firms are independent and others are subsidiaries of banks and large corporates. Think laterally about the type of private equity required. Trading partners and large corporates can be a particularly useful source of private equity, for example providing specific sector knowledge and established routes to market.

5.4 How, what and why?

(a)   *How will a liquidity strategy affect the ongoing health of the business and its stakeholders?*

Private equity provides discreet access to finance and it is aligned to the long-term needs of the business. The investment model recognises companies with hidden strategic value and can also assist with short-term liquidity requirements. It provides a currency that can be deployed for staff motivation and succession as well as acquisitions.

(b)   *What level of outside involvement is acceptable to incumbent owners and business management?*

The governance and targets introduced as part of an investment are designed to influence both the day-to-day running of the business and the long-term strategy. Families should consider whether they see this as a benefit or a hindrance. External influence will have an impact on people loyal to the family owner and sometimes a change of direction can do more harm than good to a business's prospects.

(c)   *Why is wealth required, and is the chosen method of extraction tax efficient?*

Private equity offers a flexible tool for delivering a capital sum to owners, particularly

---

5   A useful list of private equity firms (with some links to the relevant websites) in the form of a directory of members can be found on the website of the BVCA, www.bvca.co.uk.

where there might be a fragmented group of owners with different liquidity needs. As it is a transaction in the private domain, the investment can be structured as tax efficiently as possible to suit the incumbent owners, the investor and the business.

6. Using public equity markets

An initial public offering (IPO) involves selling a percentage of the business into a stock exchange by selling and/or issuing new shares. A publicly listed company has access to long-term capital from a wide range of investors, both on flotation and subsequent fundraisings.

Other advantages to a family business of following the IPO route may include raising the profile of the business, creating a market for equity participation and share trading for employees and family owners, and accessing capital for further strategic transactions (eg, acquisitions).

Potential drawbacks include the time-consuming and costly nature of the IPO process (it can take a year or so to prepare), the ongoing listing compliance obligations and the need to satisfy institutional owner objectives and transparency requirements.

6.1 Suitability

Listing a company exposes the family business to a wider profile and scrutiny by owners and stakeholders. Being well prepared and considering all the requirements of a publicly traded company are fundamental. Second chances are rare and expensive if in the public's eye a business is perceived as poorly managed. Some factors to consider include the following.

- *State of the market and investor sentiment:* in many ways beyond the control of the family owner, any public listing needs to bear in mind the sentiment of public market investors towards businesses on IPO and thereafter. Investor appetite will vary and fluctuate by business sector.
- *Use of proceeds:* stock markets will look for shareholders to limit the amount of IPO proceeds they take for themselves.
- *Size and peer group:* smaller businesses will receive reduced market coverage and investors may require a higher rate of return to compensate for this. The share price of smaller businesses can also be dictated by the performance of larger listed businesses, known as 'guilt by association'.
- *Market type and geography:* different stock markets exist to offer more flexible regulations, which can be particularly attractive to smaller businesses. For example in the United Kingdom, there are the Main Market, AIM and PLUS.[6] Consider where the business's revenue and profit is generated; for example, a UK-based business with most of its revenue in the United States might contemplate a listing in New York.
- *Track record:* does the business have a strong record of delivering profits and growth and is this sustainable? Major strategic issues and changes to the business can be difficult to explain to public market owners, particularly soon after an IPO.

---

6   AIM – Alternative Investment Market, PLUS – PLUS Markets plc.

- *Accountability and communication:* timely and informative investor communication is critical. Are the systems in place to produce relevant corporate information? If family members remain involved, are they prepared to be accountable for their actions to a wide range of investors?
- *Management team and experience:* is management unified and committed to the business for the foreseeable future and do they have the right experience? Is the board of directors suitably independent and capable of meeting public company responsibilities and accountability?
- *Loss of privacy:* are family owners prepared to allow disclosure of the business's assets, trading statements and related items (eg, directors salaries)? Accounts are published regularly (eg, six monthly in the United Kingdom) and require a sharing of information that conflicts with the privacy afforded to private companies.
- *Valuation:* a business is normally priced at a discount to the intrinsic value of the shares, otherwise known as an IPO discount. Family owners can struggle to accept this methodology.

Stock markets are often accused of placing an emphasis on short-term profits and dividend performance. Taken together with the ongoing compliance obligations inherent in participating in a stock market, a public listing can be a burden on family businesses that wish to make decisions for the long term. Therefore, some businesses simply go back to being private.

6.2 How, what and why?

(a) **How will a liquidity strategy affect the ongoing health of the business and its stakeholders?**
Public equity provides an objective market valuation for all shareholders with greater flexibility when returning capital to investors. It also raises the business's public profile and credibility. It provides a tried and tested framework for an acquisition currency and a means for all staff to participate in the business's equity. However, the business's value does become vulnerable to adverse press, short-termism and unwanted distractions.

(b) **What level of outside involvement is acceptable to incumbent owners and business management?**
The business needs to be well prepared and can ill afford not to consider the additional costs of maintaining a public listing and the need for timely shareholder communication; there are few second chances. However, for well-run businesses with a sustainable business model, the public market route can provide liquidity as well as allowing owners to retain the management of the business.

(c) **Why is wealth required, and is the chosen method of extraction tax efficient?**
Owners can stagger their exit over time to optimise tax planning as well as meeting their liquidity needs. Exposure to general public market sentiment will influence the

share price and this can be a drag on realising value. Owners need to be particularly careful not to take a company public that lacks scale; the consequent lack of an active market in the shares can frustrate the goal of extracting wealth.

7. Alternative sources of finance

This chapter has so far discussed some of the more conventional means by which liquidity events may be created for family business owners. In each case an asset is being removed from the business (cash), a liability is being created (debt) or owner control is being diluted (equity). None of these options necessarily achieves the twin primary objectives of building a sustainable family business *and* having an organised liquidity programme. Some alternative (and perhaps more strategic) means of raising finance to support a liquidity strategy are considered below.

7.1 Asset finance

Arguably a form of internal capital, the business may realise significant cash inflows from the liquidation of non-core assets. Assets to consider for disposal include fixed assets (whether by way of an outright sale, or 'sale and leaseback'[7]) and non-core subsidiaries. Alternatively, deferring asset acquisition over time through hire purchase or leasing over a fixed term at fixed interest rates can release funds.

It is common for a family business to comprise a mix of assets and business activities acquired opportunistically or developed organically. This carries strategic value; a range of business interests provides different and complementary growth and profit contributions as business cycles fluctuate. Accordingly, asset sales need to be optimised and not rushed for short-term gain.

> *Case study 4: Luxury boat manufacturer*
> - Purpose – A family owner decided to retain a luxury boat manufacturing business which had been acquired as a small non-core subsidiary of a much larger mining business.
> - Action – Incumbent management were given the opportunity to grow the business, develop the brand and strategy, and establish a strong team to take the business forward with appropriate oversight from the family owner.
> - Result – The business was sold more than 10 years later for a premium value to a trade buyer, with management all receiving equity in the business.

7.2 Joint ventures

Entering into a joint venture (or strategic alliance) involves securing a partner to develop strategic objectives around which the family business can share in future profits and revenues. For example, a business with intellectual property could find a partner to help commercialise a business opportunity. A joint venture arrangement keeps control and influence separate between the two parties; there is simply a legal

---

7   A sale and leaseback arrangement allows a business to raise money from the sale of assets, while retaining use of them, but at the cost of increasing operational gearing. The money raised from selling assets may make the company financially stronger, but is commonly used, at least in part, to return capital to owners.

arrangement that sets out how the parties will collaborate. Successful joint ventures tend to arise where there is a clear mutual benefit achieved by working together.

7.3 Franchising and licensing

It may be possible to access new markets and geographies quickly by expanding operations through franchise and licensing agreements. The business model empowers business managers with local know-how to set up operations relatively quickly. A share of revenue and/or profits provides income back to the family business. Licensing a business product or service tends to be suited to a smaller business as opposed to the management of a franchising operation.

7.4 How, what and why?

(a) *How will a liquidity strategy affect the ongoing health of the business and its stakeholders?*
Such alternative sources of finance provide an opportunity to focus and extend the business's strategy whilst crystallising funds for a liquidity strategy. However, these methods can dilute the inherently defensive qualities of a family business being closely controlled with diversified business interests.

(b) *What level of outside involvement is acceptable to incumbent owners and business management?*
Family control remains in place and the funds generated may be subject to lesser external influence. The time and cost of management of a joint venture, franchise or any other type of strategic alliance should not be underestimated.

(c) *Why is wealth required, and is the chosen method of extraction tax efficient?*
A strategic partner may be an ongoing source of liquidity, bolstering the long-term profitability of the business, reducing the need for other external finance and possibly providing an exit route. Alternative sources of finance bring funds to the business and careful timing will maximise value. The receipt and distribution of funds will require appropriate tax structuring; this might be quite complex and expensive.

8. Wealth planning

A liquidity programme may be rendered fundamentally inefficient if not enough consideration is given to maximising value after tax deductions and identifying how the wealth will be deployed. After all, wealth planning is an evolving process that needs to adjust to changes in legislation, personal circumstances and, in the case of a family business, the business's financial performance.

What exactly constitutes wealth planning? Essentially it combines three elements:

Wealth planning = tax advice + structuring + investments

Detailed analysis that attaches to each aspect of wealth planning is beyond the scope of this chapter, not least because the individual personal circumstances of each family will inevitably have an impact on the results attainable. Domestic, international and personal tax is becoming ever more complex and, whereas many business owners are often well advised with respect to their corporate tax needs, focusing on the personal tax consequences of a liquidity strategy, or indeed a disposal, may require fresh thinking. Often, taking time to deal with structuring considerations can deliver significant financial results. For example, the wide current differential between UK rates of income tax and capital gains tax will have a significant impact on planning for the extraction of wealth from a business with owners resident in the United Kingdom.

Other tax issues to be aware of and consider include those set out below. This list is necessarily generic because the specific legislation will vary from one jurisdiction to another. Thus we have:

- employment tax charges on provision of shares to employees and relieving provisions where family relationships exist;
- funding of share option plans to match corporate tax deductions and personal tax charges;
- use of government-approved option schemes to reward employee-owners where feasible;
- use of government incentives and tax reliefs to raise capital in a way that brings benefits to the investors;
- holding structures outside the business – use of trusts (onshore and offshore) and companies offshore, with the possibility of departing the country of residence and relocating elsewhere prior to any sale; and
- tax issues on 'paper for paper' exchanges on takeover/merger/demerger.

The time necessary for building a plan for investing extracted wealth cannot be underestimated. Early identification and an understanding of the risks and returns of different classes of alternative investment help to benchmark against the merits of a liquidity strategy. For example, if the liquidity strategy creates an annuity income from salaries and dividends, would the owner consider investing wealth in higher risk/return opportunities? If a lump sum is realised, how is the investment exposure spread to meet short- and long-term goals and to preserve wealth in real terms?

Careful selection of professionals to advise on these issues is critical and can take time. Family businesses may wish to explore using advisers who specialise in working with corporate and personal clients. Hiring the right set of advisers who can give constructive and independent advice should benefit the family; saving on fees can be a false economy.

9. Summary

No two family business liquidity strategies will be the same so some general messages to bear in mind are set out below.

(a) How will a liquidity strategy affect the ongoing health of the business and its stakeholders?

Arranging access to and distribution of wealth is a highly emotional affair and must be sensitively managed. An effective liquidity strategy will meet owners' wealth objectives and assist long-term business planning.

Such a strategy needs to match the business's capital requirements with the source of finance (in particular bearing in mind the exit requirement for external finance). It will ensure a family business's inherent competitive advantage is not threatened unnecessarily.

Do not neglect to consult all family members (and key management if appropriate), because being involved in the process will make them feel more comfortable about it and will help to identify any issues promptly.

(b)   *What level of outside involvement is acceptable to incumbent owners and business management?*

Internal finance retains control and offers the greatest flexibility, but it may weaken the business's trading prospects and its capacity to raise finance later on.

External finance brings outsider involvement, particularly for equity investments. Any concern about such outsider involvement needs to be weighed against the professional qualities and experience an investor brings.

The business needs to be well prepared with a clear strategic plan, proper financial records and a realistic assessment of its strengths and weaknesses.

(c)   *Why is wealth required, and is the chosen method of extraction tax efficient?*

Owners need to make a self-assessment of their personal situation and desire to realise wealth. Do they want a lump sum or annuity income, and which will be most tax efficient?

	How?		*What?*
Source of finance	*Extraction size*	*... and frequency*	*Outsider involvement*
Internal (section 3)			
Salaries etc	Small	Regular	Low
Working capital	Small	One-off	Medium
Dividends	Small	Regular	Low
Internal equity trading	Medium	One-off	Low
External (section 4)			
Private equity	Large	One-off	High
Public equity	Large	One-off	High
Debt	Medium	One-off	Medium
Hybrid	Medium	One-off	Medium
Alternative (section 7)			
Asset sales	Medium	One-off	Low
Joint venture	Small	Regular	Medium
Franchise/licensing	Small	Regular	Medium

Wealth planning will maximise value received by the owners and help them to assess the merits of a liquidity strategy.

Establishing an appropriate timeframe to address these questions should allow flexibility to make the optimal decisions for extracting wealth while ensuring the long-term sustainability of the family business. The table on the previous page highlights the key factors discussed throughout this chapter for the "how and what" questions. Tax efficiency is difficult to generalise; it will be sensitive to an individual's personal circumstances, the jurisdictional requirements and any future changes in legislation.

Selling the family business

Peter Gray
Cavendish Corporate Finance LLP

1. Introduction

The sale of a business is a complex and, in many cases, life-changing and highly emotional event. It is also generally a highly complex exercise taking at least six months – several years if one includes the preparation time that is often involved.

The complexity of a sale exercise comes from the large number of elements in a sale process: valuing the business, timing a sale, finding the right buyer, negotiating price and other terms, the due diligence process and then actually concluding the transaction sale.

Achieving a successful outcome requires excellent planning, a lot of hard work, the right advice and, often, a large slice of good fortune. This chapter aims to demystify the sale process and help the owner of a family business who has made the decision to sell achieve the best possible outcome.

2. Reasons for a sale and timing

2.1 Reasons for a sale

There are myriad reasons why the owner of a family business might consider a sale of his company. The most frequent reason given for considering a sale is to realise capital, either for financial security or for new projects.

There is, however, rarely one reason alone, but generally a combination of the following:

- a recognition that the business has reached a premium value;
- the realisation that the business cannot grow without a significant capital injection;
- the need to access new markets by being part of a large, possibly international, group;
- the business has reached a size where the owner feels unable or unwilling to manage it;
- a disagreement among shareholders that means that the business is no longer manageable under existing ownership;
- the only alternatives are closure or receivership;
- an imminent retirement/succession issue; or
- an approach has been received from a credible buyer or buyers of the business.

2.2 External factors

In addition to company-specific factors, there are a number of external factors that may have a bearing on the optimal time to sell. These include:

- a bubble in the sector has resulted in high valuations, or there are concerns that a downturn is likely to arrive in the foreseeable future;
- the acquisition strategies of major players in the sector and/or consolidation patterns that may be emerging;
- changes in technology;
- the state of the economy and, in particular, the stage of the economic cycle;
- recent or impending legislation affecting the business; and
- the strength of M&A market and the stock market.

It is important that a vendor is not coy about the reasons for sale. It will usually be one of the first questions asked by a potential purchaser and a reluctance to answer the question may make the purchaser suspicious.

2.3 Getting the timing right

In common with the sale of any investment, it is extremely difficult to pick the optimal time to sell a business. However, there are some general rules in timing a sale that should be borne in mind.

(a) Trading history

A purchaser will find a three-year profit history much more convincing than a three-year profit forecast. It is important to have a good profit track record to show potential purchasers.

(b) Tax reliefs

The current tax regime is always a relevant consideration in timing a disposal. This can be seen from the surge in company sales precipitated by the withdrawal of capital gains tax taper relief in April 2008.

(c) Critical mass

As a company grows in size, not only will it become more valuable by virtue of its growing profit stream, but it will also be accorded a higher valuation multiple. The phenomenon is demonstrated by the diagram below, which shows that on average the price/earnings ratio paid on company sales increases the bigger the deal size. The relationship can be primarily explained by two factors. First, as companies get bigger,

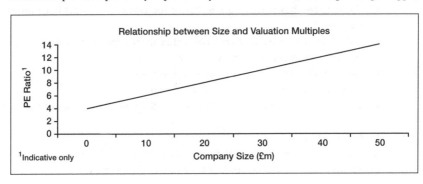

more purchasers come into play. Secondly, in general, the bigger the company the better its risk profile and earnings quality.

As companies grow, they will typically have:

- less dependence on one or two key members of management team;
- a better spread of customers; and
- less vulnerability to attack from competitors.

2.4 Have regard to market conditions

Proprietors must have regard not only to the performance of their business in timing a sale, but also to the state of the mergers and acquisitions (M&A) market in their sector. If there is a valuation bubble in a particular sector, characterised by exceptionally high profit multiples, a proprietor should consider a sale of his company even if he had not otherwise planned on selling at that stage. Valuation bubbles inevitably burst, such that even if the company's profits grow strongly thereafter, the proprietor may not achieve the same valuation for many years.

2.5 Sell when there is no need to

The one overriding rule in timing the sale of a business is always to sell at a time when there is no absolute need to do so. Buyers will quickly sense a forced sale and will use that knowledge to their advantage. History is littered with examples of proprietors who left it too late!

2.6 Timescale

Determining the optimal time to start a sale exercise will be influenced by the following timetable for a sale process, which can be used as a rough guide. The timetable also shows the demands on management time that a typical sale exercise (see Section 3 following) will impose.

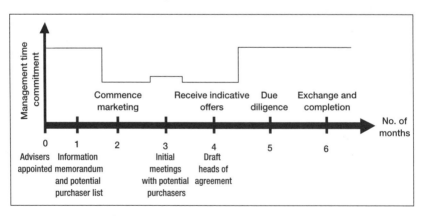

On average, a sale exercise can be expected to take around six to seven months. However, this is only a rough guide. It can take considerably longer but will rarely be significantly shorter, save in the case of a distressed sale or a 'rifle shot' exercise involving only one purchaser.

3.   Preparing a business for sale

3.1   Introduction

It will never be possible to maximise the proceeds of a company sale unless considerable time is taken before the sale commences to prepare the business for sale. A grooming exercise, which can take place over a few months or even years before a sale exercise, aims to enhance the attractiveness and value of the business to potential purchasers. This is achieved by a review covering the areas set out next.

3.2   Financial matters

(a)   *Pricing review*

Whilst a business may historically have priced its products with its long-term future in mind, and, in particular, to deter potential entrants, in a situation where a business enjoys some degree of market power, consideration should be given to enhancing margins by increasing prices in the lead-up to a sale to improve the company's bottom line.

(b)   *Review of costs*

A review should be undertaken to identify and eliminate all proprietorial costs that would not be incurred by an incoming purchaser. These include relatives on the payroll, excessive travel and entertainment costs incurred by the proprietors, and remuneration that exceeds an arm's-length level. Whilst a purchaser might be persuaded that these costs should be added back to determine the company's underlying profit, the argument is always stronger if the business can be run for a period with these costs removed.

(c)   *Assets review*

When a business has assets that might not be required or fully valued by a purchaser, such as surplus property investments, removal before a sale exercise commences should be considered.

Also, in the lead-up to a sale, working capital should be reduced to the minimum level required by the business. Policies concerning stockholding levels, debtors, and creditors should therefore be reviewed at an early stage to ensure that there is no 'fat' in working capital. If the company is sold with excess stocks or, due to poor credit collection, excess levels of debtors, the vendor is in effect gifting the excess working capital to the purchaser. Any such surplus should be eliminated and the resultant cash either stripped out or added to the purchase price.

Any hidden or undervalued assets of the business should also be identified. If the value of property assets is understated in the company's balance sheet relative to their market value, they should be revalued independently prior to a sale.

3.3 Operational matters

(a) **Management review**

The quality of the company's management team will generally be of paramount importance to a purchaser, especially where the owner/manager(s) are proposing to leave the business at the time of, or shortly after, a sale. It is important to be able to convince the purchaser that there is competent second-tier management available to assume executive control of the business following a sale. This will involve devolution of management control by the owners in the lead-up to a sale. Where second-line managers are taking executive decisions, this should be documented.

It might also be advisable for owner/managers to take an extended holiday before the sale to show the purchaser that the business can operate effectively in their absence.

(b) **Accounting policies review**

With a sale exercise in mind, a review should be undertaken of the following accounting policies, with a view to maximising stated earnings and balance-sheet values:

- recognition of profit, particularly for contract-related businesses;
- depreciation policies, both for tangible and intangible assets (they may be overly aggressive, with the resultant suppression in profits and asset values);
- provisions – excessive provisions against stock or debtors is one of the most commonly used techniques to reduce tax. In the lead-up to a sale, excess provisions should be released to boost both profits and asset values, preferably over more than one accounting period;
- valuations of properties and intangible assets; and
- research and development – where all research and development has been written off in the past through the profit and loss account, rather than capitalised, this should be identified and highlighted.

(c) **Accounting systems**

It is essential for the proprietor to start preparing high-quality monthly management accounts and put in place management information systems that track key performance indicators (KPIs) if he does not already do so. During a sale process, it is vital to have up-to-date information on the current trading performance of the company, and the purchaser will be looking for the vendor to warrant a recent set of management accounts.

It is equally important for the company to produce high-quality budgets. At a minimum, a purchaser will be looking for profit projections for both the current and the following financial year. In the case of financial buyers, a three-year financial plan with detailed supporting assumptions will be required. If the company has not had a history of producing detailed budgets (and hopefully beating them), any projections produced specifically for the sale exercise may lack credibility.

3.4 Legal review

A legal audit should be carried out in conjunction with the company's legal advisors and should, at a minimum, ensure the following have been dealt with:

- Trading contracts are examined to ensure that no change-of-control restrictions or provisions apply. Such restrictions (which, for example, allow the other party to terminate the agreement on a sale) are potentially 'poison pills' for a purchaser and to the extent possible should be resisted.
- Intellectual property rights are registered. Where overseas expansion forms a key part of the company's growth story, it significantly adds to credibility if the proprietor of the business has registered intellectual property rights in the territories he has targeted for expansion.
- Shareholder agreements and articles are examined to review provisions relating to a sale.
- Any outstanding litigation is cleared up. Even if it may be covered by insurance, major litigation can be a deterrent to a purchaser.
- To the extent possible, the ownership structure of the company is simplified. This may involve buying in minority or joint-venture interests. Purchasers value simplicity, and complex ownership structures can diminish the attractiveness of a business.
- All leases, title deeds and other key contracts are located and reviewed.

3.5 Positioning

Well before a sale exercise is undertaken, a proprietor should identify the purchasers or categories of purchasers most likely to be interested in acquiring his business and position the business as an attractive acquisition target for those purchasers. A classic example of positioning of this variety was Seattle Coffee Company. The owners of Seattle realised that Starbucks, the US market leader, would wish to enter the UK market in the near future. In order to make the acquisition of Seattle the logical means to achieve this objective, Seattle was established as a carbon copy of Starbucks' operation in the United States in terms of both store locations and the 'look and feel' of the stores. Inevitably, Starbucks purchased Seattle for a premium valuation to kick-start its UK expansion.

3.6 Corporate strategy

Before making any strategic decision, a business proprietor needs to assess whether the decision would enhance or detract from value from a purchaser's perspective. This ranges from the fairly obvious, such as not renewing a 20-year lease on the company's premises just prior to sale (as this might represent a poison pill for a purchaser that wants to consolidate the company's operations with its own), to more subtle positioning-type issues such as whether diversifying the business into related activities will make the company more or less sellable.

3.7 Environmental audit

Potential environmental liabilities will be a major area of concern for any purchaser. Depending on the nature of the business, it may be appropriate for the vendor to conduct an environmental audit prior to the sale so as to enable him to identify and remedy any potential problems at an early stage. Environmental issues coming to light at a late stage in the process have the capacity to derail a sale exercise.

3.8 Data room preparation

A data room is a key element of the preparation for a sale process. A data room should contain all key financial, commercial and legal information on the company, including detailed management accounts, copies of all contracts, particulars of all employees and properties and, where appropriate, a vendor due-diligence report (see below). The data room is typically provided to purchasers in an online format via a secure third-party data room provider.

The objective of the data room is to ensure that final offers are made on the basis of full disclosure and that as and when preferred bidder status is conferred on a particular bidder, the chances of that bidder withdrawing or reducing his offer on the basis of information gleaned during final due diligence is significantly reduced.

3.9 Vendor due diligence

Vendor due diligence involves the proprietor instructing accountants to prepare a due diligence report on the business in advance of a sale exercise being undertaken. The report is then given to potential purchasers that have expressed serious interest in the company for use in finalising their offers for the business.

The main purpose of vendor due diligence is to flush out financial, tax and other issues relating to the business at the outset of the sale process and to ensure that final bids are provided on the basis of all price-sensitive information. As a result, the chances of the deal collapsing or the purchase price being reduced once heads of agreement have been reached or a preferred bidder chosen are significantly reduced.

3.10 Appointing advisors

A specialist M&A advisor should be engaged well in advance of the sale to assist the proprietor in preparing his business for sale and acting as the proprietor's agent during the sale process itself. In selecting an advisor, care needs to be taken to ensure that:

- the advisor has the relevant M&A (and preferably sector) expertise;
- the advisor has no conflicts of interest; and
- the anticipated size of the deal means that the transaction (and anticipated success fee) will make the proprietor an important client for the advisor, as opposed to one who is at the bottom end of the advisor's deal-size spectrum.

3.11 Raising the company's profile

Potential purchasers are typically more favourably disposed to a company they have heard of than one whose name they do not recognise. Also, one of the first things any potential purchaser will do is to conduct a press search on the company. It is often advisable, therefore, to raise the company's profile prior to a sale by conducting a PR campaign, directed not at the company's customer base but at potential buyers of the business. Examples of profile PR of this nature include editorial coverage on the company in trade or financial publications. There are specialist PR firms who focus on pre-sale PR of this nature.

3.12 Conclusion

The more prepared the business is prior to the commencement of the sale process, the greater will be the ultimate valuation achieved. However, it is important not to groom a business for sale in an over-zealous fashion, or attempt to boost profits in artificial ways that will be exposed during due diligence. It is also necessary to commence the grooming process long before the sale process gets under way, principally because the impact of the steps taken to enhance profits will take some time to flow through to the company's accounts.

4. Valuation

4.1 Introduction

The actual valuation of a business will ultimately be dictated by the price that a willing buyer is prepared to pay for the company. Even though valuing a company in advance of a sale is not an exact science, the following are some of the key factors that determine a company's value:

- the company's historic and projected financial performance;
- the attractiveness of the sector in which the company operates and the strength of its market position;
- the size of the company;
- the strength of its management team; and
- the company's asset base.

4.2 Methods of valuation

Although there are a number of methods used for valuing a company, the following two methodologies are the most frequently utilised by acquirers:

- multiple of normalised earnings (typically favoured by trade buyers);
- discounted cash flows (used by private equity houses).

(a) Multiple of normalised earnings

This valuation methodology applies an appropriate multiple to the normalised earnings of a company to capitalise those earnings into a value for the company. Normalised earnings are a company's reported profits adjusted for any abnormal or non-recurrent items.

Once the normalised earnings of the company have been determined, the appropriate multiple to apply to these earnings is determined by reference to:

- the earnings multiples on which comparable quoted companies are trading on the stock market; and
- the earnings multiples on which other private companies in the company's sector have recently been sold.

On average, UK private companies are sold a discount to quoted public companies, though the level of this discount has reduced in recent years. Any discount applied to comparable quoted company multiples should be adjusted by reference to factors such as the growth profile, market share and size of the company.

(b)   *Discounted cash flow (DCF) valuations*
The discounted cash flow methodology values a business by discounting the projected future free cash flows of the company, in order to arrive at a net present value (NPV) of those cash flows. Free cash flow is residual cash after deducting all operating expenses and tax, but prior to deducting debt and equity financing payments.

4.3   Conclusion
In the end, company valuation in advance of a sale is a theoretical exercise. One will only get a good feel for the valuation that is likely to be achieved when conversations are initiated with purchasers and the level of interest in the business is determined. Ultimately, prices at which companies are sold, in common with all other prices, are largely determined by the laws of supply and demand.

5.   Identifying potential purchasers

5.1   Identifying the optimal purchaser
The optimal purchaser for a business will be one that can best meet the proprietor's price and other objectives and will deliver on the offer made for the business.
    The *ideal* potential purchaser is one that will:
- pay a premium price;
- add value to the business;
- be acceptable to management;
- not require shareholder or other approvals;
- not involve a Competition Commission referral or other regulatory issues;
- not have to raise funds to finance the acquisition; and
- have a good understanding of the business and not require extensive commercial due diligence.

    In selecting potential trade or financial buyers, regard must be had to any published acquisition criteria, their acquisition track record (if any) and their ability to finance a deal of the size in question.

5.2   Types of potential purchasers

(a)   *Introduction*
There are several broad categories into which most potential purchasers fall. These include direct competitors, overseas buyers, financial purchasers, companies in related industries and wealthy individuals.

Set out below are the main categories of potential purchasers, together with a brief description of each.

(b) Direct competitors

For reasons of confidentiality, a vendor may not wish to approach direct competitors at all. Even where information is supplied to competitors on a confidential basis, there is always a danger that competitors will attempt to use knowledge of the impending sale of the company to their advantage by disclosing that fact to the company's customers, suppliers or employees. Accordingly, even if a vendor is prepared to approach direct competitors, he may only wish to do so when he has an offer on the table from another buyer and a sale seems virtually certain to proceed. This approach is usually feasible as a direct competitor will be able to determine very quickly whether it wishes to acquire the company and, if so, the price it would be prepared to pay.

(c) Companies in related sectors

Most companies focus on their core business, with the result that diversification strategies such as those practised by Hanson and Williams Industries in the 1980s and 1990s are a thing of the past. However, companies still make acquisitions in industries related to their core business. Moreover, such acquirers will often be prepared to pay a premium price for the business as an acquisition may be the only feasible means of entering the relevant market.

(d) Financial buyers (management buy-outs)

The potential for a management buy-out of a business backed by a private equity house should always be considered. For a management buy-out to be feasible, the management remaining with the business following the sale must be sufficiently strong to assume the executive control of the business. In a situation where the management of the business has been largely confined to the vendors, this may not be the case. In such a situation, it may be that a management buy-in would be appropriate. In this situation the private equity house (or vendor's advisor) introduces a management buy-in team to take over the running of the company following the sale. The management buy-in team will take an equity stake in the business alongside the private equity house that is financing the bid.

(e) Overseas purchasers

As shown in the schematic world map on the next page, overseas acquirers account for a substantial proportion of acquisitions of UK companies, particularly larger deals. In the case of smaller companies, the due diligence and post-acquisition management costs can be prohibitive where the overseas purchaser does not have an existing presence in the United Kingdom. Overseas trade buyers will frequently outbid their UK equivalent, reflecting a preparedness to pay a strategic premium for entering the UK (or European) market.

Nationality of Acquirers (by value) 2008

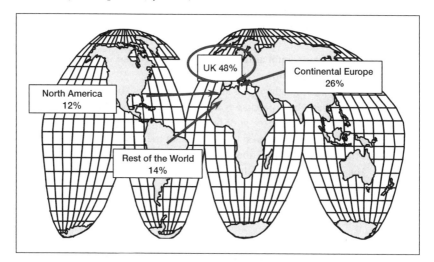

(f)   Wealthy individuals

Wealthy individuals or consortia of individuals should never be discounted as a source of potential buyers, even for larger deals. This is especially the case with prestigious 'trophy asset' businesses. Two cases in point are the purchase of Aston Martin by a consortium including a number of wealthy individuals for £479 million in 2007 and the sale of Princess Yachts for £200 million to Bernard Arnault, France's wealthiest man, in 2008.

6.   The sale process

6.1   Introduction

Choosing the right sale process is essential if a vendor is intent on maximising value. Getting the process wrong can have dire consequences from a valuation perspective and may well condemn the sale process to failure. There is no 'one size fits all' sale process. The two most commonly used processes are formal and informal auctions, but even within these two categories there are significant variations.

6.2   Formal versus informal auction

With a formal auction, potential bidders are given a timetable requiring them to give the vendor an indicative valuation by a certain date on the basis of information contained in an information memorandum. Following receipt of indicative offers, several potential purchasers are shortlisted and given the opportunity to meet management, conduct site visits and access a data room that includes a vendor due- diligence report. Following this process, they will be required to make a final binding offer for the company.

This route is only feasible where it is expected that there will be a strong level of demand for the business, allowing the vendor to dictate the sale timetable to potential purchasers. The likely level of interest in a company will, in turn, typically depend on a number of factors, including:

- the size of the company (the bigger it is the more interest it will attract); and
- the attractiveness of the sector in which it operates.

If there is any doubt as to the likely level of interest in the business, it is best to avoid a formal auction.

In the case of smaller or less attractive businesses, the vendor is compelled to run at the speed at which purchasers are prepared to respond and therefore cannot set strict deadlines for the receipt of bids. Competition between purchasers can still be generated if sufficient interest is obtained, but the resultant auction is less formalised than the process described above.

The general procedure followed in formal and informal auctions is shown in the two diagrams following.

The sale process – formal auction

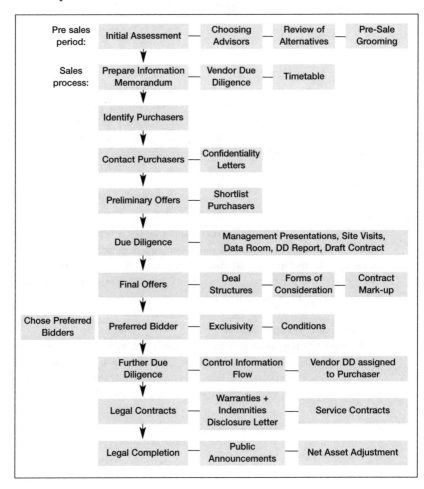

The sale process – informal auction

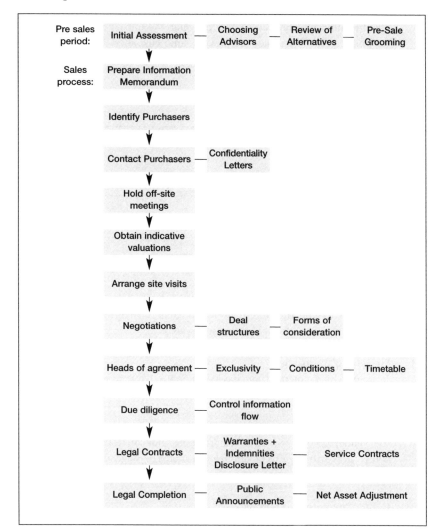

6.3 Public versus confidential auction

Before a sale process is initiated, a decision needs to be made as to whether the process will be conducted as a public auction (ie, announced to the world at large), or an attempt will be made to keep the process confidential. In making this decision, the vendor must have regard to two key factors:

- Would publicity have a damaging effect on the business? and
- What need and scope is there for the business to attract 'left field' buyers as a result of some carefully targeted publicity?

The answer to the first question is sector dependent. If it is known that a retailer is up for sale, it will have limited impact on customers, staff and suppliers. In contrast, in the case of a professional services or other business services firm, where client relationships tend to be very personal, the impact may be considerable. The possibility exists that key employees and customers will be lured away by competitors, due to the uncertainty created regarding the future ownership of the company.

Risk of publicity is sector dependent

Sector	Employees	Customers	Suppliers/Strategic partners
Retail	Fairly low	Very low	Low
Business to business services	Very high	Very high	Can be high

In terms of attracting 'left field' buyers, publicity can be particularly useful where the business in question is a 'trophy asset', that is a business such as a football club, a luxury yacht or car manufacturer, or another luxury brand name that confers status on the owner and therefore may be attractive to high-net-worth individuals who may be difficult to identify from desk research.

6.4   Staggering approaches

In approaching potential purchasers, the objective is to ensure that even where a formal auction is not being deployed, all offers for the company are received at broadly the same time.

To achieve this objective, overseas companies and potential purchasers outside the vendor's sector who will require more time to reach a decision than direct competitors will need to be approached first. The staggering of approaches can be employed, to some extent, even in the context of a formal auction.

6.5   Contacting potential purchasers

Each type of potential purchaser has its own characteristics, which will determine the preferred method of approach; but some general rules apply.

Sending out anonymous descriptions of the business to potential purchasers is not the preferred method of approaching buyers. Rather than sending out fliers and waiting for a response, it is preferable for the adviser to extol the merits of the company to the purchaser either face to face or more typically, initially, by telephone.

7.   The negotiation process

7.1   Introduction

Once potential purchasers have been contacted, the negotiation process has effectively started. Different purchasers will respond differently to different approaches and, accordingly, the approach taken must be determined on a case-by-case basis. There are, nevertheless, some general rules that should be followed in negotiations with any potential buyers of the business.

7.2 Understanding the purchaser's objectives

It is important for the vendor to understand the potential purchaser's viewpoint and to ascertain what the purchaser is seeking to achieve from the acquisition. For example, occasionally a purchaser will be interested in the business for emotive rather than strategic or financial reasons. One frequently encountered objective is status. If the target has an extremely prestigious brand name or a royal warrant, a purchaser may be more interested in the kudos attaching to the ownership of the business than its profitability. If that is the case, it may be possible to extract a higher price than the financial performance of the business would appear to merit. Similarly, if the potential purchaser is considering the acquisition of the business for strategic reasons, for example to obtain entry into the European market, it may be prepared to pay considerably more than a conventional multiple of earnings.

7.3 Reviewing offers

No two offers will ever be the same. Potential purchasers will make offers in a variety of forms, including cash, shares and loan notes or a combination thereof. It is essential, in evaluating offers, to determine the true value of each element of the consideration being offered and, in the case of consideration other than cash or bank guaranteed loan notes, to make adequate allowance for risk. Qualitatively, an offer that requires the vendor to take a significant proportion of the consideration of shares or in unsecured loan stock or preference shares is inferior to an all-cash offer, although it may be possible in certain circumstances to hedge the downside share price risk.

7.4 Bridging the price expectations gap – earn-outs

Differences in price expectations can be bridged by a number of techniques. The most commonly deployed of these is an earn-out, whereby further consideration is paid as and when future profits are earned. Vendors can often achieve a higher price via this route as they are assuming part of the risk of the future performance of the business. In effect, they are 'putting their money where their mouth is' by agreeing to link the final price to the financial projections provided to the purchaser. Earn-outs also help a purchaser pay a higher price by allowing the payment of part of the price from the future cash flows of the business.

7.5 Heads of agreement

(a) Introduction

Once all offers for the business have been tabled, the next step is to negotiate the terms of those offers. Assuming, at the end of this process, one or more of the offers is acceptable, it is then necessary to choose the offer that best meets the objectives of the vendor.

It is customary for the essential terms of that offer to be enshrined in heads of agreement. Although, save for provisions relating to exclusivity, costs and confidentiality, the heads of agreement is not a legally binding document, it should cover all of the important points of the deal. It is unwise to defer important issues for subsequent discussion for several reasons. First, the heads of agreement stage is usually a honeymoon period where good relations exist between the vendor and the purchaser. The relationship will often deteriorate once the due diligence process starts and the legal negotiations commence.

Secondly, the vendor's negotiating position is at its strongest at this stage as hopefully he will have a number of competing offers on the table to which he can revert if he cannot get the concessions he is seeking from the preferred bidder.

(b) Key issues

(i) Exclusivity

A purchaser will almost invariably insist on a period of exclusivity to enable him to conduct due diligence and prepare and negotiate the necessary legal documentation. Engaging accountants and lawyers is an expensive exercise and purchasers will rarely be prepared to do so unless they have an assurance that they will not be gazumped by a competing bidder. The length of exclusivity period is always a matter for negotiation but is generally in the region of six to eight weeks. It is in the interests of the vendor to complete a transaction in the shortest possible timeframe, not only because a transaction is disruptive to the business but also because the longer the transaction ensues, the greater the possibility that the sale will be derailed by either an external factor (eg, stock market crash, war) or internal factor (decline in profits).

(ii) Net assets/surplus cash

The typical basis of a sale is that there will be a minimum level of net assets in the company at completion. Alternatively, a company may be sold on a 'cash free/debt free basis' such that all cash in the company surplus to the working capital requirements of the business can be either stripped out prior to a sale or added to the purchase price.

(iii) Retentions/escrow arrangement

A purchaser will often ask for a substantial retention or hold-back of part of the purchase price, from which any post-completion pricing adjustment or a warranty claim can be settled. A retention is designed to provide the purchaser with security of payment of monies due from the vendor and will typically be placed in a separate escrow account, often for the duration of the warranty period.

(c) Other issues

Other key issues to be addressed in the heads of agreement include:
- terms of ongoing employment/consultancy agreements for the vendors;
- the extent of warranties to be given, the length of the warranty period and identity of warrantors; and

- the length and extent of restrictive covenants that the vendors will be required to give preventing them from competing with the business post completion.

7.6   Rules for successful negotiation

In negotiations with purchasers, the following rules should be followed:

- All information provided should be accurate and not misleading.
- It may be advisable not to reveal all of the company's attractions initially, but to hold something back in order to counteract any attempt by the purchaser to renegotiate the terms of the transaction.
- Use advisers to your best advantage. Let them pursue the hard points, possibly without the principals. The situation can always be retrieved by the principals if a compromise is necessary.
- Always consider the discussions from the other party's point of view; negotiations are never one-sided.
- Be prepared to withdraw if your objectives are not being met.

8.   The purchaser's due diligence process

8.1   Introduction

Due diligence is, in essence, an investigation by the purchaser of the business and the market in which it operates designed to ensure that the assumptions underlying the purchaser's offer are correct. Vendors often fear the due diligence process, but provided the vendor has not withheld any crucial information concerning the business, it should not give rise to any unpleasant surprises.

8.2   Types of due diligence

There are several types of due diligence. These can be categorised as set out next.

(a)   Financial due diligence

Financial due diligence involves a detailed examination of the financial affairs of the company with particular focus on the historic, current and projected performance of the business. Financial due diligence will generally take the form of a lengthy accountants' report. One of the critical roles of the reporting accountants will be to test the assumptions underlying the profit projections of the business because it is the future profit stream of the company that forms the essence of what the purchaser is buying.

(b)   Market/commercial due diligence

If the purchaser is not already familiar with the market in which the vendor is operating, it may undertake some market due diligence either in-house or by commissioning external consultants. Commercial due diligence of this nature is not only concerned with the future of, and underlying trends in, the market in which the company operates, but will also assess the company's position within its market and how competitive influences are likely to impact on its future performance.

(c)   ***Customer due diligence***

Where appropriate, a purchaser will wish to speak to the company's major customers to assess their level of satisfaction with the company and the prospects for their continued patronage. The vendor should insist that this be left to the very end of the process, when the deal is virtually certain to proceed.

(d)   ***Management due diligence***

Financial buyers will generally wish to carry out due diligence on the senior management team as well as meeting them on an individual and collective basis. This due diligence generally involves taking up personal references from former employers and business associates, checking for any previous bankruptcies or criminal records and, in some cases, psychometric testing.

(e)   ***Legal due diligence***

Legal due diligence focuses on key contracts and other legal documentation of the company. The company's exposure to litigation or other contingent liabilities and ownership of assets, including its properties and intellectual property rights, will also be reviewed.

9.   Conclusion

Each business is unique, and each vendor has his own unique characteristics and objectives, but certain key rules nearly always apply in achieving a successful sale:

- determine the objectives of the sale exercise and ensure that they are agreed and understood by all of the company's shareholders;
- start preparing for a sale exercise well in advance of a sale;
- set realistic targets, both for timing and price, and regularly review the position;
- think laterally in identifying potential acquirers; and
- be prepared to walk away from the deal if your objectives are not being met.

Selling a business is a complex, time-consuming and in many cases emotional experience for a vendor. Moreover, a sale process may involve considerable risk as a result of an unwanted leak. It should therefore never be embarked on without very serious intent on the part of the proprietor. Even so, a sale of a company still represents the most common way of realising value for a business and if the guidelines outlined in this chapter are followed, the vendor will maximise his chances of achieving a successful outcome.

Conflict management and dispute resolution

Ian Marsh
*family*dr

Family conflict is one of the biggest challenges facing those seeking to build a multi-generational family business. Conflict risk is more manageable than many other types of risk, yet it is still relatively unusual for families to take steps to manage it, or to seek professional help in doing so – until, of course, things 'go critical' and they reach for their litigators.

As we shall see, conflict is an inherent part of the human condition. It is neither good nor bad. What matters is how people deal with it. Handled well, it can lead to invention and innovation, and to both personal and corporate growth. Handled badly, it can all too easily lead to entrenchment, polarisation, demonisation, even addiction, and ultimately to the destruction of family, fortune and business.

This chapter looks at how families deal with conflict, and suggests what they might do to manage their conflicts well – to keep their conflict circle virtuous.

1. What do we mean by 'conflict'?

There are many definitions of 'conflict' in the literature, but one that I find particularly useful in the business family context is that first given by Wilmot and Hocker in 1978:[1]

> *Conflict is an expressed struggle between at least two interdependent parties who perceive incompatible goals, scarce resources, and interference from others in achieving their goals.*

In other words, I am in conflict with you if I believe that you and I have incompatible goals, and that your actions will interfere with me achieving mine, and I cannot just accept that.

It is not difficult to predict the likely battlegrounds for business families, for example:

- siblings competing for their parents' favours, for entry to the boardroom and, in time, for ownership or control of the company;
- children pressing their parents to hand over the reins sooner rather than later, while parents, particularly founder parents, are reluctant let go;
- those running the business expecting their relatives to stay invested whatever the return, while those investors may feel their 'executive' relations are

---

1   WH Wilmot and JL Hocker, *Interpersonal Conflict*, 1st edition (1978) – but see now 7th edition (2007) – McGraw Hill.

somewhat overpaying themselves;

- children pushing for (sometimes being coerced into) management roles for which they are totally ill-suited;
- professional managers being hired to run the business, but judged on their ability to finesse family politics; or
- not to mention value questions such as "Are we a business family or a family business?", "What is the family – do we include the in-laws?", "Is this a multi-generational business, or are we serial entrepreneurs?", and so on.

2.   It is never 'just about the money'

But there is more to it even than that. All conflict has its irrational/emotional component but in families, as in many tribal/international disputes, the emotion behind the conflict often has little to do with the events actually complained about. So, for example:

- shareholder sibling rivalries often turn out to have their roots in early childhood – "You always got a bigger slice of cake than I did" – however old the siblings are when things finally explode;
- pushy children may be driven by off-hand comments their parents never gave a second thought to – "One day, my boy, all this will be yours" – or even by an unspoken family tradition of primogeniture;
- the sister who alleges her brother takes an excessive salary from the business may be angry that, as she sees it, her sacrifices as primary carer for their parents go totally unrecognised; or
- arguments between step-relations very often turn out to be about the (now adult) children's unresolved issues from their parents' divorce.

Sometimes, of course, these conflicts pass down the generations, 'the cause' becoming everything and the roots of the original falling out lost in family mythology.

I have worked with families where, despite pages of detailed legal argument, there turned out to be no hard, substantive, issues between them at all; and once the soft, emotional, issues were dealt with, all the other complaints fell away. I have never, however, seen a case where there were no soft issues at all.

3.   An anatomy of conflict

Of course, every case is very different but, before we look at what might be done, it is useful to have even a stereotypical view of how conflict can develop.

You think someone stands between you and your goal. If you can just accept that, and let go, the tension passes. If not, and it starts to affect what you say (or do not say) or what you do (or do not do), you are in conflict with your perceived competitor, even if he or she remains blissfully unaware of it. And so it begins.

An obvious first step would be to check whether your concern is justified. All trainee mediators are told 'the orange story': two ladies (sometimes, companies) argue over a crate of oranges (a whole crop for companies); they are invited to share it 50:50, but each insists they need all the oranges; in fact one is interested only in producing orange juice, and the other only in the flesh and rind for marmalade – the classic win-win solution, if only the parties can get there.[2]

In fact, you probably just assume you know both what is really eating you, and where the other person is coming from. You feel threatened, so they must have intended to threaten you. You go in 'all guns blazing' and, perhaps not surprisingly, they go on the defensive. From their perspective, they did not intend to threaten you; therefore you should not/cannot feel threatened.[3] You both go into broken record mode, neither listening to the other, and emotions keep on rising – a problem in any conflict, but all the more so in the family scenario where emotions always run high and even the briefest phrase, pause or gesture, can carry decades, if not generations, of baggage. For all you may both have started out intending to solve a problem, you have only succeeded in making a bad situation worse.

You may both just try to get on with your lives, rubbing along as best you can, but any trust between you has now pretty much evaporated, barriers have gone up, and your ability to communicate effectively – the key to solving the problem – is at an all-time low.

You look for support from those around you, each building alliances where you can. When you tell your story, your natural tendency is to exaggerate both your innocence and your hurt, and with it the guilt, as you see it, of the other person. Those closest to you 'stand by their man', agreeing that you have been terribly treated, and that seems somehow to confirm the rightness of your story. So, when you retell it to the next person, you tend to exaggerate still further. Of course, it is no different for them. And so it goes on, as you each become more and more convinced of the rightness of your cause, and increasingly entrenched in your positions. Meanwhile, those around you are feeling forced into one camp or the other, or risking alienating both sides by their neutrality: "You're either with us, or against us", as someone once said.

Then something happens to change the dynamic: the death or divorce of a senior family member, perhaps, or a takeover bid for the company, although the mere threat, or rumour, of such a change – "Did you know Dad has changed his will?" – may have just the same effect. Suddenly, both in a state of grief for what was, all the pent-up emotion explodes and you go to war.

Sadly, that just seems to prolong, if not suspend, the grieving process, almost guaranteeing that no one is in a fit state to make the decisions they must to resolve the issues between them. At this stage, as Kenneth Cloke puts it:[4]

Many people fantasise secretly about revenge. Few carry it out. Most hire lawyers instead.

It is, perhaps, the obvious next step. Where else do people go for help with a problem like this? But going to law is an escalation of enormous proportions and likely to be seen as such by all parties, particularly in those families that have

---

2   R Fisher and W Ury, *Getting to Yes: negotiating an agreement without giving in*, 2nd edition (1991), Business Books Ltd.

3   D Stone, B Patton and S Heen, *Difficult Conversations: how to discuss what matters most*, 1st edition (1999), Penguin Books.

4   K Cloke, *Mediating Dangerously: the frontiers of conflict resolution*, 1st edition (2001), Jossey Bass.

traditionally settled their differences in private.

This is the point at which direct communication between the principal actors typically comes to and end. Family gatherings for important social and cultural events may be suspended, and younger generations are often discouraged – if not forbidden – from seeing each other. Where the principals are both active in the management of the business, the effect on morale throughout the business can be catastrophic and, usually, something will have to give.

Drastic though that is, the involvement of lawyers can have an equally fundamental impact on the conflict. Not surprisingly, they tend to reframe it in terms that they understand and can deal with. What was "a problem with my [expletive deleted] cousin" becomes "a claim under Section 23(2)(b) of the 2006 Act", or whatever it might be.

The whole conversation becomes focused on legal rights and obligations. The lawyer's client becomes 'the claimant', an innocent victim, and her cousin, forever now 'the defendant' or 'the other side', a wrongdoer, perhaps even a perpetrator. Classic demonisation of the enemy, which reinforces still further the claimant's sense that this was all her cousin's fault, implies that it is he who must put things right.

Instructing lawyers also introduces new dynamics – those between the lawyers and their clients, and those between the lawyers themselves – into the equation. The lawyers too have interests: earning fees, managing risk, and so on, all of which inevitably impact the way they manage their cases. Any advice on the merits – the likelihood of success in court – inevitably depends on the information available on which to base it; the most information will be available after disclosure/discovery and there is a tendency therefore for negotiations to be deferred until that point in the process. Unfortunately, in the meantime, the principals become increasingly polarised and entrenched as they each hone and rehearse statements supporting their positions in law, and the prospects of a resolution that addresses the original issues between them recedes still further.

The lawyer can also become another constituent of the client, another gallery to whom the client feels obliged to play. I mediated one case where the single biggest stumbling block to settlement was one party's desperate desire not to disappoint their lawyer by accepting too low an offer.

Sadly, I have also mediated cases where the major obstacle was that one party, typically the youngest child in the family (and usually by many years) had never felt so important before in his life. He said "jump" and his many lawyers – and to a degree even his older siblings – said "how high?" He saw any settlement as ending this state of affairs, which he had no intention of doing.

By this point, what brings people to the table is the uncertainty of trial (one recently retired English High Court judge has put the chances of winning an "absolute no lose case" at no more than 70%), the fact that the costs are likely now out of all proportion to the amounts allegedly in dispute, and the risk (in England and Wales at least) of being ordered to pay the other parties' costs if they refuse. Mediation can be very successful in these circumstances, but it does then tend to focus on settling the legal claim rather than addressing the underlying issues, which often remain unspoken, like a volcano lying dormant … until the next eruption.

4. Contain if necessary; resolve if possible; best of all prevent[5]

The challenge then, if I may paraphrase William Ury, is to find ways of preventing outbreaks of destructive conflict, and of containing, and hopefully resolving, those that do break out.

If most disputes flow from miscommunication, unmet expectation, disappointment and frustration,[6] the answer surely lies in engagement, dialogue and collaboration – and in a willingness to be first curious (ie, to accept that you may not have all the answers) and then confused (when you begin to learn what answers others might have).[7]

If you do think someone stands between you and your goals, a good starting point is to check what your goals really are. Do you really want to sell your shares in the family company, or do you just want your income to be independent of your cousins who control the board? And why is that independence important to you? Perhaps you have some other project you are desperate to pursue that might add value to the family business if it was encouraged in the right way?

Is it actually about the income? Or is it about your relationship with your cousins? Is it about your self-image, the fact that you have the name but are not involved with the business? Or, do you just need what you see as a fair process through which all these things can be discussed? Quite possibly, a combination of all four.

And what of your cousins' goals? Try and put yourself in their shoes. How do they see things? They may not feel comfortable with what they see as a threat to their authority in the business. They may be fearful of having to lay staff off if you force through a sale of your shares, and they are unable to refinance. Or they may just feel you are taking advantage of difficult times to bully them into doing what you want, regardless of the consequences for others. In fact, they will probably each see things differently from one another, and are quite likely never to have discussed things between them in this way.

With all this in mind, now is the time to have the conversation with your cousins, not with a view to persuading them you are right but with a view to understanding how they really do see things. Not because their views take precedence over yours, but because you want them to do something they are not doing now, and you are unlikely to be able to change their minds without first knowing what is in them.[8] You may also find that if you approach the conversation as an active and effective listener, your cousins' approach is likely to change considerably. We all need to feel heard and are much more amenable to the concerns of others once we are.

All of this is, of course, much easier said than done, particularly where emotions are already running high. Over the longer term, these are skills that can be learned,

---

5   W Ury, *The Third Side: why we fight and how we can stop*, 2nd edition (2000), Penguin Books.
6   E Carroll and K Mackie, *International Mediation – the art of business diplomacy*, 1st edition (2000), Kluwer Law International.
7   R Ready and K Burton, *Neuro-linguistic Programming for Dummies*, 1st edition (2004), John Wiley & Sons Ltd.
8   R Fisher, E Kopelman and AK Schneider, *Beyond Machiavelli: tools for coping with conflict*, 1st edition (1994), Harvard University Press.

like any other. In the shorter term, why not consider engaging a skilled, neutral, third party to mediate the conversation? After all, if you had a tax problem, you would soon phone your accountant, and you were very close to calling your lawyer anyway, so why not speak with a professional facilitator?

5.   Good governance and effective conflict management

Experience shows that those who agree when things are going well how they will deal with any differences that may arise between them in future stand a much better chance of keeping their conflict circle virtuous. Good governance is crucial to effective conflict management; equally, good conflict management is a fundamental part of effective governance.

There are many sound models for governance available. These range from the use of family elders, non-executive directors, non-family trustees and protectors, and so on, through to family councils and family charters/constitutions.[9] All of these models can be extremely effective but, to give them – and, in particular, their conflict management provisions – the best possible chance of success, they do need to be tailored to the needs of the family business concerned; all other things being equal, the bespoke solution will always outperform 'one size fits all'.

Designing such a system requires a great deal of information about the family business system:[10]

- Who is involved, what are their various roles in both the family and the business? And what are the relationships, and the dynamics, between them?[11]
- What do they tend to fall out about? What are their various 'hot buttons'?
- Why do they think this happens?
- When does it tend to happen, and how often?
- What processes (formal or informal) exist for dealing with these situations?
- Are there any family myths about past conflicts and how they played out? Are there any family traditions about dealing with conflict?
- How do those involved prefer to deal with conflict? Who tends to walk away? Who just sulks? Who just cannot keep quiet? Who sees everything as a competition? Who wants everyone to pull together? And who are the bridge builders?
- How happy are they each with the way things tend to work out. If they are not, what would they need to be different to make them happy?
- And what does all this cost, not just in terms of money but in terms of wear and tear on individuals and their relationships, on morale in family and business, and in missed opportunities?

Of course, it is often the case that the head of the family thinks there have rarely been any conflicts in the family worth the name, or that there was a huge fight a

---

9   See the earlier chapter in this publication on "Governance and management".
10   WL Ury, JB Brett and SB Goldberg, *Getting Disputes Resolved: designing systems to cut the costs of conflict*, 1st paperback edition (1993), PON Books.
11   It may be useful to plot this information on a genogram. See M McGoldrick, R Gerson and S Petry, *Genograms: assessment and intervention*, 3rd edition (2008), WW Norton & Co Inc.

long time ago but that they have all learned their lesson since and any differences now are resolved on an entirely consensual basis. Heads may nod in an open family meeting but in private, with a trusted neutral, where people feel free to speak the unspeakable, other views often emerge.

If it is to work, whatever system emerges really must be seen by everyone to serve them all. Otherwise, the danger is that people sign up but do not actually buy into the deal. They may be afraid of some sort of reprisal if they do not fall in line. They may interpret their parents' unhappiness with dissent as meaning they are "a bad son". Or they may just be unable to overcome a traditional/cultural belief in putting (the appearance of) family unity first. Either way, they have no faith in any 'new deal', so they never invoke its terms. The dominant individuals take that as assent, and carry on as before – until something happens to trigger the explosion. In many ways, this is the worst of problems, because everyone has convinced themselves they have fixed the problem, so the explosion, when it comes, is all the worse.

It is absolutely crucial, therefore, that both the process of developing the conflict management system, and the system itself, exhibit fair process behaviours,[12] that is to say they:

- give all stakeholders the opportunity to speak – to tell their story – and be heard, and create the perception that each can make a difference to the outcome;
- offer timely and accurate information to all concerned about family and business issues;
- apply rules in the same way to all concerned;
- require all concerned to be willing to make adjustments to their arrangements based on new information or changing situations; and
- require all concerned to practise fair process in all their dealings with each other.

The possible outcomes of this process are as varied as the families who start down the road, and will tend to range in complexity with the stage the business has reached. Is it an owner-managed company, still run by its founder, or has it evolved into a sibling partnership, or a cousin consortium?[13] Is it a single family business or a multi-family business? Have divorces intervened to complicate matters with first family/second family dynamics? And so on.

In smaller or simpler situations, it may be that all differences of opinion can be aired at a family meeting, albeit one that might be facilitated by a neutral third party. At the other end of the scale, perceived grievances may have to be taken to a particular person in the first instance, perhaps with capital/resource, power/control, employment and culture/value issues being referred to different individuals. Those individuals may be able to undertake informal mediation between those in conflict, or they may have power to bring in a neutral third party to do so. If that fails to

---

12   MFR Kets de Vries and RS Carlock with E Florent-Treacy, *Family Business on the Couch: a psychological perspective*, 1st edition (2007), John Wiley & Sons Inc.

13   P Leach, *Family Business: the essentials*, 1st edition (2007), Profile Books Ltd.

resolve matters, there may be a referral to the company's board, or to a family council, or even to a full family meeting, again typically facilitated by an outsider. Should even that fail, there may be a formal set-piece mediation as a last best hope for peace before parties are free to take an adversarial stance and delegate the decision over their futures to judge or arbitrator.

There is also the issue of what sanctions should apply to those who fail to follow the rules. Many will say that the courts will not entertain a claim until the earlier processes have been exhausted and, for them, that is enough; but I have also seen it suggested that those in default should cease to benefit from family trusts that are the direct owners of the business and the custodians of the family wealth.

Finally, one might hope that there would be a moratorium on commencing proceedings while the agreed processes are followed through, as well perhaps as a moratorium on lobbying/alliance building within the family business and, for those with a higher public profile, press briefings, leaks etc. Some families, however, particularly those with a tradition of communicating through the media, may feel that goes too far. The role of the process designer is to help the stakeholders to identify options, but it must always be the stakeholders' choice as to which option (if any) they adopt.

Having said all that, a good conflict management system should provide more than mere process. Ideally, having identified the stakeholders' hot buttons and their preferred approaches to conflict, such a system should be able to provide early warning of issues that are likely to 'go critical', so that they can be dealt with before they get out of hand – and perhaps even by a different process than less sensitive issues.

Perhaps even more importantly, however, the system should provide the resources and motivation needed to ensure all concerned will use the process.[14] If some feel they do not have the skills to use the process well – and are unlikely therefore to use it – they should be given the necessary training. If they need support in using it, they should be provided with coaching. If the process calls for facilitators or mediators, or is sufficiently complex to require ongoing administration, everyone must be comfortable that all that is needed will be provided on a timely basis. There is also, of course, the question of how all this will be paid for. Can funds be set aside just for the purpose? If so, who will administer them? Who can call on them? When? And how? Perhaps needless to say, if funding is dependent only on some of the stakeholders, and they are likely to be key players in any dispute, there is a fair chance that others will see that funding becoming conditional on some particular outcome, and that will affect how they view the whole process.

6. Dealing with existing conflicts

Almost by definition, most family conflicts will not take place within the confines of such processes. Yet there is still much that can be done to prevent, and hopefully to reverse, entrenchment and escalation.

The key is to be very goal oriented. Focus on fixing the problem, rather than on

---

14   *Getting Disputes Resolved*, see note 10 above.

settling a legal claim; and, as we have already discussed, that means being very sure what it is you are trying to achieve, and why; how much of that you can achieve without any input from those you are in conflict with; and what exactly it is you need them to do for you to achieve your goal.

Be very clear also what your best, and worst, alternatives are to a negotiated agreement.[15] Your worst may be to walk away, and to accept what is. Or it may actually be to litigate and lose: spending a fortune on lawyers, and then having to pick up the other side's bill too; spending months, possibly years, committed to a process that never has certainty; enduring the wear and tear and the missed opportunities; and, very possibly, all the while watching the family business fail because those who should be running it are too intent on fighting one another. Your best alternative may be to litigate and win. The costs situation will be very different – at least it will if you can actually get yours back from the other side – but otherwise the experience may be very much the same. If litigation is both your best and worst option, consider very carefully the respective chances of each coming to pass.[16]

Before you engage, try and put yourself in the other person's shoes. How do they see things, not just in terms of the substantive issues but also in terms of the communications between you? You know what you meant to say but, when you try to adopt the other person's perspective, what do think the message they received was? What was its impact on them? Why do you think they have not responded positively to any offers you have made? Would those offers go any way towards meeting their objectives as you now understand them? If not, why would you expect them to say "yes"? Would saying "yes" cause them to lose power, or standing, with some important constituency? Perhaps they think that something better might come along, and they can always change their mind later; that saying "no" keeps their options open? Perhaps they do not realise that this is a fading opportunity?[17]

Think also about who else has a stake in the outcome of this conflict, whether directly or indirectly. That is very often a much larger group than would be party to any legal proceedings, yet all may play a useful – perhaps critical – role in bringing about a durable resolution. What are the principal actors' constituencies, the galleries they play to, the people whose opinions matter to them? 'Face' plays an enormous role in business family conflicts and particularly in those that have become intractable, perhaps even the stuff of family legend, and it needs to be dealt with.

And consider other 'centres of influence' – people with no stake in the outcome but who, through their relationships with a particular person, or perhaps through their standing in a particular community, might influence a key player, not necessarily in relation to the substance of the dispute but at least to come to the table.

Take responsibility for fixing the problem. Most people need to feel heard before they can hear what anyone else is saying to them. If you are going to make progress, someone has to break that impasse and there are considerable benefits from being the person who does. For one thing, you are likely to learn where the other person

---

15   *Getting to Yes*, note 2 above.
16   See, for example, D Chalk, *Risk Assessment in Litigation: conditional fee arrangements, insurance and funding*, 1st edition (2001), Tottel Publishing.
17   *Beyond Machiavelli*, see note 8.

is really coming from, what is most important to them, and what they need in order to be able to draw a line under the conflict and move on. For another, you may well draw them into a state where they not only want to understand where you are coming from but are much more minded to work with you to solve your shared problem. And to those who say to me, "We've done all we can. The ball's in their court now," I say, "Why are you giving them the choice of whether you solve the problem or go to war? Don't you want a say in that?" That is not to say that they should bid against themselves, but rather that they should redouble their efforts to understand why what has been proposed does not work for the others involved.

None of which is to say that this is an easy, or a speedy, option. If you take this route, it will take time and persistence. You will likely hear things that you do not want to hear, and just as likely hear them expressed in ways that you find offensive. So too may everyone else involved, but it is generally only through this that the most fundamental issues between you will get on the table, and if they do not get on the table they will never get resolved.

Given the strength of feeling that is likely to be involved on all sides, particularly where a conflict has become intractable, this is a process that generally requires skilled facilitation; it needs to be mediated. The mediator can provide an environment in which all parties feel comfortable telling their stories – speaking the unspeakable, if you will. If necessary, the mediator can work with them confidentially, in private, coaching them how best to do that, to make sure that all that needs to be said *is* said. He can also bridge the communication gap between the parties, making sure the message sent by one really is the message received by the other. When the time is right, he can bring the focus from past to present and, hopefully, get the parties working together on where they go next. And when the principals' energy and commitment flags, he can keep things moving forward.

7. **When you have to park the tanks on the lawn**
Of course, it would be naïve to suggest that all business family conflicts can be resolved without litigation; sometimes it may be necessary to 'park the tanks on the lawn'. It is beyond the scope of this chapter to discuss the strategy and tactics of such litigation, let alone the procedures involved. It is, however, worthwhile trying to put litigation into a broader conflict-resolution, problem-solving context.

As I have already noted, the outbreak of litigation generally marks the end of direct communication between the parties, at least about the issues in dispute between them. Typically, there will be no negotiations between the lawyers until each side has set out its case in some detail, and often not until after disclosure/discovery and any interrogatories have been completed.

Understandable as that might be, I do find it rather strange. If one looks at international conflict, for example, talks virtually never stop. Whatever preparations are being made for war, the diplomats stay hard at work to avert it. When diplomatic relations are broken off, talks generally continue through the good offices of other countries, or through agencies such as the United Nations. Even when things are at their darkest, the rhetoric at its highest, and some "will never sit down with the men of violence", somewhere behind closed doors and far from the cameras, someone will be working to try and get the parties to engage and, once engaged, to build a dialogue.

The stakes will be less in the typical business family conflict (although it may not seem that way to those involved), but why take such a different approach? In my experience, whilst it is as yet by no means commonplace, involving a mediator at as early a stage as possible and on an ongoing basis, rather than just for the stereotypical 'one day, last best hope for peace' set-piece mediation in the run up to trial, has a great deal to recommend it.

That set-piece model comes from the world of commercial litigation and is used for business family disputes partly because they are litigated under the same procedural rules and partly because the majority of the available mediators are commercial mediators. It is a highly successful model, yet I believe it can be improved upon in relation to family conflicts generally and business family conflicts in particular.

These conflicts are almost always multi-party, often with shifting alliances between the parties. Numbers of those parties may be elderly, and many will not be business people. Some will find even a one-hour meeting in a strange setting stressful. To bring them to a setting famed for running into the small hours of tomorrow does not, in my view, create the best chance of a durable resolution. The 'pressure cooker effect' has its uses, but sometimes the pressure can be too much.

Because of the level of emotion, the effects of family myths and legends, and so on, many family members really do need to be able to tell their own story, in their own words, and in their own time, before they are going to be ready to draw a line under the past and move on. Mediation is the only form of dispute resolution that really allows that, but it does take time even when they are prepared to do so in the presence of other parties. Very often it is something that has to be done first in private session and only later, perhaps after some coaching, can the parties come together and share their stories in a productive way. All this takes time and, with multiple parties, there may simply not be time in one day to do what is necessary. Either the storytelling is curtailed, or the parties spend most of the day in their own rooms wondering what on earth is happening. Either can be extremely counterproductive.

It is far better in many cases for the mediation to be an ongoing process, with the mediator free to meet with each of the parties at a time, and in a place, where they feel comfortable. He can flush out the parties' interests and their underlying wants and needs, and he can identify the soft issues that may be preventing them from resolving things between them. He can also identify the hard issues that can only be resolved by negotiation or by litigation, so that the lawyers can then focus on those issues. The mediator can also come in and out of the process as needed, to break the log-jams along the way, perhaps over the provision of documents or information, or fresh outbreaks of high emotion following some uncomfortable disclosure, or an impasse in negotiations.

At the end of the day, if there is still need of a last-best-chance-for-peace meeting, he can mediate that in the usual way, but with the focus now almost entirely on the negotiation phase and on the mediator testing the reality of the parties' positions (what I like to call 'speaking truth to power'), so that they can each make a fully informed decision as to whether the best deal they can negotiate is good enough, or whether they prefer the costs and risks of a trial.

And just a few final words for those who would choose the latter:

- It is highly unlikely, in my experience, that sitting through a trial will bring any party to a realisation that the other was right; more likely that the loser will come to see that the judge too was wrong;

- The objective truth (if indeed such a thing can ever be known to mere mortals) will not emerge: the judge will simply determine what, on the balance of probabilities, and on the basis of the evidence presented to him on the day, he thinks most likely happened; and

- The judge's order is unlikely meet any party's needs, unless those needs are no more than to have their rights as set down in law – which in my experience is rarely the case.

Managing succession, managing wealth

Joan Major
Alex Scott
Sand Aire Ltd

1. Introduction

Successful family businesses have the potential to generate wealth for all stakeholders. As the business matures or passes from family hands to subsequent owners, wealth management becomes a more pressing issue than was the case during the wealth-creation phase of the business family's evolution. Over time, it is possible that the liquid or external wealth owned by the business family will become as substantial as the illiquid wealth represented by shares in the family enterprise. This chapter is concerned with the considerations a family will face with the former category.

Since most successful enterprises take several years (if not decades) to reach a cash-generative stage in their evolution, decisions regarding wealth management tend to be taken toward the end of the entrepreneurial phase of a founder's life, or perhaps will be taken by subsequent generations who have either harvested or built upon the founder's business achievements. The decisions faced by families who continue to own an operating business and those who have sold it are markedly different.

For a business-owning family, the efficient management of the wealth lying outside the family business is simply a matter of expediency: when investments and chattels are of a significant breadth and scale, coordination of their oversight, control and management is a sensible development of the family's activities. This activity may be carried out within the existing family business (usually overseen by a trusted financial lieutenant) or, in a subsequent iteration, a dedicated family office.

For a family whose members have sold their operating business, the choice is inevitably starker: should they remain connected through the coordinated management of their liquid wealth or should they pursue separate destinies? It is clear that there is no objectively appropriate solution: each family member will pursue the path that they believe is right for them. The route they choose is likely to be influenced by the events that led to the sale of the business, the scale of the assets they have realised and the degree of commitment and loyalty they have to the family as a unit.

Research has shown[1] that there are potentially three frequently trodden paths to the sale of a business. It is possible to infer from the path the family has followed (willingly or not) whether the result will be a coherent and coordinated response to wealth management or an independent, individualistic one. Businesses tend to be sold because:

- they have been expropriated by non-family directors;

---

1   2005 Sand Aire/INSEAD Dr Sabine Klein.

- they are part of a planned entrepreneurial project carried out by the business founder; or
- the family has made a strategic decision to exit.

In the first case, the business is likely to have been run by non-family members, because the owning family is no longer willing or able to provide coherent ownership and governance. The resulting vacuum tends both to encourage and enable non-family management or directors to pursue a strategy that might lead to a sale. The impact of this process on a family can be devastating, both to their inter-family and personal relationships and to their willingness to continue to operate in any way in conjunction with their family. Dr Sabine Klein again:[2]

What became clear from the three cases of expropriation in this study is that only a family group that is able to communicate is able to stop the tendencies of non-family managers or board members to get control over the Company."

In contrast, the family that has pursued a strategic sale is much more likely to have followed this route because the family members hold a shared vision about their future and how they should interact for the collective good, whilst the entrepreneurially led family is likely to remain together because of the binding power of the wealth creator who is very much still in control of the family's financial destiny.

A collaborative approach to wealth management is therefore most likely to be undertaken by a family whose wealth is either held within, or is generated by, a continuing business and those who have realised the value of their family business through either strategic or entrepreneurial intent. Subsequent sections of this chapter deal with the mechanics of the process they are likely to follow so as to ensure they do this most effectively.

The character and behaviours of the families who decide to act together in management of their wealth will in many ways be unique to their own circumstances and background, but they may also exhibit certain shared characteristics. Having expressly or unconsciously made the decision to remain connected through a shared approach to the management of their wealth, it is likely that they share a strong degree of loyalty to each other and to their family's legacy. From an initial base of agreeing to act cohesively, they will over time develop a family wealth strategy that will give shape and meaning to the route that they pursue.

Underlying this conscious approach to wealth management may be:

- a sense of *mission* regarding what they are trying to achieve (such as safeguarding their inheritance, acting as responsible (wealthy) citizens and providing a solid financial base from which this and subsequent generations can develop meaningful and successful lives);
- an approach to *governance* that recognises that as a family grows in size and complexity, it will need increasingly sophisticated decision-making structures to ensure efficiency and involvement and to demonstrate fairness in process – family members may be involved either at the heart of matters or more distantly depending on their experience and capabilities, but it is important

---

2   *Id.*

that they remain involved and recognise their responsibility for doing so;

- an awareness that *power and control* will need to be managed and delegated consciously and carefully; and
- above all, an appreciation that whilst extraordinary efforts were required to build a great and successful business in the first place, that effort will need to be sustained, refreshed and renewed if the family is to continue to be successful into the future.

2.   The family office

It is thought that the term 'family office' was first used as a descriptor in the United States early in the nineteenth century when wealthy traders and merchants had a trusted adviser to oversee their home-based assets and wealth whilst they were away. Some family offices in Europe have their origins in merchant banks set up by the merchants of the time, whilst family offices in the United Kingdom often developed out-of-estate offices (and in fact still exist in that guise) where, once again, a trusted adviser or employee expanded on their role and became responsible for a family's entire asset base.

Whether or not the formal title of 'family office' is used, the means whereby a family coordinates its financial affairs can be conveniently described by this name. Whereas each family's approach to the management of their wealth will be dictated by their own needs and circumstances, it is likely that consistent characteristics will be observed. A family office, once in place, can provide a customised, dedicated and cost-effective service to the family.

Families that are in business together are successful if they hold a shared vision and aim to grow their business whilst staying together as a cohesive group. They know that the succession of a business or family legacy must be planned and managed. The same applies to the establishment of a family office.

The need or wish for a family office is usually driven either by a requirement for coordination of the liquid portion of wealth or by a significant increase in family liquidity and the desire to retain some degree of control of the management of the proceeds of that occurrence.

Thoughtful decision making during the initial development and planning of the family office is essential. As with a family business, the distinction between ownership and management must be thought through and defined.

The needs of the wealth creator and the family are at the heart of the focus of a family office and will determine its design. Family dynamics will shape the family office structure. A family office can respond to the needs of the family, ensure the issues of stewardship and the challenges it poses are addressed and, where operating companies continue to exist, form either an essential link or barrier between the family and the business. A family office is a way for a family to maintain control over the manner in which they preserve and grow their wealth whilst at the same time being a focal point of contact for the family and their numerous advisers.

In many cases, a family may already be benefiting from some of the services it would seek from a family office, with these being provided from an office within an existing operating business. The move to formalise and separate the service provision into a family office marks an enhanced focus on these services and a recognition that they are appropriately provided separately. This may be as a result of a change within the governance of the business, the way in which the business is managed, or a branch of the family having sold their holding in a way that gives rise to the understanding that it is no longer viable or appropriate for family members to continue to be served privately by employees of a business.

3.   Family office choices

When confronted with a liquidity event or a need to separate a service provision, a family will face a number of choices. First and foremost, the wealth creator and family must come to a decision as to the degree of control they wish to retain with regard to the management of their liquid and other assets and whether they wish to establish a team to manage their requirements and at what level to engage or own a professional wealth-management and/or administration operation.

The establishment of a family office is not necessarily the most appropriate route for all families and there are a number of approaches that can be considered – each with differing levels of service, control, confidentiality and responsibility.

This chapter focuses on the establishment of a 'single family office' (an office serving one family – see Section 4 following), but other alternatives are explored briefly below. Each has its own advantages and disadvantages. In each case, appropriate legal and tax advice should be sought from the close advisers that will, in many cases, have been working with the wealth creator or family members for a number of years. These professionals will be able to provide a useful and constructive insight into the ways in which the family operates and how the different structures would deliver family requirements. In many cases these advisors will continue to have an important role and will be able to provide valuable ongoing advice.

The available forms of family office

3.1   'Do it yourself' (DIY)

If the wealth creator (or other family member) wishes to retain absolute control of the investment of the liquid funds and has some level of investment experience, they may want to take on the role of investment manager and have responsibility for all of the investment decisions, potentially assisted and advised by consultants, with the input of an investment committee made up of investment professionals known to the family. For the family member involved, this will be a time-consuming and challenging role, although for the right individual it will be stimulating and will continue to give a focus and purpose following the sale of a business.

However, the complexity of today's investment markets mean that expertise is not necessarily readily available within a family, particularly if the original family business was not one involved in financial services. Outside consultants may have to be engaged to look at asset allocation, manager selection and monitoring, risk management and generation of income. Reporting to family members will be complex and time consuming. A further consideration will be that, if family assets are held within a trust structure, trustees may find it difficult to delegate responsibilities to the DIY model unless appropriate professionalism can be demonstrated.

In this DIY scenario, the family member becomes the investment family office and the establishment of another structure will not be necessary or warranted. This type of setup will not necessarily be configured to provide the family with any administrative or accounting services.

Example of a DIY structure

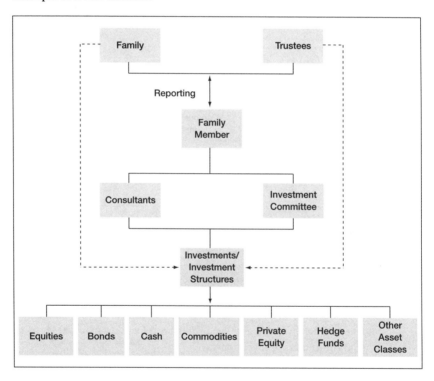

3.2   Single or multiple banks/asset managers

This approach encompasses the delegation of investment management either to one or a number of different firms to manage separate portfolios. The wealth creator/family member can have a level of involvement of their choosing, but the approach requires someone to fulfil a role of coordination, reporting and oversight. In the case of multiple managers, it is unlikely that any one of the providers will provide consolidated reporting or oversight of the whole; therefore, reporting services will either have to be sourced or developed. An existing advisor (such as an accountant) may be in a position to fulfil this role. As with the DIY route, the outsourcing of the investment to multiple managers does not allow for the provision of other services unless these too can be provided by the reporting advisor.

As with the DIY model, consultants (and an investment committee) can be involved to oversee strategy and asset allocation policy. Families may see this model as one that allows a level of diversification. However, care must be taken to ensure that this is the case and that the different portfolios do not have too high a degree of overlap.

Example of a structure using single/multiple banks

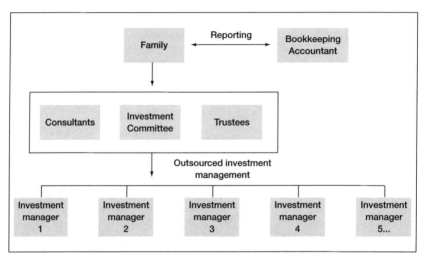

3.3   Multi-family office

For those who do not wish to engage in the expense and ongoing administration involved in creating their own family office, an alternative can be found in a multi-family office. Most multi-family offices are developed with the principle of diversifying investment management to multiple providers and as a result the majority are independently owned and operated. Multi-family offices come in a number of different guises and most will have a focus on investment management, either as consultants or practitioners.

A multi-family office will serve a number of clients and this model gives families, who either do not have the necessary level of wealth to warrant the creation of a single family office or do not wish to build a family office, the opportunity to delegate the creation of a personalised asset allocation and investment strategy designed to meet the family's needs and deliver other services as available. Unlike the two previous examples, multi-family offices will often have access to administrative and management skills that are attractive to individuals and family members and as part of their business model provide these (alongside the investment management services) to the families for whom they work.

Many of the advantages of a single family office are evident in a multi-family office. The key difference is that service will be provided by a team working for a number of families. However, most multi-family offices endeavour to provide highly customised services, tailored to each individual client's needs. The compensating factor is that the skills available to client families are correspondingly broader and deeper and the cost is spread over a larger asset base.

As illustrated in the diagram below, the structure and relationship of a single or multiple family office to a family is very much the same – the differences will lie in the range of services provided and the fact that a multiple family office will serve a number of families.

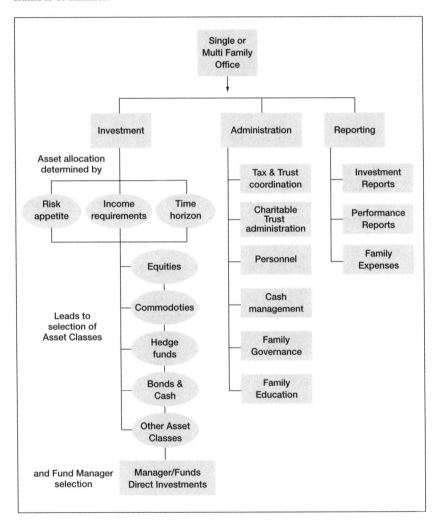

4.   Setting up a single family office

We will now look at the key considerations for the establishment and ongoing management of a single family office that provides both investment and other family services and the transition from a family business to a family office. Although the following focuses on both investment and administrative functions, many family offices may only require partial provision of the functions. For instance, there are cases where a family office is set up to provide only the administrative and reporting services required by the family, with the investment function being outsourced along the lines of one of the above examples.

An important factor will be the level of costs incurred in relation to the results and service achieved. As has been established from 2008 data:[3]

A recent study by Merrill Lynch/Campden Research has shown that a single family office can cost anything between 3 and 120 basis points of assets under management with an average of just over 62 basis points. The research also found that single family offices with an internal management function need to have at least €250m to €300m in assets under management to justify the cost. Single family offices that outsource the investment management function can be supported by a lower base of assets under management (circa €50m to €100m).

Family Office Exchange[4] has also carried out research into the cost of family offices and it similarly calculates that for assets of between €251 million and €1 billion, the cost of a family office is around 48 to 57 basis points. It can therefore be concluded that at the very least the sum of €50 million of liquid assets is required (for the simplest of offices) and that although the costs of such an operation will be dependent upon the service required, they may amount to several million euros.

Analysis of viability and desirability is not only related to level of wealth but also to family interest, family expertise (the sector in which the family fortune was made or in which family members have gained experience) and the degree of drive or energy the family have to support the new enterprise.

The advantages and disadvantages of owning and operating a single family office are numerous and not all will be of concern to every family. The advantages are that the office will be bespoke and highly flexible, independent and private. On the downside there will be challenges of recruiting, motivating, managing and retaining staff, the risk and potential of becoming over-reliant on one or two members of staff, and a continuing need for family cohesion and oversight if the office is to be able to fulfil its mission and function effectively.

Once a family has weighed up all the options and made the decision to form a family office, the following issues will need to be addressed. Decisions should be made in conjunction with family advisors, who will often be able to add much value to the process having had experience of the family dynamics and expectations over a number of years. The issues are:

- assets for management;

---

3   "Preserving family values. The changing role of the family office", Merrill Lynch/Campden Research European Single Family Office Survey 2008.

4   See www.foxexchange.com.

- business plan;
- service requirements (either in-house or outsourced);
- structure;
- implementation and staffing; and
- reporting.

4.1 Assets for management

The primary objectives for the establishment of a family office will be a key decider for the manner in which the office is staffed and constructed. The determination of the key responsibilities will have a significant bearing on the success of the resulting operation and thereby the success of the family in the context of its wealth.

Examples of the assets that can be managed by the family office in addition to the core liquid family balance sheet are:

- Operating companies – if there is a continuing operating business, will some management of this entity be included in the remit of the family office?
- Land – does the family own estates or other land that will need oversight?
- Property – are there numerous personal properties in the country of residence and/or overseas? If so, will there be a need for active management, rental management, repairs and personnel management?
- Personally held financial investments – do family members have individual investment portfolios that they would wish the family office to oversee and advise on?
- Private equity, special situations, direct investing – what is the family's approach to ad hoc investments and direct investing: do individual family members have an area of special interest or a need for personal investment?
- Cultural assets – (art, cars, wine and so on) – will staff be required to manage special collections, what level of expertise is needed, and how will each asset be managed?
- Sporting interests, bloodstock – will specialist knowledge be necessary?
- Aircraft, yachts – will there be charter requirements, staffing, repairs, insurance?

4.2 Business plan

Once the assets under the management of the family office have been defined, the business plan can be drawn taking into account costs, structure and ownership. Before its creation, and in addition to putting in place the resources for the oversight and management of the assets mentioned above, the following will need careful thought:

- creation of a holding structure for the office;
- implementation of a governance plan for the office – consideration of the need for a board and its appropriate composition;
- creation and definition of a mission for the office. It may be useful to draft a mission statement for the office to detail its role and the family's goals. For example, will the mission be to develop, evaluate, implement and monitor objectives of the family and if so what are those objectives?
- overall plan and objectives for the wealth (eg, investment objectives, philanthropic strategies, individual spending requirements, risk parameters);

- confirmation that all family members are in agreement with a collective approach to the management of their wealth/business;
- determination of whether it is possible and desirable to have a collective investment policy (this is of particular importance with regard to income requirements of different family members);
- agreement on the sharing of costs. It is very important that there is agreement on how the family office is to be funded and how each family member will be charged for the service they receive. Where there are multiple generations and family branches, it is important that the cost-sharing arrangements are clearly defined;
- agreement regarding the role of family members within the office structure. Will there be requirements for family members to have gained relevant expertise before being employed within the office. Will a family member chair the office?
- determination of office location – location is likely to be agreed upon according to the responsibilities allocated. The office may need to be accessible for some or all family members, located close to family or business assets, or positioned wherever the local workforce has the appropriate skills;
- agreement on technology requirements – this will depend on and be driven by the sophistication of the operation and the requirements of the family for reporting and other IT support;
- establishment of remuneration strategy for employees. As well as assessing the going rate for the skills required, the family will need to consider whether it is appropriate to create an incentive plan for senior personnel to reward results and behaviours that are in line with the family's objectives; and
- creation of a personnel policy.

When each of these issues and any others that are personal and pertinent to the family have been addressed, a clear idea of the appropriate personnel and physical infrastructure that is desirable can be established. Once the financial implications have been calculated, a business plan and budget can be developed to encapsulate the services the office will offer, its governance and its likely costs.

4.3 Services

With a business plan approved and in place, the family and its advisors will enter the initial development and planning stage. At this juncture, that there will need to be a focus on the investment and administrative functions the office will be asked to carry out, since requirements for these services are likely to have been the drivers of the decision to form an office in the first place.

(a) *Investment*

One of the key decisions in this context will be that of whether the central investment function is to be in-house or outsourced and, if so, to what degree. The list below outlines the key responsibilities with regard to investment:

- asset allocation;
- manager and stock selection;

- manager monitoring (due diligence and compliance);
- portfolio management;
- dealing;
- trade settlements;
- performance analysis;
- quantitative and qualitative performance assessment;
- risk analysis and management;
- fund creation and management;
- management and initiation of ad hoc investment initiatives; and
- reporting (covered in more detail later in this chapter).

(b)   *Administration*

Careful thought should be given concerning the degree to which the family wishes to be reliant on the family office for administrative functions. There is a trade-off here between the provision of effective support to allow family members to live their lives successfully without multiple distractions and the risk of creating overdependence on these same services. In practice, families will have varying approaches to this issue and some will implement support services that others might see as risking the establishment of a dependency culture within the family, particularly in the case of generations who are following the original wealth creators. Some may feel a degree of self-sufficiency is appropriate and necessary to ensure family members remain connected with everyday life and take responsibility for some aspects of their existence. Others will prefer to avoid what they consider to be unnecessary distractions.

Areas of responsibility that are often delegated to a family office are detailed below and the following points should be taken into account:

- Family forums – will the office be responsible for implementing and arranging family meetings?
- Education – is the office expected to have an active role in the education of family members (and in particular the younger generations) with regard to investment, governance, family protocols?
- Philanthropy – are there family charitable foundations and will the office take an active part in family philanthropic initiatives? Will the office need to handle applications, the administration of grants and follow up on charities supported?
- Family governance – will the family office be expected to put in place family governance plans, liaise with family councils, produce family newsletters or act as a conduit for other family governance issues?
- Tax, trust and structures – will the office take responsibility for all tax and trust work? Will this be a coordinating or advisory role?
- Legal – will the office need legal representation – will it be expected to give legal advice, work on legal documents or act as a conduit for other legal initiatives?

In addition to the above, examples of administrative functions often undertaken by family offices are:

- family personal assistant/secretarial support;
- financial record keeping;

- bill paying;
- tax and trust coordination (if not a main function of a member of staff);
- private expense budgets;
- personal cash management;
- security;
- audits;
- charitable foundations – management, reporting, review;
- family expenses – for example, monitoring building work;
- personnel – recruitment, payroll, staff performance and education;
- yacht and aircraft management;
- family coaching;
- insurance;
- property inventories;
- personal property management – management of estates, staffing, etc;
- renewals of licences, passports, credit cards;
- monitoring family travel expenses (and those of the office);
- travel arrangements;
- shipping, transport expenses;
- management of household expenditure (eg, oversight of nannies, housekeepers); and
- keeping family records.

4.4   Structure

The business plan and services required will determine the structure the family office adopts and what external advice will be necessary and advisable. A key decision in this context is whether the responsibilities and activities of the family office are to be carried out by in-house professionals or outsourced to others. As illustrated below, the family office will be at the centre of these activities whether or not the responsibilities are outsourced or staffed internally.

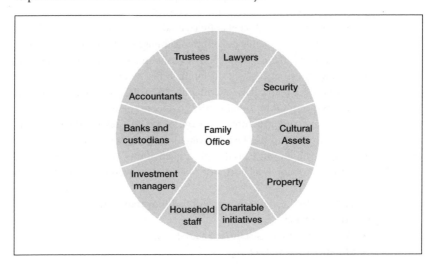

In addition, structures will vary depending on the family's legal jurisdiction(s). A thorough understanding of all of the family's estate and tax-planning complexities is essential and will drive the decision process. Each family will have different requirements, and appropriate advice should be sought taking into account possible future family movements, present location, different tax status and domicile where relevant. As wealth and investment structures become increasingly complex, so will tax planning. Ensuring proper use is made of skilled professionals to advise on structures is of utmost importance. There are many incidences of families who have been badly advised and subsequently faced difficult tax issues or whose structures have been found to be too inflexible to meet long-term family needs and changes.

Examples of top-level structures are:

- limited company;
- limited liability partnership;
- partnership;
- trusts; and
- protected cell company.

Structure will clearly influence the manner in which different assets are held. As with the structure of the office itself, those for the underlying assets will also need to be considered in conjunction with any differing tax rules, family requirements, the restrictions that some of the structures may impose and the implications for liquidity for individual family members.

Examples of structures which can be used are:

- collective investment vehicles, in which all family members can have an interest;
- limited liability partnerships for private equity, private investments;
- offshore holding vehicles for aircraft, yachts and so on; and
- insurance wrappers.

Requirements will vary from family to family and family advisors, in conjunction with family office personnel (if already appointed), will play an important part in determining the optimum arrangements in each individual case.

4.5   Implementation and staffing

Once the business plan, structure and range of services have been determined, the implementation of the plan and the establishment of the office and the employment of family office personnel can commence.

The most important considerations when hiring family office staff are confidentiality and trust. Many families commence the establishment of their family office by hiring someone who has either been known to them or has worked with them for a lengthy period (eg, an individual they have worked alongside in an operating business or on legal and accounting matters). This person may also have contributed to the business plan. Whilst the chosen individual may not have the precise skills required for the new venture (particularly if the family is moving from a business-owning family to becoming a financial family), the knowledge they have of the family and the trust with which they are regarded is often an overriding qualification.

Notwithstanding the presence of a trusted employee, the establishment of a single family office requires the acceptance by the family that they will be revealing and allowing access to detail regarding much of their lives to one or more people. In order to mitigate the risks associated with employment of people who will have access to this information, the recruitment process should be carefully managed and extensive personal due diligence carried out.

The decision on appropriate qualifications and expertise of the staff to be employed will depend on the complexity of each family and the business plan developed for the family office. In the case of a family with, or planning to have, a number of different domiciles, thought will need to be given as to how the family will be advised. It is unlikely that one person would be able to service all the different needs, and inevitable that advice on technical planning issues will need to be outsourced. In contrast, bookkeeping and some degree of accounting together with investment reporting are functions that are likely to be both a firm requirement and capable of being centralised in the office.

Alongside these services may lie a requirement for investment management skills. Financial services professionals tend to be concentrated in certain areas and the likelihood of attracting appropriately skilled employees will be a function of total assets under management (which will influence remuneration) and location. Given these prerequisites, the calibre and quality of the individual will be driven by the extent of autonomy that the family is prepared to grant in this arena. The greater the autonomy granted and the more responsibilities delegated, the more the requirement will be for an experienced investment professional. Job specifications will need to be clearly articulated for at least the lead investment professional, who might then be expected to develop specifications and requirements for a support team.

In order to ensure an appropriate forum for both the setting and oversight of investment targets and subsequent monitoring results, most families put in place an investment committee, the membership of which can be determined according to their own preferences. Generally, these will consist of family members with or without outside advisers. The investment committee would meet with the investment team on a regular basis (at least quarterly) and the meetings would be used for an exchange of information on the progress of the investment portfolios as well as changes in family requirements. This forum is most likely to focus on strategic oversight, rather than on the more tactical issues that tend to be delegated to management.

The most important drivers of investment performance are asset allocation, manager selection and portfolio construction and it is probable that investment professionals will be asked, possibly supplemented by outside consultants, to concentrate on these areas and have the appropriate skills to take responsibility for the delivery of these disciplines. Individual stock selection will generally be delegated to outside managers unless the family office is of a very significant scale. Exceptions often observed in this context are the purchase and management of government debt and the management of family legacy holdings.

It follows that investment professionals will require clear guidelines and understand the family's specific areas of interest and enthusiasm. The discipline with which both the family and the investment team pursue investment strategy will have a significant impact on the results achieved. Some would therefore argue that ad hoc investment initiatives driven by specific family interests should be kept to a minimum.

One final consideration is whether the family office investment operation needs to be regulated. Whilst it may not be absolutely necessary, advice should be taken. In addition, although regulation can be costly, investment management personnel may be keen to retain their regulatory registrations, which could lapse if they were employed in a non-regulated business.

4.6   Reporting

The family office will be the central point for reporting (and accounting) and will be expected to give timely and accurate information on accounts, performance, costs and so on. Be it at individual or family level – local or global – the reports should meet the requirements of those to whom they are being presented and the family will have the opportunity to express what such reports should measure and monitor. The resulting reports must be accessible and comprehensible to all stakeholders.

The content of reports will be dependent upon the assets held, structures in place and the way in which the family wishes to obtain the information, whether it be by:

- quarterly investment reports;
- quarterly (or other) meetings – this will require family representatives, either family members or those engaged to represent the family (investment committee), to ensure the investment management is adequately monitored;
- annual family meetings;
- formal annual reports for a holding company or collective investment vehicle; or
- an annual family newsletter.

Information to be included in the reports can include:

- investment portfolios, valuations and performance data;
- special investments;
- values of properties;
- values of cultural assets/chattels (art, wine and other collections); and
- details of expenditure and costs.

4.7   Education

One further role a family office can carry out is that of a resource for knowledge and education, related to its investment activities and beyond to philanthropy and governance.

Education at all levels is important and older family members may also find it useful if the family office is able to provide an adult education programme. Many fortunes are made outside the financial markets, making it likely that all participants (from the wealth creator down) will need to acquire, and continue to develop, insight and knowledge. Specialised education programmes can help non-financial family members to gain an understanding of investment, learn about the different asset classes, investment strategies and styles and what they should be looking for and expecting from the family office. Undertaken effectively, this will allow family members to become knowledgeable and effective owners and thereby be appropriately equipped to take on the challenges implicit in overseeing significant family wealth.

The family office can either play a pivotal role or assist in the outsourcing of the education of members of the family and be a point of contact and source of support that the younger inheritors may not seek from within the family.

Education programmes might involve all or any of the following and be carried out by personnel within the office, or in conjunction with trusted advisors such as lawyers and accountants and outsourced specialists:

- investment and financial education – a basic introduction to the financial markets and terminology;
- the importance of stewardship – how the family wealth has been derived and passed down through the generations;
- the responsibility of wealth and ownership – how wealth might enable philanthropic initiatives, and so on;
- governance – the way in which the family governance structures have been developed and are managed, and the governance structures for businesses and the family office;
- family continuity and owner education;
- an understanding of structures/trusts etc – the way in which the different structures function and the ultimate ownership of those structures and underlying investments; and
- the way in which the family office works and the services it offers.

5. Conclusion

Family offices are increasingly being considered as an option for the integration and management of financial assets and other matters for families with significant wealth. They come in several guises, and for families with a cohesive and strategic approach to their wealth management they represent one of several possible choices.

Nevertheless, they are complex to create and manage and they should not be undertaken without due care and consideration.

A 10-step programme for protecting family wealth

Jordan M Atin
Hull & Hull LLP
James MacBride
Landmark Advantage
Patricia A Robinson
Goodmans LLP

Introduction

Business families are unique in that techniques and strategies used in traditional estate planning often do not identify and integrate 'family issues' with the issues of the business and the concerns of the owner(s). Nowadays, if you work with families in business, technical expertise in one's field is a professional responsibility and is expected by owner/clients. However, many advisors are uncomfortable, unwilling or incapable of leading a conversation and coming to terms with the 'family' issues that are often critical to the success of the technical solutions.

Creating solutions that work for families in business requires sensitivity to the underlying values, beliefs, experience and expectations of all family members impacted by any formulated plan. This requires practitioners to expand their inquiry and develop special skills that will facilitate a deeper understanding and appreciation of the complexity of the issues owner/clients face. As successful practitioners, we can become entrenched in the traditional approach of providing technical solutions and send clients away unaided to sort out the family issues with instructions to "get back to us when you are ready to complete the plan".

Many owner/clients also dismiss or do not feel the need to address 'family' issues and are often not aware of them or the risks they pose. They just want a solution! Today, the complexities of the family business system require integration and insight from the family and from advisors from a variety of disciplines in order to help the family safeguard its wealth.

This moves us toward an interdisciplinary, collaborative approach involving experts and specialists in the legal, accounting, financial, behavioural science and management science fields. The process of sharing knowledge and building consensus can assist owner/clients in managing unforeseen risks and obtaining better results.

Let us now consider the following case study, which will be used for illustrative purposes throughout the description (forming the bulk of the chapter) of the 10 steps towards an effective wealth protection plan.

Case study 1: Harvey Counter makes his plans

Harvey Counter is 87 years old and excels in the real estate development business. As a young man he started buying houses, renovating them, and reselling at a profit. Over the years he built a multi-million dollar enterprise in land development and home building. Harvey is a powerhouse and a forceful personality who usually gets his own way. He likes to be in control and is not keen on paying professional fees.

When he started out, Harvey's friend Gerry was also starting out as a young lawyer and Harvey asked him to do his legal work. When Gerry recommended that Harvey should have a will, Harvey got his will done by Annie, the 'estates lawyer' at Gerry's firm. Over the years his will has been revised on several occasions to meet his changing circumstances.

Twenty years ago Harvey did an estate freeze,1 so that the future growth in his $20 million company (let us call it FamilyCo) would accrue to a trust for his children (He complained vociferously at the time about the professional fees.) Subsequently, the trust was distributed and Harvey chose not to ask Annie for advice when the shares were transferred on the books of FamilyCo. Each of Harvey's three children (Gen2) now owns a third of the shares of FamilyCo. Harvey still holds voting control through a separate class of voting shares.

Seven years ago, Harvey had Annie revise his will once more, to include bequests to grandchildren (Gen3) and that was the last Annie heard from him. Gerry has since retired and Harvey now has Craig, a local lawyer, dealing with his real-estate matters. Harvey asked Craig to draft a codicil to his will two years ago, providing that the shares of another company (LandCo) be distributed to his children unequally when the last of Harvey and Rose, his wife of 65 years, passes away. His will continues to provide for equal distribution of FamilyCo.

The codicil provides that the oldest son, Bruce, who works full-time in the business, is to get 50% of LandCo. Sue, the youngest, who works part-time in the business and gives a lot of support to her parents, is getting 30%. Peter, not working in the business, gets 20%. Somehow, Gen2 found out about the codicil and now Peter and Sue are upset with Harvey and are not talking to Bruce. Other issues are beginning to come up with Gen2 and Rose is getting quite upset. Harvey has come back to Annie to discuss what to do!

Annie reviews the existing will, asks Harvey for a copy of the codicil and a corporate diagram identifying who owns what. She then meets with Harvey. Annie discovers that because LandCo is a subsidiary owned by FamilyCo, Harvey does not own the shares and therefore cannot leave them to anyone in his will, making the codicil irrelevant. Harvey has difficulty understanding this, even though it is clear on the corporate diagram.

Harvey returns to Annie's office twice more to discuss some other issues regarding Gen2 – once on his own and once with his accountant. In those discussions, Annie surmises that Bruce is asking Harvey to make some special

---

1   An estate planning technique to limit the growth in the value of a client's capital property. Post freeze, the future growth in value of the frozen property is transferred to the client's heirs and limits the client's tax liability at death.

provision for him because of the responsibility he has in the business. It appears Bruce is afraid that after Harvey is gone, his siblings, representing two-thirds of the shareholders of FamilyCo, may gang up on him and fire him; Harvey is worried about this too. Bruce is now 58, has always made a very good living from the family business and has a lavish lifestyle to sustain. Annie suspects that Bruce's influence is strong and that he is pressuring Harvey to 'take care of him'.

Harvey sides with Bruce in that he believes Bruce has made the most significant contribution to the business. He says Peter and Sue work hard too "but not like Bruce". He says Peter owns a dry-cleaning business and in any event "his wife is rich". Annie knows for a fact that Peter has a pre-nuptial agreement that provides Peter with no claim against his wife's wealth, but when she suggests this possibility to Harvey he simply dismisses it. Annie finds this a little ironic since Harvey was very concerned about Sue's common-law partner making a claim against her inherited wealth and insisted on a very tight cohabitation agreement, which is now in place!

Harvey proposes giving Bruce a $500,000 'bonus', which Harvey suggests he pay with personal funds. This may help Bruce in the short term, but it does not seem to address the possibility of Bruce being fired by his siblings. Harvey also realises that if the other children find out about the bonus they will think it is Bruce's doing and will demand equal treatment. The first meeting ends with no resolution, except for the fact that it is agreed that Harvey's power of attorney will appoint Sue and Bruce acting together (before it was Bruce only). Harvey hopes this will ease the suspicions and hostility among the kids.

After the first meeting, Sue calls Annie who becomes concerned about an attack on Harvey's competence as a result of the line of Sue's questioning. Harvey is a bit forgetful sometimes, but otherwise he seems to be in total control of his faculties and in Annie's opinion there is no question about his testamentary capacity. She prepares a lengthy memo to file, documenting her observations of Harvey and her conclusions about his competence and the situation in general.

At the second meeting, Harvey appears to be getting impatient. Harvey's accountant suggests an employment contract with a large severance payment. After much discussion, Harvey rejects this. Annie senses that he just wants the uncomfortable feelings to go away and expects he will take some action to placate Bruce and once again implement a solution without consideration of the current family dynamics. Since she last spoke with Harvey, she has been thinking a lot about the family and how stressed Harvey and Rose are.

1. The traditional estate plan will not necessarily protect family wealth

Now, we fast-forward to a year after Harvey's death. Sadly, Rose predeceased him. Annie is beginning to hear more about the fighting going on in the family. In reflecting on the situation, Annie feels that she developed a solid plan, documented the circumstances and the decisions made and drafted a good will that would make the transition of the wealth to Gen2 simple to execute. Harvey's will appointed Bruce and his accountant as the trustees and divided his estate equally among his three children with specific bequests to Gen3. However, because of concerns Harvey developed about Peter's financial situation (Peter had to declare bankruptcy after divorcing his wife), he put Peter's share in trust.

Harvey never let any of his kids know about the will. "It's none of their business and they will find out soon enough," he believed. When the kids received a copy of the will, they did exactly what most children do: they looked to see if the will confirmed their own perception of their family and their role in it.

So what does the will say to each of them? To Bruce, the will confirms the trust Dad had in him throughout his life. Dad put him in charge because he knew that Bruce was the most responsible. Dad was smart to put a limit on Peter's inheritance because of Peter's demonstrated lack of success with money. "Dad wants me to protect him now."

To Peter, the will reinforces that he is not to be taken seriously and that he cannot be trusted to make his own decisions. It was that way growing up and it is still that way even though he is 55 years old. "Dad never trusted me and he is showing it again by putting Bruce in charge ... He is not going to tell me what to do!"

Sue has already started getting calls from Peter about how unfair the will is to them. She is also getting calls from Bruce who wants her to support him in his decision not to give more money to Peter. "Why would Dad do this when I have no one to support me?", she asks, " I have enough problems of my own."

The will released all the emotions and feelings that had been bubbling under the surface for all those years. Things were always taken care of the way Dad wanted and now no one was around to fix it. That intangible 'lid', which often kept the issues and emotions in the family firmly in place, was no longer present, now that both parents had died.

How do siblings justify fighting each other over their parent's estate? It is a rare occasion when a party will admit that he or she is fighting only for the money. Instead, when an estate dispute arises, children justify their involvement in one of two 'principled' ways:

"It's not what Dad really wanted!"

For example, in a will challenge, the challenger will justify the challenge by alleging that the will does not reflect Dad's true intentions because he lacked testamentary capacity or was unduly influenced. The children supporting the will justify fighting by protecting Dad's true wishes as expressed in his will.

"It's not fair!"

This justification might be used when assets are transferred *in specie* and those assets that once had similar value are now disproportionate.

In Harvey's case, the fight is started by Peter. For him it is about "righting the wrongs of the past". Peter challenged the validity of the will, sought an accounting of it and applied to remove Bruce as a trustee of Peter's trust. Peter is determined to prove that he is equal to his siblings. Bruce feels the need to protect himself and will fight back, all the while telling everyone that he is "just carrying out Dad's wishes".

The goal of protecting the family wealth was not met in any sense. The lack of effective communication, the unmet expectations and the children's surprise as to what was in the will all contributed to a foreseeable dispute. Annie wonders what could have been done to prevent this situation from developing.

2. Families in business are distinct

Successful families in business blend complex family dynamics with business strategies, leadership decisions and long-term planning. Harvey's forceful nature, hard work and discipline served him well in taking advantage of opportunities and managing the risks necessary to build the family business. If Harvey understood what makes families in business unique from those not in business, he may have been moved to consider a new approach that would not have left the family wealth to chance.

According to the Aspen Family Business Group,[2] families in business differ from other families in at least three important ways:

- Communication is more complicated when ownership and management considerations overlap with family dynamics;
- There is a more complicated web of relationships that surrounds and influences the family; and
- The decisions that are made by families in business are more frequent and of greater consequence than those of non-business families.

From the business perspective, governance of a family business is also more complicated because of the central role of the family that owns and typically leads the business.[3]

Professional advisors who have family business clients know that identifying and addressing critical issues for these families is challenging and goes beyond any one area of expertise.

3. Start at the beginning

Like any other estate-planning client, owner/clients have goals they expect to achieve in planning their estates. Irrespective of where the client begins in the process, identifying those goals and drawing them out from the client, has an important place at the start of discussions.

Often owner/clients, because of the very traits that made them successful, come to advisors with the specifics of what they want in their estate plan. "Put this asset in trust", "Pay my son $X per year", "All spouses are excluded" they tell us, having already figured out how the estate plan is going to work. But that is putting the cart before the horse. Family businesses face special challenges when they deal with intergenerational issues, and involving all of the stakeholders in the estate planning process is an opportunity to uncover insights into family relationships that may arise from discussing sensitive issues and allow families to deal with them wisely to achieve the outcome they seek.

Without first identifying the family goals, values and objectives, advisors cannot fully use their experience and expertise to preserve the value of the estate. Each owner/client's goals and priorities create the prism through which the estate plan is conceived. When asked about goals, many clients will speak in generalities – "Provide for my spouse", "Make sure my kids don't lose all the money" or "Keep the

---

2   The Aspen Family Business Group is an international consulting resource for families in business.
3   "Governing the Family-Run Business", John Davis, *Harvard Business Review*, September 4 2001.

business going". An advisor's job is to drill down to the core values and to help the client articulate them.

Pulling it all together, interviewing family members and other stakeholders as well as gathering information and gaining insight from other advisors helps ensure greater success in achieving protection of the family wealth over the long term.

Ultimately, when the time comes to start preparing the estate plan, the advisors will want to be in a position to test the estate plan against the stated goals. Does the plan accomplish all of the goals articulated? Were the goals achieved in the correct priority? What were the trade-offs inside the family or from a financial perspective that had to be made to satisfy the goals?

4.   **Understanding family dynamics**

In helping Harvey articulate his goals concerning the protection of the family wealth, Annie may have considered gaining additional insight into the family dynamics by asking questions such as:

- Has Harvey discussed these goals and his plan with Rose and what are her views?
- What is Harvey's relationship with each of his children? Does Harvey or Rose have a perceived favourite? Do their children perceive a favourite?
- What are the family communication patterns? Do they talk about these things with open dialogue? Does dialogue occur one to one, or in group settings?
- How do Gen2 get along with each other? Are there special alliances? Are there any exclusionary or conflicted relations?
- To what degree are in-laws included in family discussions? How are they informed? What is the family's relationship with in-laws?
- Has Harvey asked Gen2 how they see their future and the future of the business when he and Rose are gone?

Some advisors determine this to be a separate role depending on how deep the enquiry goes.

If Annie did not feel qualified or was uncomfortable herself, through dialogue she may have been able to create an opening for Harvey and his family to agree to engage a behavioural science expert to support them in addressing the family issues before proceeding. (See step 7 – Dealing with resistance.) Getting Harvey to consider bringing in another advisor may be dependent on Harvey and Rose's understanding that the families' goals in protecting their wealth may only be realised once unresolved conflict has been identified and addressed. A helpful tool to assess a family's readiness for open communication can be found at: www.fambus.com (Choose "Free Biz Tools" then "Quick Test – Family Firm Succession Readiness").

5.   **Protection of family wealth**

"Why protect the wealth?" This is a question that should be asked of an entire family and relates to the family's goals and values. In this regard, James E Hughes Jr's book *Family Wealth: Keeping It in the Family* is most helpful in articulating why most families want to protect their wealth. According to Hughes, most families seek to "enhance each individual's pursuit of happiness in the overall pursuit of long-term preservation of the family".[4] Preservation of the family wealth is an integral part of achieving that purpose.

5.1 What wealth?

When advisors seek to understand what wealth needs to be protected, most planning that is done, as in Harvey's case, focuses on the financial capital[5] and how to preserve it, particularly from taxation. When Harvey did his traditional tax planning years ago, not all aspects of the wealth he was trying to protect or the inherent threats to the family were considered. Since one of Harvey's goals was to "make his family happy", Annie may have helped Harvey reframe his definition of wealth to include his family's human capital[6] and social capital.[7] He may then have begun to explore the value all of the family attributes in the context of family wealth and how they might best be employed.

For example, if Harvey had been more open about Bruce's contribution to the business and the value he added, perhaps the other children would have been more amenable to an arrangement whereby Bruce was awarded for his performance.

Similarly, if the family had been encouraged to share their visions of their future, Peter might have discussed his business plans with Harvey and had the benefit of Harvey's experience and wisdom. Peter might have avoided some of the pitfalls that ultimately resulted in his bankruptcy. Harvey would also have been aware that Peter had a marriage contract that excluded him from sharing in any of his wife's family's wealth, and this might have informed his thinking about Peter and the provisions he made for him.

Finally, discussions with Sue might have resulted in more effective tax planning for her and her disabled daughter.

5.2 Protection for whom?

The term "shirtsleeves to shirtsleeves in three generations" is widely known. A multi-generational perspective is very often necessary when planning to protect family wealth. Owners like Harvey are often distracted by the immediate demands of the business and expectations of Gen2, particularly once Gen2 reach adulthood and become more aggressive about advancing their own interests and needs. Helping Harvey and Gen2 gain a multi-generational perspective of the collective family wealth would help shift their focus from the current 'Gen2 issues' to the broader and longer-term considerations that need attention.

Another helpful perspective for the entire family is demonstrated by the three-circle model.[8] The three-circle model illustrates the interaction between the family

4   Hughes, James E Jr, *Family Wealth: Keeping It in the Family*, page v of Preface.
5   Financial capital is purchasing power in the form of money available for the production or purchasing of goods, etc. For wealthy owner/clients the question is often, "How does the wealth become a blessing to my family and not a curse?"
6   Human capital in this context is the development of skill, knowledge and wisdom by an individual or family in the pursuit of purpose and meaning in life.
7   Social capital describes the connections within and between social networks, as well as connections among individuals, and the inclinations that arise from these networks to assist each other.
8   The three-circle model, Tagiuri and Davis, 1982.

system, the ownership system and the business system and the competing needs and interests of each (see the first main chapter of this publication). Some family members are part of each system and some are not. Therefore, what trade-offs will be necessary in order to balance the competing needs and interests of each system?

5.3 Protection from whom?

When asked "from whom" the family wealth requires protection, most owner/clients would identify tax authorities as the primary threat, then spouses, creditors and other external threats. It is rare that an owner/client will identify immediate family members as a threat to the family wealth and yet, as is apparent in Harvey's case, that seems to be the source of the primary threat.

In some ways, Harvey's planning created an environment for potential disputes, some of which could have been anticipated and possibly pre-empted at various times during the planning stages. For example, the three children are now shareholders of FamilyCo and there is no mechanism (such as a shareholders' agreement) to organise and govern their relationship.

Each child's own family situation poses inherent concerns and fears. Everyone, for example, is aware that Bruce's wife is a concern. She is accustomed to a lavish lifestyle and is making huge demands on Bruce. Bruce has no marriage contract and is rightly worried what a break-up in his marriage could mean for the business. They are all aware that it is impossible to put a marriage contract in place at this stage.

Peter had a marriage contract with his wealthy wife whose family demanded that her family wealth be protected. He is now divorced and his inheritance is managed by Bruce. He is not happy with that arrangement and does not believe Bruce should be investing his money and doling it out to him. The situation is intolerable.

While Sue has a cohabitation agreement, she also has a special-needs child who takes a lot of her time and energy and who needs expensive long-term care. She not only worries about a fight between her brothers, but also regrets that she did not talk to her parents more about her own situation and the planning that could have been beneficial to her.

The children are all at a loss to understand what exactly this plan their parents put in place was supposed to protect them from.

6. Engaging stakeholders and other advisors

In working with family business owner/clients, it is imperative that we identify all the stakeholders. Who are stakeholders? The answer is anyone who has an interest in the affairs of the family is a stakeholder. A child, a spouse of a child, even a long-time friend of the family or a key employee can be a stakeholder. It is also important to understand each of their roles and how they can influence the decisions being made whether or not they are 'at the table'. A well graphed family genogram[9] is helpful to gain insight into identifying all of the stakeholders and their relationships within the family.

---

9   A genogram is a pictorial display of a person's family relationships and medical history. It goes beyond a traditional family tree by allowing the user to visualise hereditary patterns and psychological factors that punctuate relationships. It can be used to identify repetitive patterns of behaviour and to recognise hereditary tendencies.

Learning to address difficult issues, developing strategies to overcome obstacles and creating effective family communication are integral to protecting family wealth. In a complex, multi-million-dollar family business environment such as Harvey's, engaging stakeholders, keeping the lines of communication open and promoting trust and understanding using a family council[10] and family charter[11] may be appropriate. Peter and Sue's suspicions concerning their parents' estate wishes might have been avoided and Bruce's employment contract could have been resolved had a family council and a family charter been in place when these situations arose.

As discussed earlier, a high degree of interaction with advisors and experts in different disciplines is also valuable. There are two important challenges when collaborating with other advisors:

- getting all advisors to support owner/clients to slow down and engage in a process that will help them make better decisions, fully understanding the long-term impact of the strategies and solutions they choose in protecting their wealth; and
- tracking data and getting relevant information to the correct person at the correct time to ensure nothing significant is missed and thereby preventing assumptions being made that might put the family or business at risk.

A statement of net wealth gives a complete financial picture that Annie could have used to raise important issues such as beneficiary designations on life insurance, the impact of personal debt used by Harvey and Rose to finance the business, and the tax and estate settlement implications of the foreign property. The statement of net wealth can also be used as a tool for providing disclosure of family assets and helping inform the family and advisors of what is at stake.

An advanced genogram[12] may have prompted Annie to ask Harvey whether he wanted some assistance to address issues such as the alliance that Sue and Peter formed to the exclusion of Bruce after the codicil came to light. It may also have prompted Annie to ask about provisions for Sue's special-needs adult child and 'what if' questions related to Bruce potentially deciding to bring his children into the business – the genogram shows he is the only sibling that has the opportunity to involve his children.

7.   Dealing with resistance

When faced with difficult decisions, owner/clients will often present conscious and unconscious barriers to change. In attempting to make a change, it may be that

---

10   The Aspen Family Business Group defines a family council as a group of adult and older-teenage family members who meet regularly to deliberate, make agreements, share understandings, make plans and develop the next generation for the ongoing stewardship of family assets.

11   The Aspen Family Business Group describes a family charter as a guide for a family council that articulates the purpose, goals and values of the family; provides guidelines that anticipate predictable 'tough' issues; defines how the council will support continuous development and education of family members; creates a context that fosters harmony, and establishes policies and plans regarding family assets.

12   An advanced genogram demonstrates: communication patterns and directions, special alliances, favouritism patterns, exclusionary relations, conflicted relations, emotional cut-offs, emotional triangles and Myers-Briggs cognitive types.

Harvey is caught in a competing commitment[13] – a subconscious, hidden goal that conflicts with his stated commitments. Change involving a competing commitment is a challenge to one's longest-held beliefs and requires empathy and skill. Conversely, Harvey may consciously resist taking a new approach in developing his estate plan as he attributed much of his success to the old way of doing things. ("I am successful, why do I need to change?")

Resistance can be a useful source of information for practitioners, which when skilfully dealt with can lead to concrete strategies that will help owner/clients move forward. Some owner/clients resist taking a new approach or idea because they feel:

- fear of the unknown or an expectation of loss (ie, the business has a reputation and brand to protect and someone may see the less pleasant side of them or their family);
- change may imply that previous behaviour was somehow wrong – the need to protect their ego;
- they will have to involve family members more intimately than ever before – uncertainty and fear about issues they are being asked to explore; or
- worried about the added time and cost of involving new advisors to the mix – the cost is too high, the benefits are too low.

Understanding the importance of resistance in the families we work with requires that we actively strategise and address the resistance in a manner appropriate to our training and experience. Practitioners should make sure of involving professionals with sufficient psychological training when the resistance seems to be psychological. The resistance may well be from the fact that the family is secretly dealing with issues such as addictions, depression or other illness.

Overcoming resistance from clients requires building trust, using effective communication strategies and developing action plans for clients and advisors to ensure everyone is moving forward together with the family's best interests in mind. Thinking back, Annie felt she could have helped Harvey with what "might happen" if she had been better prepared to discuss his options when he asked, "Why should I change?"

It is important to link change with positive results early in the process. Some of Harvey's concerns may easily have been addressed by taking one or more of the following actions:

- Test client goals against expected results without involvement of the family and have them reflect on whether or not the plan actually achieves the goals in the long term. For example, knowing one of Harvey's goals was to "keep the family happy", he may consider asking the family whether his assumption that the business would stay in the family for future generations was correct.
- Provide 'what if' scenarios for Harvey. What if Gen2 agreed they wanted to explore other options? What if they would rather sell the business and take the money to keep the family intact?
- Discuss with Harvey how unmet expectations and surprises account for most

---

13   "The Real Reason People Won't Change", Robert Kegan and Lisa Laskow Lahey, *Harvard Business Review*, November 2001.

estate disputes. Sue and Peter may have been more supportive of Bruce's stake in the business if their needs were considered and could be met in some other way. If asked, they might have felt relieved they were not asked to take on additional responsibility.

- Provide a 'big picture' view – examine the real value of what is being protected. Annie remembered seeing a presentation on the benefits of working with a multi-family office,[14] where they described how they take the 'whole family' into consideration and can provide, among other things, consolidated financial reporting as well as formal family communication and access to expertise such as intergenerational counselling to help realise the full potential of the human capital in families.

8.   Developing the plan

At this point, the client has, at least notionally, bought into the idea of involving other stakeholders in the discussion about estate planning. Now how do we go about involving those stakeholders? At what point in the process should we be recommending that the client sit down with those stakeholders?

Creating an estate plan is, in some ways, like constructing a family home. In the traditional approach, the parent believes that because it is his land and his money that goes into the construction of the house, he is going to decide how it is going to look, how many bedrooms, how many bathrooms, whether there is going to be a finished basement, and so on. When the family moves in, the house is already complete.

If the whole family is to live there, does it not make sense to let them have some input on how it is designed? Maybe two of the kids do not mind sharing a bedroom, or for one of them it is very important that they have a specific workspace so they can pursue a hobby. If the parents design the house based on what they want and on what they believe their children want, they may unnecessarily have put extra rooms where they were not needed and overlooked a simple inexpensive option that would have made a positive impact on all the children. By having the children involved, the parents might just as likely have been able to achieve their goals in the design of the house while, at the same time, supporting the rest of the family in achieving their objectives in life.

How and when should the involvement of family members occur? Should the involvement be done in a group setting or individually? The advisor can canvass the benefits of both options.

Turning to Harvey's situation as an example, what could have avoided the problems over his codicil? Aside from not seeking comprehensive advice, Harvey chose to keep the matter secret from his children. When the children ultimately find out, they are suspicious and angry with one another and their parents. Perhaps, had Harvey sought professional advice, the advisor would have suggested a group meeting including Sue, Peter and Bruce, where each could have had a chance to

---

14   A multi-family office (MFO) is a team of independent and objective experts dedicated to the success of wealthy families. Services provided by MFOs include: intergenerational counselling and family communications; integrated tax, legal and financial advice; monitoring of third-party service providers; consolidated financial reporting; risk management; family governance; and philanthropy.

express their thoughts and feelings.

One of the benefits of the group setting is that the same information is provided to everyone. One of the big causes of unrealistic, and often unmet, expectations on the part of children is a parent telling each child something different (or the children hearing it differently because of their own agendas and experiences in the family). Parents, if pressured, often tell their children what they want to hear in order to avoid confrontation and conflict. They do this often with the best intentions but without an appreciation of the long-term impact. This is exactly what Harvey did with Bruce. Families may just find, by talking with each other openly, that a more creative solution and the likelihood of consensus building and 'buy-in' will be increased.

On the other hand, it may be best for the owner/client to get a feel for the reaction of the individual stakeholders in private before all appear in a room at the same time. This is especially important where there is concern that openness may harm the family if input is gathered through a group setting. Having the process turn into a free-for-all is a significant fear of clients and advisors alike. Experts in facilitation and communication are commonly brought in to help in these situations.

Through discussions with Harvey, Annie may have surmised Bruce's true concerns about losing his employment with the family company. Addressing this privately with Bruce and Harvey alone may have resulted in a different strategy that could have avoided the problems with the secret codicil. Owner/clients will need the assurance that family input is solicited with the understanding that the client's goals are paramount.

Emotions may be running high in business families as they attempt to resolve differences that may arise as events (either planned or unforeseen) occur around them. Effective family communication and management of conflict require special attention to help these families face their fears and overcome years of entrenched family dynamics. For an overview of a facilitated process in managing conflict, review www.familiasco.com (Choose "Resources" then "Conflict in the Family Firm").

9. **Keeping it in the family**

Once the stakeholders have been consulted and the plan has been developed and effectively communicated so that everyone is satisfied that the issues have been addressed, the traditional tools must be relied on to implement the plan. These include the will or multiple wills (eg, for different assets and/or different jurisdictions) and powers of attorney or substitute decision-making documents. There may also be a need for trusts, either *inter vivos* or testamentary. These can include insurance trusts, family trusts, trusts for special-needs children or grandchildren, and life-long testamentary trusts for both tax-planning and creditor-proofing purposes. Will planning for Gen2 should also be addressed.

With the whole family being part of the process, there can be frank discussions about the need to protect family wealth from the ravages of divorce. All children should be encouraged to enter into marriage contracts or pre-nuptial agreements as early as possible to protect inherited wealth. For children who are already married, applicable legislation in some jurisdictions will exclude inherited property from a division of property. In others, steps may need to be taken to afford maximum protection where a contract is not a viable option.

With respect to the business, employment contracts for key employees (whether family members or not) are appropriate in many circumstances. Shareholder and/or buy/sell agreements should be put in place, so that a set of rules is established to govern the children's relationship as shareholders, once the parents are gone.

Had Harvey engaged in open communication with his family and the advisors, he might have been able to take advantage of several traditional planning techniques well suited to their situation. For example, the benefits of a testamentary trust for Peter could have been explained to him (eg, protection from creditors), and Peter could have been a co-trustee so that he felt he had some control. A discretionary trust could have been created for Sue's daughter to take advantage of tax rules for disabled persons. Bruce might have also been encouraged to have a marriage contract if there had been dialogue about the impact of family law. A shareholders' agreement could have been put in place when the trust was distributed and many issues could have been addressed at that time. Perhaps some retirement planning vehicles could have been put in place with the company to aid all the children in their longer-term planning.

Finally, a comprehensive family business record is a useful resource for the whole family. This record should include the relevant corporate documents, corporate chart, planning memorandums, copies of family council meeting minutes or other decision documents and agreements such as employment and shareholder agreements. It is also a useful tool for all future advisors when questions are invariably asked about what was done and why.

10.   Protecting the advisor

When something does go wrong, advisors – whether they be lawyers, accountants or other professionals – are increasingly being looked to as being the cause of the problem. The deep pockets of the advisors' insurers become increasingly attractive. What can advisors do to avoid being turned on by their former clients and their families?

In our experience, business owners often do not have a firm grasp of why certain planning steps were taken. When asked to recall why they undertook an estate freeze reorganisation, for example, they often respond with "to save tax". They will be shocked (honestly or less so) to learn that as a result of the tax-saving technique their children, and not they, own much of the value of the family business. Detailed reporting letters to clients about the pros and cons of the transaction, why it was done and the fact that the children now have legal rights in the business that cannot be taken away are just some of the issues that should be confirmed in writing.

Many negligence claims revolve around issues that 'fell through the gaps'. Clients anticipate that their advisor is taking care of all issues. On the other hand, the advisor has not expected, and may not even be competent, to take on responsibility for issues outside the advisor's profession of origin. In today's era of specialisation, the 'gaps' have become numerous. The key to avoiding these types of claims is to limit one's retainer specifically to an area of expertise. Whether we are restricting our advice to, for example, will drafting or specific tax advice on a single transaction, failure to ensure that the client understands those limits can lead to finger pointing when things go wrong.

Similarly, the retainer should also be limited in respect of the persons for whom the advisor acts. This is especially common to family businesses where an advisor is seen as acting for 'the family'. If an advisor is acting for more than one stakeholder, it should be made clear how confidential information is going to be treated and what will happen in the event of conflict between the two or more stakeholders.

It becomes even more concerning when the beneficiaries seek to challenge the estate plan and the client is no longer around to tell his side of the story. Detailed notes and reporting letters become even more important in these situations. A rule of thumb is to document the file expecting that you will be a witness in a proceeding concerning the client's intentions in 20 years' time. Will your file have sufficient notes to permit you to stand up to cross-examination about an event that you have little actual memory of? It should.

Conclusion

There is no one correct approach to protecting family wealth, just as there is no one solution to solving technical problems in family business. It is imperative, however, that the challenges unique to families in business are understood and addressed. With this understanding, the risk of unhappy family members sabotaging the plan and family relationships being harmed is minimised.

It takes work by everyone involved, including advisors, educators, the owner/client and the family, to implement and monitor an effective wealth protection strategy and to ensure that family wealth and harmony created in this generation is preserved for the next. It does not just happen!

About the authors

Jordan M Atin

Senior Associate Counsel, Hull & Hull LLP

jatin@hullandhull.com

Jordan Atin was appointed as one of Ontario's first Certified Specialists in Estates and Trusts Law.

Jordan is the immediate past chair of the Ontario Bar Association trust and estates section and a full member of the Society of Trusts and Estate Practitioners (STEP). He was the inaugural winner of the Hoffstein Prize in recognition of his contributions and achievements in the area of wills, trusts and estates.

Jordan is a frequent presenter and Chair of Continuing Legal Education programmes on estate matters. He is a contributing author to the well known text *Estate Litigation* and his articles are referred to in many of Canada's leading estates texts.

Jordan's book for non-lawyers, *The Family War – Winning the Inheritance Battle*, has been featured on TV, radio and newspapers across North America.

Christine Blondel

Adjunct Professor of Family Business at INSEAD; Founder and Advisor, Family Governance

Christine.blondel@insead.edu

Christine Blondel is Adjunct Professor of Family Business at INSEAD, the global business school in France and Singapore: she teaches and co-directs the seminar "The Family Enterprise Challenge" and was appointed as the first executive director of the Wendel International Centre for Family Enterprise. She regularly speaks in conferences, organises training programmes and has written extensively on the topics of long-lasting family firms, succession, women in the family business, the sale of the family business, and governance.

She advises business families on issues linked to generational transitions and governance of the business and the family. Her approach is to foster 'fair process' through participative communication methods and adequate governance structures.

Christine is actively involved in the Family Business Network (FBN), the International Family Enterprise Research Academy (IFERA), and the Family Firm Institute (FFI).

Joanna Boatfield

Manager, Dixon Wilson

joannaboatfield@dixonwilson.co.uk

Joanna Boatfield is a practising accountant at Dixon Wilson chartered accountants in London. She is a member of the Institute of Chartered Accountants in England and Wales. Her role at Dixon Wilson involves acting for a number of families and their businesses, advising on all areas of the family business including succession planning, business structuring, raising external financing and taxation matters. Since joining Dixon Wilson, Joanna has been involved in establishing or reorganising the ownership structures of a number of family businesses, with a particular emphasis on the role of trusts in these ownership arrangements.

Richard R Brass
Client Director, Schroders Private Banking
Richard.Brass@schroders.com

Richard Brass joined Schroders Private Banking in 2008, having spent much of his career in investment banking where he specialised in providing corporate finance advice to private and public companies. Richard previously worked for Compass Advisers, an international investment banking partnership, where he co-founded the European office. He joined Schroders from Montpelier Asset Management, an emerging markets fund. He began his career with KPMG in 1994, where he qualified as a chartered accountant before moving into its corporate finance team. He has a degree in mathematics from the University of Sussex.

Malcolm D Burrows
Head of Philanthropic Advisory Services
Scotia Private Client Group
malcolm.burrows@scotiatrust.com

Malcolm Burrows is head of philanthropic advisory services at Scotia Private Client Group, which is the largest national provider of services to private foundations in Canada. Prior to 2004, he worked for major Canadian charities over a period of 13 years. He is well known as a writer and educator in the charitable sector, and he has worked extensively as a volunteer with the federal government on charitable incentives and regulatory issues.

Stephen F Cutts
Managing Director
Rawlinson & Hunter SAM, Monaco
stephen.cutts@rawlinson-hunter.mc

Stephen Cutts is managing director of Rawlinson & Hunter, Monaco, setting up and administering international structures and trusts for private clients.

He has 20 years' experience providing succession and private wealth planning for clients with both significant operating investments and private assets, including a number of years as CEO of a family office.

Stephen is a UK-qualified accountant and chartered tax adviser, and a member of both the Society of Trust and Estate Practitioners (STEP) and the International Tax Planning Association (ITPA). He is also a member of the STEP International Business Families Group and an expert adviser to the Lebanese American University. Stephen worked with the Dubai International Financial Centre (DIFC), drafting the policies for the world's first legislation for family offices that was enacted there in 2008.

Nan-b de Gaspé Beaubien
Co-Chair, The de Gaspé Beaubien Foundation

Nan-b de Gaspé Beaubien is co-chair, with her husband, Philippe, of The de Gaspé Beaubien Foundation, a family foundation based in Montreal. She incorporated her study of educational psychology into a successful career in human resources management and, with her husband, helped build their company, Telemedia, into one of the top multimedia companies in Canada.

She is a founder of the Canadian Broadcast Institute and founder and co-chair of the Business Families Foundation (BFF). BFF is a non-profit foundation devoted to helping business families and the professionals who serve them, to provide the education and support they need to better understand their issues and face their challenges. Since its inception in 1993, the de Gaspé Beaubiens have helped found and support seven family business university centres across Canada.

Nan-b has sat on many for-profit boards, such as Four Seasons Resorts and Hotels Inc, Imasco Inc and Campbell Soup (Canada), as well as on the boards of non-profit organisations such as the Harvard Business School Board of Dean's Advisors, the Institute for Research on Public Policy, the National Centre for Research and Development and the Terry Fox Humanitarian Committee. She is a recipient of the Canadian Centennial Medal and a member of the Canadian Broadcasters' Hall of

Fame. Nan-b and her husband are the first couple to be inducted into the Canadian Business Hall of Fame; they are also recipients of an Honorary Degree from the University of British Columbia.

Mary K Duke

Managing Director, Head of Global Wealth Solutions – Americas, HSBC Private Bank
mary.k.duke@hsbcpb.com

Mary Duke is a managing director and head of global wealth solutions for the Americas at HSBC Private Bank. She is responsible for the trust and fiduciary businesses, philanthropy, and family wealth advisory and private-client insurance throughout the region, including Bermuda and the Caribbean.

She is an expert in integrating cross-border transfer of wealth strategies, family business succession planning, next-generation leadership, global philanthropy, family office solutions and governance for multigenerational families. She is an author and lecturer, often quoted in *Barron's, Financial Times, Forbes, The Economist, Institutional Investor* and *Worth*.

Mary is a licensed attorney and certified accountant and former head of two private family offices. She was a financial services consultant with Arthur Andersen & Co and practised law, specialising in closely held corporations, estate planning, real estate and tax.

Louise Fisher

Consultant, Family Business Solutions Ltd
lfisher@familybusinesssolutions.co.uk

Louise Fisher is a consultant with Family Business Solutions Ltd, an independent consulting, research and teaching organisation. To date she has concentrated on helping family businesses and business families, through transitions in ownership and leadership and through implementation of systems of governance. Louise is particularly interested in working with next-generation members of business families who are contemplating a life in the family business as a manager, owner or leader.

Louise has worked with Scottish Enterprise on its Enterprising Glasgow Initiative to ensure that family business entrepreneurship remains to the fore. During 2008, Louise delivered a number of training programmes for government organisations and professional advisers, with the aim of increasing their understanding of the challenges that family businesses face and helping them deliver a better service to their clients.

With the help of the Family Firm Institute's Certificate in Family Business Advising, Louise has developed a deep understanding of family systems theory, adult development theory and family business governance.

Peter Gray

Partner, Cavendish Corporate Finance LLP
pgray@cavendish.com

Peter Gray is a partner with Cavendish Corporate Finance LLP. Cavendish is currently the United Kindgom's leading specialist adviser to vendors of family-owned companies, having acted on the successful sale of some 400 companies since its inception in 1988. Peter joined Cavendish in 1995, since which time he has been personally involved in the sale of more than 50 companies, including a number of household names such as Avent Baby Products and Antler Luggage.

Prior to joining Cavendish, Peter worked as a lawyer with Clifford Chance in its management buy-out group. He has degrees in Law and Economics from the University of Melbourne and an MBA. He is a frequent lecturer on the subject of selling private companies.

Judy Green

Executive Director, Family Firm Institute Inc
judy@ffi.org

Judy Green is executive director of the Family Firm Institute (FFI) where, since 1992, she has led the international professional membership

273

organisation through significant organisation and programmatic growth. FFI is now the premier international body for advising and research in the family business and family wealth fields.

During Judy's tenure, FFI has grown to more than 1,500 members with 35% of its membership now based outside the United States; strengthened its global reach to markets in Western Europe, Asia, Australia, Latin America and Canada; established two professional certificate programmes to uphold and promote standards of best practices in the field; and deepened the Institute's commitment to cross-disciplinary education among various professions within FFI's core disciplines of behavioural sciences, finance, law and management science.

In 2008, Judy received the Barbara Hollander Award, which was created to honour the Institute's founder and first president.

David Harvey

Chief Executive
Society of Trust and Estate Practitioners
david.harvey@step.org

David Harvey is chief executive of the Society of Trust and Estate Practitioners, the professional body worldwide for lawyers, accountants and others who advise on the responsible stewardship and structuring of assets and on planning by today's complex families. During his tenure, STEP has doubled in size to 14,500 members worldwide in more than 70 jurisdictions. STEP won national UK public affairs awards in both 2007 and 2008.

David is a former president of the Institute for Small Business and Entrepreneurship and a visiting fellow at Kingston Business School. He speaks and writes widely on family business issues. He is a member of the Council of the Centre for Policy Studies, a chartered accountant (FCA FCCA) and a public relations practitioner (MCIPR). David has also worked on a range of UK government and EU working parties looking at small and family business issues. He was educated at Mansfield College Oxford.

Jane Hilburt-Davis

President, Key Resources, LLC
j.hilburtdavis@comcast.net

Jane Hilburt-Davis is an experienced family business consultant and president of Key Resources, LLC, a Boston-based consulting firm. She is the founding chair of the innovative Certificate for Family Business Advisors, an FFI Fellow and president emeritus of FFI. Considered a leader in the field, she received the 2008 Richard Beckard Practice Award designed to recognise outstanding contributions to family business practice. Jane is the author of many articles and case studies, and she has trained, mentored and coached hundreds of family business advisors. She is co-author of the widely acclaimed book, *Consulting to Family Businesses*. She serves as consultant and advisor to family businesses, and closely held companies, throughout the United States, and has lectured and taught in the family business field in the United States, Canada, Europe and Australia.

Ivan Lansberg

Senior Partner
Lansberg, Gersick & Associates LLC
lansberg@lgassoc.com

Ivan Lansberg is co-founder and a senior partner of Lansberg, Gersick & Associates LLC, a research and consulting firm specialising in family enterprise and family philanthropy. Ivan is also in the faculty of the Northwestern University's Kellogg School of Management and co-director of the Center for Family Enterprises. Prior to his involvement at Kellogg, Ivan was a professor of organisational behaviour at the Yale School of Organization and Management for seven years. One of the founders of the Family Firm Institute, Ivan was the founding editor of the *Family Business Review*. He has written widely on family business issues, including *Succeeding Generations* (1999) Harvard Business School Press, and *Generation to Generation: Life Cycles of the Family Business* (1997) Harvard Business School Press. His most recent article, entitled "Tests of a Prince", was published in the *Harvard Business Review* (September, 2007). Ivan holds PhD, MA, and BA degrees from Columbia University.

Francine RS Lee

Senior Vice President, Head of Family Wealth
Advisory Services for the Americas
HSBC Private Bank
francine.r.lee@hsbcpb.com

Francine Lee is a senior vice president and head of family wealth advisory services for the Americas at HSBC Private Bank. She is responsible for delivering specialist advisory services to the Private Bank's ultra-high-net-worth families, focusing on philanthropy, family governance, business succession planning, next-generation training, and family office advisory services.

Francine was formerly with the Goldman Sachs Family Office, where she led complex large-scale wealth transfer strategies, advised on tax-sensitive capital markets transactions, and developed a suite of wealth management services. She founded the alternative investments group at Prudential Securities and also developed hedging, diversification and liquidity strategies for concentrated equity positions. Francine was a tax attorney at Lehman Brothers and spent several years in private practice.

James MacBride

Director of Communication
Landmark Advantage
jamie@landmarkadvantage.ca

James MacBride has been advising families in business for more than 10 years. He is co-founder of Landmark Advantage, a multi-family office operating in Markham, Ontario, Canada since 2001.

Landmark takes an integrated approach to managing complex, multidimensional family and technical issues in supporting business families to reach the full potential of their human and social capital.

Prior to co-founding Landmark Advantage, James was an investment advisor and financial planner in a wealth management practice that specialised in family business clients.

In 2006, he joined the steering committee and became a founding member of FFI Ontario chapter responsible for bringing the Family Firm Institute (FFI) to Canada. This was first FFI branch outside the United States. His commitment to continuous education in the family business consulting field allows him to remain at the forefront of the interdisciplinary approach to advising families in business.

Ian Macdonald

Partner, Wright Johnston & Mackenzie LLP
IM@wjm.co.uk

Ian Macdonald is a solicitor in Scotland; he is a partner in Wright Johnston & Mackenzie LLP based in Glasgow and Edinburgh and specialises in tax and estate planning and trusts. He has worked with family businesses for 15 years and is particularly involved in advising on the best structures to hold family businesses and other family enterprise assets. Ian is Deputy Chairman of the STEP Business Families Group, one of the consulting editors of this book and a Council member of STEP Worldwide.

Ken McCracken

Director, Family Business Solutions Limited
ken.mccracken@wjm.co.uk

Ken McCracken is a founding director and consultant with Family Business Solutions Limited (FBS, www.familybusinesssolutions.co.uk). FBS is a leading international consulting and training organisation that works with enterprising families and their family businesses and family offices.

In his consulting work, Ken has particular expertise in family enterprise transition planning and complex governance issues. He works with families whose interests span a variety of types of business and other assets through which their lives are connected.

Ken also provides training and strategic advice to advisers and groups such as professional associations, educators and trade bodies. As an enthusiastic champion of family entrepreneurship, he is actively involved in lobbying political, educational and other influential bodies with the aim of improving the overall awareness of the economic and social contribution made by enterprising families.

Paul McGrath
Partner, Withers LLP
Paul.mcgrath@withersworldwide.com

Paul McGrath is a partner at Withers LLP and jointly leads the funds, investments, tax and trusts practice group. Paul specialises in company and partnership law, mergers and acquisitions, joint ventures, corporate reorganisations and employee share schemes.

Paul trained at Withers, joining in 1995. He is a member of the Association of Partnership Practitioners and is a co-editor of the employee trusts section of *Practical Trust Precedents*. Paul has recently lectured on family businesses, in conjunction with the Institute for Family Business.

In his spare time, Paul is a volunteer reading partner at a local state primary school.

Joan Major
Director, Wealth Management
Sand Aire Ltd
joan.major@sandaire.com

Joan Major is director of wealth management at Sand Aire Ltd with responsibility for client relationships and services. With a background of roles within family businesses and financial market firms, Joan has more than 15 years' family office experience and was previously head of family services for a single-client family office.

Joan works closely with Sand Aire clients in the areas of charity and foundation administration, tax and trust coordination, and a

wide range of special projects. She has a Certificate in Family Business Advising from the Family Firm Institute (FFI) and is actively involved with the organisation.

Ian Marsh
Founder, *family*dr
imarsh@familydr.co.uk

Ian Marsh practised law for more than 30 years and was a private-client partner with law firms in London and New York for 16 years, before founding *family*dr Limited in June 2006.

During that period, he acted as trusted adviser to a number of successful families and their business and philanthropic interests. He advised them how to organise, manage and preserve their wealth, and how to resolve issues of governance and succession; he became trustee (or protector) of their family and charitable trusts, and director of their companies; and he was instrumental in resolving a number of complex multi-party, multi-jurisdictional family wars.

Through *family*dr, Ian now acts variously as facilitator, mediator and conciliator to family enterprises and their advisers, to help them manage change more effectively, to deal with difference more constructively, and to resolve the crises that inevitably erupt from time to time.

Maria Dolores Moreno
Senior Associate
Lansberg, Gersick & Associates LLC
moreno@lgassoc.com

Maria Dolores Moreno is a senior associate with Lansberg, Gersick & Associates, a research and consulting firm specialising in family enterprise and family philanthropy. Before becoming a consultant, she was the chief financial officer of a major family enterprise in Central America. She has worked extensively over the last 25 years on family business ownership structures, financing, mergers and acquisitions, financial restructuring, dividend policies, stock ownership programmes and executive compensation. She has been actively involved in continuity planning in large cousin consortiums and has been responsible for coordinating among family members, external advisors and legal counsel the design and implementation of ownership and governance structures, estate plans, shareholders' agreements, succession plans and retirement plans.

Maria Dolores is a Fulbright alumna and holds an MBA degree from the Peter F Drucker Graduate School of Management.

Jason Ogelman

Associate Director, John Lamb Partnership Ltd
jasonogelman@johnlamb.co.uk

Jason Ogelman is an associate director of John Lamb Partnership Limited, which has provided independent financial advice in London for half a century and was recently awarded chartered status by the Chartered Insurance Institute.

Beginning his career at Norwich Union, Jason has been an independent financial adviser since 1996. He specialises in advising owners and managers of small to medium-sized companies on all aspects of the provision of employee benefits. This includes company pensions, group life, critical illness, long-term disability, dependants' pension and medical insurance schemes. He firmly believes that well-informed, open communication is the basis for long-term client relationships.

Jason's professional qualifications include FPC and CeMap and he is currently completing his DipPFS qualification. He is a member of the Personal Finance Society. In his spare time he actively engages in charitable fundraising and has a love of anything with four wheels.

Andrew Parsons

Manager, Dixon Wilson
andrewparsons@dixonwilson.co.uk

Andrew Parsons is a manager at Dixon Wilson Chartered Accountants and a member of the Institute of Chartered Accountants in England and Wales. He joined Dixon Wilson in 2003. Andrew works primarily with private clients, advising on tax and related matters. His current position at Dixon Wilson involves acting for a number of families with significant family business interests, which range in size from small privately owned companies and partnerships, to a listed group. Andrew is involved in providing succession and capital tax planning advice to the owners of these family businesses at all stages in their development.

Ian Perrett

Solicitor, Boodle Hatfield
iperrett@boodlehatfield.com

Ian Perrett's main areas of practice include wills, trusts and estate planning. He trained with Boodle Hatfield and joined the private client and tax team after qualifying in 2006.

Aron R Pervin

Chair, Pervin Family Business Advisors Inc
apervin@pervinfamilybusiness.com

Aron Pervin, CMC, ICDD, TEP specialises in the resolution of complex family enterprise and ownership situations, and business and family interaction.

Aron collaborates with business family members and celebrates how they regulate their emotions, perform and feel worthy, deal with belonging, rejection, self-control, irrationality and self-destructive behaviour and observes how they recognise, choose, apply and maintain new habits, including the stress related to choice and change. Simply, he examines the productive and destructive impact of these thoughts and behaviours on the individual, family, business, board and/or foundation and employs beneficial positive, achievable and sustainable outcomes.

Aron works with business families at the founder stage and typically consults to successful second-, third- and fourth-generation leaders and business families that require and demand *results and not recommendations®.*

He is the Canadian leader and international pioneer in the field of family business management, organisation and governance, private foundations and business family relationships.

Jonathan Riley
Partner, Michelmores LLP
jjr@michelmores.com

Jonathan qualified as a company/commercial lawyer in the City of London in 1994. Following six years practising company/commercial law, Jonathan changed the emphasis of his practice and now advises individuals and families as to the protection of their family wealth.

Jonathan heads Michelmores' families in business team and his areas of expertise include the protection of family wealth and succession, the mitigation of UK capital taxes and the creation and operation of family settlements. Jonathan's commercial and private-client background provides him with a valuable perspective when advising business owners.

Jonathan is a member of the Society of Trust and Estate Practitioners and sits on its families in business committee.

Patricia A Robinson
Senior Partner, Goodmans LLP
probinson@goodmans.ca

Pat Robinson heads the estates, trusts and charities group at Goodmans. Her practice focuses on all aspects of personal tax, retirement and estate planning, and estate administration. Pat's clients are high-net-worth individuals with a variety of domestic and international holdings. Pat combines the traditional tools of estate planning, such as *inter vivos* and testamentary trusts, shareholders' agreements and domestic contracts, with a creative and multi-generational approach to wealth protection and succession planning. Pat is also a senior member of the Canadian

charities bar and advises charities regarding structure, registration, donation agreements and compliance.

Pat has lectured at the University of Toronto and University of Windsor law schools on will drafting and estate planning and writes on estate planning, wills and trusts law, and charities law.

Simon Rylatt
Partner, Boodle Hatfield
srylatt@boodlehatfield.com

Simon Rylatt is a partner at Boodle Hatfield and specialises in UK and international tax and estate planning for individuals and trusts, as well as advising on high-value, contentious trust and estate disputes for both onshore and offshore clients. He additionally advises on estate planning strategies for wealthy families and their businesses (including wealth protection structures, governance, divorce issues, pre- and post-nuptial agreements and generational succession planning). Simon joined Boodle Hatfield in 2000, becoming an associate in 2003 and a partner in 2005. He is also a member of the Association of Contentious Trust and Probate Specialists (ACTAPS) and the Society of Trust and Estate Practitioners, where he sits on the editorial board for the STEP journal.

Alex Scott
Chairman and CEO, Sand Aire Ltd
alexander.scott@sandaire.com

Alex Scott is chairman and CEO of Sand Aire, a company he formed in 1996 after leading the sale of his family's business, Provincial Insurance, in 1994. Sand Aire is a full-service multi-family office, delivering investment and family office services to wealthy families.

Alex is a director, co-founder and past chairman of the not-for-profit Institute for Family Business (UK) and has served as a director of the Family Firm Institute. He speaks regularly at family business and family office conferences and is a director of several private companies and a trustee of the Francis Scott Charitable Trust. He has an MA from Oxford University and an MBA from IMD, Lausanne.

Jonathan Sutton
Chartered accountant and tax adviser,
Dixon Wilson
jonsutton@dixonwilson.co.uk

Jonathan Sutton is a chartered accountant and tax adviser. He is a partner in Dixon Wilson's private client practice in London. Mr Sutton advises UK and international families and their businesses on their financial, taxation and wider affairs. He is deputy chairman of the STEP Business Families Group.

Charlie Tee
Solicitor, Withers LLP
charlie.tee@withersworldwide.com

Charlie Tee is a solicitor in the family and business planning group of the wealth planning department at Withers LLP.

Charlie has worked closely with a number of business families, advising on existing structures set up for the management and governance of the family business, its interaction with family trusts and associated estate planning measures.

Charlie also advises UK-based and international clients on their personal tax, estate planning and trust matters. A particular area of expertise is advising on and setting up family offices and related structures to help ensure the preservation of the family business for future generations.

Matthew Woods
Solicitor, Withers LLP
matthew.woods@withersworldwide.com

Matthew Woods is a solicitor and partner in the family and business planning group of the wealth planning department at Withers LLP. Withers LLP is a leading international law firm specialising in advising private individuals and their businesses on governance, management and succession issues.

Matthew advises on suitable structures to manage family wealth and on the mitigation of inheritance and capital gains taxes, particularly for landed estates and owner-managed businesses. Matthew is also joint head of the firm's landed estates group and has considerable experience in advising on the long-term devolution of private wealth.